The Paradox
of Jesus
in the Gospels

The Paradox
of Jesus
in the Gospels

by
Charles W. F. Smith

THE WESTMINSTER PRESS
Philadelphia

STANDARD BOOK No. 664–20853–3
LIBRARY OF CONGRESS CATALOG CARD No. 69–14201

PUBLISHED BY THE WESTMINSTER PRESS ®
PHILADELPHIA, PENNSYLVANIA

PRINTED IN THE UNITED STATES OF AMERICA

To Ivy

Preface

These chapters were not designed to be a direct contribution to what, elsewhere, I have called a "debate about a debate," namely, the search for a "historical Jesus" and the "legitimacy" of such an undertaking. They are concerned rather with one area of "the phenomenon of the New Testament"—a phrase Prof. C. F. D. Moule used as the title of the first monograph in the Second Series of Studies in Biblical Theology.

No direct reference is intended to the debate because it moves in largely technical language and I have been as much concerned for the preacher in his pulpit and among his people as for the scholar in his study and among his students. What is attempted here is the exploration of a concern, arising from exegesis among English-speaking students, that the Gospels be allowed to explain their existence. It is my point that they can do this only as paradoxical documents in which both the Jesus who lived and died and the Jesus Christ who is worshiped and served are realities that operate in constant tension. Attempts to resolve such a paradox fail to explain the shape of the Gospels as they stand.

The long period during which this material has been developed has been occupied by detailed studies (the ones in print are referred to) and by discussion with students at the Episcopal Theological School. To them I offer my thanks. I would thank others also who kindly listened to some of it on our visit to the Orient in 1965 when the subject "Christology and Commitment in the Gospels" was explored. I am grateful to the staff and students of the Central Theological College and the Christian Studies Department of Rikkyo (St. Paul's University) in Tokyo; to the Cathedral authorities, to clergy and lay people in Hong Kong; to Trinity Theological College and especially to Dean Frank Balchin, in Singapore; to the faculty and student body, and to the then Bishop Lyman Ogilby and Dean Ezra Diman, at St. Andrew's Theological Seminary in Quezon City, Philippines; and finally to the Principal, Dr. William Stewart, theological faculty, and students of Serampore University in West Bengal—where, in the last two places, longer visits enabled me to participate in courses.

I offer this work as a tribute to my wife, who not only shared these interests and journeyings and endured the preoccupation its reduction to writing has involved, but has always been to me a living exponent of a follower of the way of Christ.

Miss Marcia Holden and Miss Marjorie Zerbel contributed skills, in the niches of their work at the Episcopal Theological School, in preparing some of the material at various stages for class use, and have earned my gratitude. Miss Zerbel has prepared the final manuscript, and I am thankful for intelligence and patience beyond the call of duty. To the Trustees of the School thanks are offered for a generous policy of Sabbatical leaves, and to my colleagues who have patiently read some of the chapters.

The preacher has been in mind most of the way, but not as the recipient of directly preachable material. Rather, it is the hope that he (or she) may be stimulated to turn again to the Gospels as the deposit of the preaching and teaching of the early Christian church. There he may find content and method developed before the systematizing of its theology too formally dictates his options.

C. W. F. S.

Cambridge, Massachusetts

Contents

PREFACE   7

One
    THE PARADOX OF THE GOSPELS   11

Two
    THE BAPTIZER WHO WAS BAPTIZED:
       I. JOHN'S PROPHECY   29

Three
    THE BAPTIZER WHO WAS BAPTIZED:
       II. THE BAPTISM OF JESUS   50

Four
    THE UNIVERSAL SAVIOR WHO WAS
       A PROVINCIAL PREACHER   73

Five
    THE ETERNAL SON WHO MUST DIE   99

Six
    THE KING WITHOUT A THRONE:
       THE TEMPLE WITHOUT A LORD   134

Seven
    THE FINAL PARADOX:
       THE SAVIOR WHO COULD NOT SAVE   158

Eight
    THE PARADOX IN RESURRECTION AND RETROSPECT   182

Postscript
    LIVING WITH THE PARADOX, THEN AND NOW   213

INDEXES   229

One

The Paradox
of the Gospels

How are we to take the Gospels and how judge the place of Jesus in them? As preachments of the Christian church concerning one in a heavenly state of existence who is the object of the church's worship? Or as factual accounts of the public life and tragedy of an old-time amateur rabbi and the good advice he gave? To phrase the questions in these ways makes it clear that neither will lead us to the answer. How, then, shall we go about reading the Gospels? Shall we take all the tools of modern criticism and, starting from the beginning, dissect out the core of historical fact and on this residue build a faith? Or shall we work backward from the proclamation of the resurrection of Christ, and seek for a theological Savior, warned in advance that no salvation lies in history critically sifted? We could do either, for both have been done to some advantage. But in each case we shall feel uneasy with the Gospels themselves, as though we were reading them in two dimensions, without that third dimension which gives depth to the perspective and bodies out the figures in their own peculiar landscape and so outlines the sharpened form of the central Figure of all.

Two Symbolical Stories

Instead, we might try to look at these much scrutinized documents to see if they offer any clues to their own apparent inner contradictions. As an approach we consider two stories in the Gospel of Mark which, though they have some superficial resemblances, have also inherent and fundamental differences. Both take place on the Sea of Galilee and both concern the disciples of Jesus afloat on the lake. In each, there is a storm and in each, Christ plays a vital part in saving the situation. Apart from that they differ in significant respects. Each story is, quite obviously, written after the death of Jesus, so that both are the product of the tradition of the church. But one story starts with the preresurrection situation, the other with the resurrection experience itself. To put it more simply yet at the same time more profoundly, one starts with *Jesus*, the other starts with *the Christ*. Here is the basic paradox that has determined the nature of the Gospels—they are about Jesus Christ, or Jesus the Christ, or Christ Jesus.

The stories are in Mark 4:35–41 and 6:45–52. Each is the sequel to a crowded scene, and we find the disciples working a boat through the waves of the lake. So far the setting is similar. In the first, Jesus has spent the day teaching the multitudes by parables from the boat just off the shore; in the second, there has been the "feeding" of five thousand men by the lakeside. Beyond that both stories are symbolical insofar as they involve events outside of normal experience and have a function in the development of meaning in their respective locations in the Gospel. By this it is not meant that the disciples or the boat or even the storm are not real, or that the incident is not based on a recollected happening—only that its treatment is symbolical.

It is the case with symbolical stories of the Bible that they yield their meaning only if they are taken seriously. That is to say, the symbolical value depends upon our taking the event as described and re-creating it in our imagination so that its circumstances and its progression are thought of as really happening. To do so does not commit us, one way or the other, to a judgment about the historical facts involved. We are not here asking, Did it happen like this? or, Could it have happened just so? We ask only what, taken on its own terms, its meaning is. We shall therefore take each story initially as it stands, constructing the scene as best we can from the text given us. To do so is, in fact, one method of demythologizing the stories.

THE STILLING OF THE STORM

In Mark 4:35–41, the day's teaching over, Jesus proposes that he and the disciples "go across to the other side." They leave the crowd and take Jesus "just as he is" in the boat. Here Jesus is given transportation in the boat which in v. 1 he has used as a platform. To the disciples who man the boat he is their well-known leader, the popular teacher, the carpenter-rabbi who has held the crowds with his homespun stories. True, they are already aware that there are dimensions to these stories beyond what is easily grasped—or so Mark would have us understand. Hitherto the disciples have been listeners and spectators in the realm of Jesus' competence. Now, as the boat puts out to sea, he has entered their realm of competence; he is their passenger and there is nothing for him to do or to concern himself with. Tired by his teaching of the crowds, he goes to sleep on the cushion in the stern (v. 38). Their roles have in a sense been reversed. Jesus is in their hands; they are able to serve him.

In a few words in v. 37 Mark calls up vividly the emergency that arose. We see the wind suddenly gusting, as it does on a lake set among hills, and in spite of all their efforts, the waves are beating into the boat, so that it is "already filling" and threatens to founder. Jesus is apparently undisturbed, still asleep, unconcerned. Perhaps we would not be wrong to see in this his complete confidence in them as they ply their natural occupation and operate competently in their own sphere. They, at least have so far made no objection to his complete relaxation and disassociation from the business in hand.

Now, suddenly, all is changed. In danger of disaster, there can be no passengers. Everyone must do what he can if the boat is to ride out the storm, so they wake Jesus. The question they put to him is not a query so much as an expostulation, even a rebuke. His rest, which while all went well they accepted, now becomes an affront. With urgency they exclaim, "Don't you care if we perish?" It is no time for idle hands; every hand must be bent to shortening sail, to pulling an oar, to bailing, to shifting weight, to doing whatever experience or desperation counsels. Yet it is difficult to see what Jesus could be expected to do, since he was no fisherman at home on the water—unless indeed, like Jonah, he might plunge overboard to lighten the ship.

The significant thing to be noticed, apart from speculation, is the complete familiarity with which the disciples in this story address Jesus, the freedom with which they treat him. True, they address him as "Rabbi" (Luke has used the Greek term for "teacher"; Matthew has heightened the address to "Lord") but the tone of their rebuke suggests a complete absence of awe or of religious reverence. The voyage is the realm of their competence, and Jesus is properly under their orders. They may reasonably object that to sleep at this juncture appears to show a lack of concern which may be fatal. We are thus presented so far with an entirely human situation. Jesus is a man among men and they treat him as one of themselves, indeed, as one who seems to lack appreciation of the emergency in which they together exist.

There may indeed be little that Jesus can do as far as the boat is concerned or its handling in a crisis. In fact he makes no attempt to do anything about the navigation. According to the story, Jesus does nothing about the boat but attends to the conditions under which the boat exists—or threatens no longer to exist. He gives no command to helmsman or oarsmen but addresses himself to the cause of their problem. It lies, after all, not in their tactics but in the conditions outside them. The wind that causes their distress he "rebukes." To the waves whose turbulence imperils their lives he speaks as to a person,

"Peace! Be still!" The conditions immediately respond. The boat now floats in a calm that gives them leisure to put all in order and in due course to proceed according to their plan.

In so great a transition no one can proceed as though nothing had happened. Is it after all true that the problem lay entirely with external conditions, not with the people involved? First Jesus speaks to them. It is his turn to offer a rebuke, not, of course, to their ability as seamen, but to their spiritual condition. "Why are you afraid?"

"Have you no faith?" is addressed to their condition too. Not perhaps that they should have believed they would pull through without disturbing him; after all, Jesus is not peevish. Rather, in waking him why should they reproach him as if they really thought he did not care and might be unwilling to help in whatever way he could? In the same way the leper had questioned Jesus' willingness and aroused his emotion in Mark 1:40 ff. In this tale also the question concerning faith seems to apply to intention rather than to fact. In the case of the leper, the reader of the preceding items might feel that the leper's plea was justified, "*If you will*, you can make me clean." In v. 41 there is a reading in the Western text which depicts Jesus' anger (in our text compassion is expressed—Matthew and Luke avoid the word). It is as though the questioning of his willingness disturbed Jesus more than doubt about his ability would have done. In the calm after the storm (Mark 4:40) it is less easy to see why there should be a rebuke, unless indeed Jesus preferred to have his ability rather than his intention questioned. Perhaps so, but in any case it heightens the effect of his intervention and prepares the way for their response. Now, in complete contrast to their previous familiarity and freedom with him, they stand in awe and begin to say to each other, "Who then *is* this?" In this *change of attitude* lies the import of the tale. It is one whom they know well, with whom they have stood on common and familiar terms, who now presents to them a mystery and who fills them with questioning awe.

Before we can appreciate the full meaning of this story and

its function in the Gospel, we must examine the other tale, so similar in its setting, so very different in its impact and purpose.

THE WALKING ON THE WATER

In Mark 6:45–52 we are again with the disciples afloat on the lake. But now Jesus is not with them. In fact, according to Mark's link between this tale and the preceding incident, Jesus has made the disciples depart in the boat and leave him behind on shore. There he dismisses the throng who have shared in the "meal" he has provided and goes into the hills to pray (vs. 45 f.). So it comes about that the disciples in the boat are well out in the lake (literally, "in the middle") without Jesus and he is alone on the land, and evening has come (v. 47).

Our attention is first directed to Jesus, since we are told that it is he who observes that they are in distress, trying to row against the wind. Here also we find a difference from the previous story. Now the initiative lies with Jesus; they are no longer able to call on him. It is well into the night before Jesus approaches, coming toward them as though walking across the water. Yet he designs (as the Greek puts it) to pass by them—as if upon some voyage or purpose of his own. We learn no more than that, for attention is now directed to the disciples who see the figure "walking on the sea" and think it a *phantasma* (the Greek word) and so cry out. They call out, not for help but because, as the text says, "they all saw him, and were terrified." We can hardly fail to note the difference from the previous story. Here Christ is not someone well known whom they can rebuke, but only a terrifying apparition. Their fear is the terror aroused by the unknown.

There can, then, be no question of an appeal for help, much less a demand, for they have no initiative—it is his alone. So once more the attention shifts and the apparition (whom the readers, but not the rowers, know to be Jesus) speaks to them. When he says, "Take courage. It is I. Do not be afraid," they should know who it is. He then joins them in the boat and his presence with them is enough to change the situation completely. Once again the wind ceases, now, because he is with them. There is no rebuke to the wind nor is there, this time, to them. We are told only that they were astounded. The Evangelist adds his comment, again tying the tale to the incident of the feeding, that "they did not understand about the loaves, but their hearts were hardened" (v. 52). *The New English Bible* interprets the Greek aptly when it renders it: "For they had not understood the incident of the loaves; their minds were closed." The connection implied here will be discussed later.

THE NATURE OF THE STORIES

We can be too easily attracted by the similarities of the two tales as "miracles," even as "nature" miracles involving wind and boat, endangered disciples and a magical Jesus, to note the quite remarkable differences. In the first tale, Jesus is with them; here he is not. In the first, he is completely human in his need for rest and their readiness to complain to him; here he is quite unrecognizable, unapproachable, the initiative his, not theirs. There they can ask him for help, in effect, demand it; here they can do no such thing. Jesus comes to them in their need, not they to him. In fact the apparition adds to their dread instead of raising hopes of rescue. Recognition comes only by his self-disclosure, by his words *egō eimi* (literally, "I am" but idiomatically, "It is I") and by his presence with them in the boat. This solves their nautical problem—once again by a change in the conditions, not in the handling of the boat—but does nothing to change fear to familiarity. The quality of their astonishment is changed, but they could hardly be called at ease with their unexpected and previously unrecognized helper.

Of course not. This is not Jesus. This is the Risen Christ. That is the basic difference in the two stories. This is a resurrection story. The other was about Jesus and his days among them as a man, an epiphany story perhaps, but not a resurrection story as this is. C. H. Dodd has drawn attention to the characteristic form taken by the narratives of the resurrection (see "Notes to Chapter One," par. 4). Basically, its stages are: the situation in which Christ's followers are shown "bereft of their Lord"; the Lord appears; he gives a greeting; there is recognition; the climax is often a word of command or a commission. Other resurrection stories show a development of this basic structure by the addition of more vivid narrative material. Dodd points out that the tale we have been reviewing has all the resurrection features except for the final command (he deals especially with the version in John 6:16 ff.). It has some features that bring it closer to the more fully narrative type. We might disregard Dodd's further analysis, which roots the story firmly in the Galilean ministry of Jesus, since the placing of it is more dependent on Mark's design and message than on a historical sequence of events.

It seems clear that in essence the walking on the water is a resurrection story. The Jesus who appears here, as in the Easter stories, takes the initiative, comes to the disciples who are without him and who, because they are without him, cannot succeed in their task. He comes, moreover, unrecognized and has to disclose his identity. His word or, in this case, his presence effects both recognition and the solution of their problem. Their attitude toward him is not, even then, that of men to a man, but one of awe and wonder. He is indeed one who has "come to them." In the Matthean version this has been heightened in conformity with a more advanced Christology; those in the boat worship him and confess him to be indeed "Son of God" (Matt. 14:33). Matthew has also added the theme of Peter's attempt to walk on the water, which leads him to introduce here also the theme of doubt or of insufficient faith as it is not introduced explicitly in the second story in Mark (see Chapter Eight, below). In Mark there is no final command because it is closely knit to its context by Mark's editorial work and his theme of the hardening of the disciples' hearts (Mark 6:52).

The conclusion Mark has provided is a cryptic comment on the feeding story with which we shall deal later (see Chapter Five, below). We can perhaps see that the differences between the "walking on the water" and the "stilling of the storm" stories are basic not just in form and fact but also in purpose. In the first story, Jesus is one with the disciples, human enough to need sleep, a man with whom they can be familiar, from which familiarity they are led, however, to wonder and speculation. In the second story, the Christ is not even recognized, he does not appear to them as a man at all; he has to disclose himself to them; they begin in fear and end in astonishment. If it were not for the connection with what follows, this might have been worship, as in Matthew. The latter Evangelist has not cared so much to preserve the connection and seems to feel no incongruity in proceeding in the chapters which follow as though this revelation had not even happened.

THE PARADOXICAL NATURE OF THE GOSPELS

It has been necessary in the above to use the term "Christ." That is another way of marking the contrast. One tale is about Jesus, the other about Christ, the Risen Lord. Yet both tales, in Mark, are set within the Galilean ministry before crucifixion and resurrection. How can a tale about a clearly human Jesus and a tale about a clearly supernatural Christ be a part of the same basic account? To ask the question expresses the peculiar character of the Gospel narrative. It is *paradoxical*. It is at one and the same time about the historical Jesus and the Risen Christ. It is about two attitudes toward him. In one *they* seek to understand who he is, though already known to them; in the other *he* reveals to them who he is, though unrecognized by them. The one story moves from the basis of historical recollection, the other from the basis of the gospel proclamation. Yet we cannot distinguish them absolutely in this way. There are elements of each in both. The stilling of the storm has elements in it of a proclamation of the gospel. The walking on the water also proclaims the gospel but has realistic and natural elements in it. This is the essence of the paradoxical nature of the Gospels. The point that will interest us is that what is true of the Gospels is also true of Jesus (or of the Christ) who is himself the paradox behind the paradoxical.

Both the boat tales are symbolical. In the second tale, clearly a resurrection appearance, it would be futile to ask what the facts are about Christ's walking on the water. The Risen Christ may walk on the water as readily as he may appear within closed doors (John 20:19, 26) or disappear from the supper table (Luke 24:30 f.). In the earlier story, there is a miraculous element, the stilling of the storm, but it is effected by the human Jesus whose power to accomplish this arouses the speculative wonder of his followers who had (in the story) been disposed to treat him all too familiarly. It is symbolical of all the aspects of the experience of both the disciples and the people in their contact with the actual Jesus. Concerning what some of those aspects of wonderment were which prompted men to ask, "Who then is this?" we must inquire further.

We have then, in the two tales, two aspects of the Christian experience. There is the wonder, the mystery, which arises from the activity as well as from the teaching of Jesus in his life as this, transposed into the key of the gospel, is set forth by the Evangelists in various ways. Sometimes it is done by a symbolical tale as here, sometimes by a narrative, a parable, a discourse, each of them modified to serve the propagation, the exposition, or even the justification of the gospel. Sometimes it is done by an equally symbolical representation of the resurrection experience and the words of the Risen Christ declaring Who He Is, modified by being transposed into his lifetime to establish the connection between this Christ and that Jesus.

Further evidence of the transition involved is found in a striking manner in Luke 5:1–11. There (vs. 1–3) we have a situation akin to the setting which in Mark is the prelude to the stilling of the storm—teaching the people from the boat. In

Luke, however, it does not introduce the calming of a storm (which occurs in Luke 8:22 and is introduced by a vague, "one day") but a particularly Lucan passage combining elements of Mark 1:16–20 and, surprisingly, John 21:1–17. However, Luke's version differs from both these connections. It differs from Mark in that instead of a call to the brothers Simon and Andrew, and to James and John who work with their father Zebedee, Simon (Peter) is, in Luke, the center of interest (Luke 5:3–5, 8, 10–11) and it is he who is specifically commissioned. John's story has the same interest in Peter (John 21:3, 7, 11, 15 ff.) and again he is commissioned, or recommissioned, this time not as a fisher of men but as a shepherd of sheep. The Johannine story is like the Lucan story in being concerned with their inability to catch fish until Jesus intervenes. Both stories have to do with a recognition of Christ, John's being explicitly a resurrection story, but Luke's a combined story of precrucifixion and resurrection motifs.

When we compare Luke's story with the two boat stories, we discover the similarities and differences are a combination of the two types. In the Lucan scene, Jesus is also known to Peter (especially) as the teacher of the crowds. Jesus is a person to whom Peter can reply with the expostulation, "Master, we toiled all night," and to whom he can make the concession, "But at your word I will . . ." (Luke 5:5). The word that Luke uses for Peter's address to Jesus is *epistata* ("Teacher"). No disclosure is involved, for recognition is already there— on one level, familiarity. After the marvelous catch of fish, however, all is changed. Simon is now (v. 8) referred to as Simon Peter, he falls before Jesus in an attitude of worship, he recognizes in the presence of Christ his sinfulness, and he no longer addresses Jesus as "Teacher" but as "Lord" (*kyrie*). The other three men are made subordinate to Peter.

We have, therefore, a combination of motifs made into one story; an incident that begins with Jesus "in the days of his flesh" and moves on to a recognition scene which has distinctive marks of a resurrection appearance. In John, ch. 21, it is a resurrection appearance, for there the "beloved disciple" mediates to Peter the recognition that the *unknown* figure on the shore is "the Lord" (v. 7). The subject in Luke is the change in the skeptical Simon's attitude to Jesus brought about by the resurrection, after which he is Peter who recognizes Christ as Lord. We shall see the story of the change in Peter, here condensed, worked out in more detail in the chapters below. The Evangelist has moved a resurrection experience of Peter back into the Galilean setting and combined it with the call to be a fisher of men. Luke has done this probably for several reasons, not the least of which is that the resurrection appearances he has used otherwise take place in Jerusalem. Hence, here, at the level of recognition and disclosure, which in Mark is dealt with from two angles by two stories, we have a combination of familiarity leading to awe and of disclosure producing worship. It is marked by the significant change of address from "Teacher" to "Lord," which signifies the resurrection experience of those who had known Jesus in the flesh and so were able to receive the disclosure of himself in his risen form, in the Spirit.

The similarities and contrasts of the two Marcan stories likewise suggest a phase of gospel development which becomes more apparent as we go on. First, however, we turn back to the story of the storm and ask whether we can see what experience underlies the question to which it leads.

"Who Then Is This?"

The stilling of the storm prompted the sense of mystery among the disciples, and stands as a symbol of all those things about Jesus which caused his contemporaries to ask this question. The symbolical element in the story is the means of pointing to a situation, arising from events, which demanded reflection and response, a situation to which the response itself could only be given in symbolical or "religious" terms, though its issue would be a new course of action.

Equally it suggests that the same experiences prompted

others to reject the question and substitute their own answer, ultimately in the form, "Crucify him!" The essence of this paradox is that it was within human acquaintance with Jesus that both the query and the repudiation arose. Both were, to use a phrase that will later claim attention, *kata sarka*, "according to the flesh." What people saw and heard was a man whose antecedents could be traced, whose kinfolk some of them knew (Mark 6:3), whose interests and needs were theirs also, who was involved in the turmoil in which they were all embroiled, and who was vulnerable to restriction, repudiation, and death, as well as capable of success and applause, just as they were. At the same time there was, on further acquaintance, something about him that inevitably gave rise to questions, to an astonishment that called for an answer to the question, "Who then is this?"

It was easy to dismiss Jesus as a relative of people who could be interviewed, as the son of an artisan, himself a worker, who had turned to a career of itinerant preaching, who was treated by his followers as a rabbi and by the crowds as a prophet. Yet even within this casual and everyday assessment there were disturbing features. There was, among those who associated constantly with him, the imperious nature of his invitation to them, having the overtones of a compelling demand rather than a permissive invitation (Mark 1:16; 2:14). Who was this who commanded a following of men without previous debate, without coming to terms, even without prior acquaintance? Moreover, he appointed delegates, as though he were in himself an authoritative center, a one-man "Sanhedrin" entitled to send deputies to the people (Mark 3:14; 6:7). Who was this itinerant who behaved as if he were Jerusalem itself?

He was, for a while at least, invited to speak in the synagogue. Once seated, he made use of the opportunity as if he were one who needed no further credentials but might teach without reference to precedent or predecessors (Mark 1:22, etc.). He spoke as one who decided what the interpretation should be without known support of ordination or delegation. Who, then, was this who spoke with an authority unlike that

of the scribes? The manner of his teaching, scornful of any
visible place, commission, or precedent that justified it, could
cause only offense, so that all were bound to ask, "Who?"

This sovereign assurance we note also in his parables, which
venture to draw analogies in almost entirely secular language
from the ordinary experiences of men—domestic, commercial,
pastoral, agricultural, familial, and social—of the nature of
God in his dealings with them. The impact of these parables
upon the delicately poised situation of the times, their timing
in relation to impending crisis, their power to compel a judgment, were so shrewdly aimed that there was bound to arise
the demand, "Who then is this?" What was the nature of this
authority, this implied claim to be in himself a sign of the
times?

The same disturbing question about the recognition of a
critical turn of events is found elsewhere in his teaching. The
implication can scarcely be avoided that the time had come
to a critical moment by virtue of his presence in it and what
he was doing. It may well be that the stories of his wonderful
deeds—his healings, his exorcisms, even his "nature" miracles—
owe much to the formulations of the church, which used
Jewish or Hellenistic methods to tell wonder tales. It may
even be that other men were able to do similar deeds. What
creates speculation and offense, however, is the disdain for
publicity and for accepted methods. The connection made
between these deeds and the critical turn of events to which
his teaching points forces the question, "Who is this?"

Along with this immediacy goes also the demand for commitment, a commitment complete, instant, and final. There has
to be a decision for or against, but one freely taken, compelled
neither by the premature revelations made by demons nor by
any kind of "sign" that would disclose in advance any credentials he might be expected to claim. The decision had to be
arrived at and the commitment made with no other evidence
than the presence of Jesus and what happened when he was
present. It would seem, rather, that his way and his demand
were one and the same and could, as such, do no more than
prompt the question, not define the answer.

Associated with the demand for active commitment that admitted of no way back went two other features of teaching and ministry. There can be little doubt that the impression the Gospels give of a consistency between Jesus' teaching and action, of the dependence of the one on the other and their interaction, preserves a basic recollection of the effect Jesus created and of a notable cause for disturbance. We find it reflected in two aspects of his teaching which were always attributed to him. One is Jesus' insistence that a thing is to be judged by its function (as we see more clearly when we come to the parables). The other is that where there is a claim to faith or righteousness, there must be the product, active expression. This stress on function and production sounds surprisingly modern, even commercial, but it need not for that reason be suspect. The New Testament contains in its vocabulary a number of words of secular or business provenance in process of becoming "religious." Jesus' insistence is prophetic and realistic rather than modern.

In this connection we meet the clearly attested attitude of independence which he adopted toward some aspects of the law. We do not find him engaging in philosophical discussions of the basis of the regulations that dominated Jewish life at the time, but raising questions of their purpose and their effect in the situation. His means of discrimination was whether the rules provided an immediate answer to the human need that faced him or were a hindrance to its being met. He pointed to a contrast between the attitude of his critics toward economic interests and their attitude toward people. That is why the Sabbath is the usual point of contention. But if one were so to defy established convention, reinforced by economic pressures and sanctioned by religious pronouncements, he must indeed raise the question, "Who then is this?"

The correspondence between word and act that Jesus demanded is the clue to his own words which in themselves have the effect of action, illustrated vividly in exorcism and healing, but no less in his willingness to bear the consequences, to support action by justification of the acts, and to express teaching in acts that gave it body and form. Hence arose the debate about him which demanded proof of authority rather than of the power he exercised.

Finally, nothing could be more clearly attested in the Gospels than the tradition of Jesus' concern for the outcasts, those who, for various reasons, were excluded from the fullness of Israel's life, religious, social, or economic. Whether the causes of their separation were hygienic (as with lepers) or ritual uncleanness (the term "sinner" being applied to those unable to keep the law because of their occupations), whether they were actually immoral or heretical or subversive, whether they were in an inferior position because of sex or by designation 'am ha'aretz, seems to have made no difference to Jesus' response. He did not undertake this approach lightly, for it entailed the criticism and opposition of many who were most likely to be in a position to lend him support with both the authorities and the people—most prominently and crucially, the Pharisees. So much of his vindication of his own practices is associated with this issue that it is unlikely the vindication is altogether the creation of the later church, even supposing the church's inclusion within its fellowship of all who responded to the gospel needed such justification. For one like himself, lacking official standing, vulnerable to the charge of lack of antecedents or weighty credentials, so to risk censure and repudiation for his acceptance of the unacceptable was bound to give rise to the demand, "Who then is this?"

As we shall see, there is a good deal in the gospel presentation of Jesus which does not instantly or unequivocally fit the demands of the first-century church's task apart from some actual recollection of Jesus and use of that memory. When scholars talk of an "incognito" or a "hidden revelation," it is presumably this that they have in mind. We have found it put symbolically by Mark in his pictures of Jesus in the boat; well-known and recognized, yet unexplainable without further question; or, from the other end, the revealed and Risen Christ explained by his ambiguous existence before the resurrection. From one "boat" the revelation lies ahead; from the other "boat" it lies behind. It is difficult to state a paradox of this kind, the paradox which determines the form of the Gospels, without seeing it at work in the Gospels. It is that to which we now turn to examine some other examples of how it functions.

NOTES TO CHAPTER ONE

1. A useful summary of the debate about faith and history with references to important literature will be found in Carl E. Braaten, *History and Hermeneutics* (New Directions in Theology Today, Vol. II; The Westminster Press, 1966).

2. See also the following in the series Studies in Biblical Theology (London: SCM Press, Ltd., and Alec R. Allenson, Inc.): James M. Robinson, *A New Quest of the Historical Jesus* (No. 25; 1959); Ernst Käsemann, "The Problem of the Historical Jesus," *Essays on New Testament Themes*, tr. by W. J. Montague (No. 41; 1964); and Ernst Fuchs, "The Quest of the Historical Jesus" and other essays in *Studies of the Historical Jesus*, tr. by Andrew Scobie (No. 42; 1964).

3. For an overall view of Jesus and his impact similar to that given in this chapter, see Günther Bornkamm, *Jesus of Nazareth*, tr. by Irene and Fraser McLuskey (Harper & Brothers, 1960). For another treatment of the first story, see his "The Stilling of the Storm in Matthew" in G. Bornkamm, G. Barth, H. J. Held, *Tradition and Interpretation in Matthew*, tr. by Percy Scott (The New Testament Library, The Westminster Press, 1963).

4. On the characteristics of the resurrection narratives, see C. H. Dodd, "The Appearances of the Risen Christ: An Essay in Form-Criticism of the Gospels," in Dennis E. Nineham, ed., *Studies in the Gospels* (Oxford: Basil Blackwell & Mott, Ltd., 1955).

5. On the call of the disciples, see C. W. F. Smith, "Fishers of Men," in *Harvard Theological Review*, Vol. 52, No. 3 (1959). For a full hermeneutical treatment of the metaphor, see Wilhelm H. Wuellner, *The Meaning of "Fishers of Men"* (The New Testament Library, The Westminster Press, 1967).

6. For further reading on the relation of Peter to the resurrection narratives, and on the consistency of word and act in Jesus as a retrospective judgment, see Chapter Eight; the same for the temptations.

7. On the relation of the parables to Jesus' times, see C. W. F. Smith, *The Jesus of the Parables* (The Westminster Press, 1948).

8. For an independent view of the development of the New Testament which gives weight to the historical factor, see, with reservations: C. F. D. Moule, *The Birth of the New Testament* (Harper's New Testament Commentaries, Harper & Row, Publishers, Inc., 1962); *The Phenomenon of the New Testament* (Studies in Biblical Theology, Second Series, No. 1).

Two

The Baptizer

Who Was Baptized
I. John's Prophecy

Jesus was a figure of paradox from the very beginning. He is likely always to be a disturbing element in human history, whether that history continues in some sense to be Christian or whether it becomes increasingly secularized and agnostic. Not only Christians find Jesus disturbing. In fact, Christians are not often enough aware that they are or ought to be disturbed. There are those who become Christians because they have found Jesus' existence to be a disrupting factor in their lives. The elements of paradox, moreover, keep Jesus from being "captured" by the church or by anyone who would neatly dispose of him in a closed theological system or by those who would make use of him for their own purposes. Yet this paradoxical element is not a feature imposed on the Gospels as a theological device, nor is it found in isolated places or in strands which can be completely isolated. It meets us at the outset and continues throughout.

THE PARADOX OF THE INCARNATION

In dogmatical language the paradox comes to full expression in the doctrine of the incarnation, the assertion that Christ was one with God and "came down" (in at least the metaphorical sense) and became fully man: in actual nature, God; in actual nature, man. The paradox of the incarnation is stated

in the New Testament in striking ways, though the extent to
which it finds explicit statement (especially in the Synoptic
Gospels) can easily be exaggerated. We find the expressions:
"Though he was rich, yet for your sake he became poor"
(II Cor. 8:9); "who, though he was in the form of God . . .
emptied himself, . . . and became obedient" (Phil. 2:6–8);
"the Logos became flesh and dwelt among us" (John 1:14);
"Jesus, who for a little while was made lower than the angels,
crowned with glory and honor because of the suffering of
death" (Heb. 2:9). The fact that to the natural eye Christ
appeared a human being has given rise to the idea of "the
divine incognito." His disguise, however, could not in fact be
penetrated because it was not a disguise at all. The incarnation
was a real becoming-man, unless, as the New Testament sometimes unwarily seems to suggest, it was a real becoming-God.

We do not find the theological concept fully developed in
the Gospels; hence their paradoxical nature. They are not
"dogmatic" in the sense that the Christian creeds or the statements of the Councils of the church are dogmatical. Yet they
are Christological. That is to say, they are not merely historical records of a period of time or of a human career. Their
purpose is to set out the Christian gospel. They can be shown
to have arisen in large measure from the preaching and teaching by which that gospel was propagated and made a way of
life. Further, perhaps not enough allowance has been made for
the effect that the apologetics occasioned by its defense has
had upon their shape. Their paradoxical nature arises out of
these issues, that they deal, ultimately, with a historical situation but they deal with it religiously rather than historically.
They present historically conditioned religion and religiously
conditioned history. Hence their central figure is, as we have
seen, presented in paradoxical ways. Many years ago Dibelius
went so far as to call the paradox "monstrous." He used the
expressions: "the monstrous paradox of Jesus' earthly existence," and "the monstrous paradox of the death of Jesus"
(see "Notes to Chapter Two," par. 2). It becomes apparent
that the paradox normally starts from the assumption that we

know Jesus to have been divine and have to find out in what sense he was human. Is this assumption supported by the Gospels as they developed?

The essential paradox becomes apparent in the place at which all the Gospels, in agreement, begin. It is a paradox revealed throughout by the manner in which the Evangelists have been compelled to deal with the tradition.

The Beginning of the Gospel

The gospel as story begins essentially with a paradoxical fact. A man named Jesus came from Galilee to Judea and was baptized by John the Baptist. This is treated as a fact which has to be accepted. It immediately presents a paradox because Jesus (or the figure with whom he was identified) was expected to baptize, not to be baptized. The one who was to dispense baptism received baptism. The paradox is the more paradoxical because it turned out that the church was unable to present the baptism which Jesus offered in terms of the expected baptism which was foretold. This double paradox is inescapable and quite fundamental to the story for two reasons. It stands as the agreed opening of the Gospels and it provides a crucial area of interpretation. Because it begins the story we must examine the treatment given it by the Evangelists. Because it is important for interpretation, we must, more than in other cases, ask what early Christian writers made of it both within and beyond the New Testament.

When we examine passages in Acts which attempt to describe the essence of the gospel proclaimed in and by the primitive church, we find that they cover a normative period which is either known or made known and to which witness is given. To be able to testify to it made one, for the author of Acts, a "witness to his resurrection." So in Acts 1:21 f., the requirement for candidates for the vacant place of Judas, to restore the number of the Twelve, is to be able to testify to "the time that the Lord Jesus went in and out among us, beginning from the baptism of John." Whether this is reliable history or dependent on a primitive source, or is a Lucan construction designed to establish the concept of a "college of apostles," is not important. It is a first-century definition of the limits of a common testimony. In a sense, the later it is, the more interesting its existence becomes. Nor does it stand alone.

"This Jesus" who was crucified (Acts 2: 23 ff.) is described (v. 22) as "Jesus of Nazareth, a man attested to you by God with mighty works and wonders and signs which God did through him in your midst, as you yourselves know." The opportunity to "know" this is described in the Gospels as the time following John the Baptist's baptism of Jesus, not before. In Acts 3:13 the reference to God's "servant Jesus" is confined to the trial before Pilate (cf. chs. 4:10; 5:32). In ch. 4:13 the "boldness" of otherwise undistinguished men like Peter and John is attributed to their having been companions of Jesus— a case of guilt by association. In v. 27 of the same chapter, however, the baptism of Jesus is referred to in the words of a prayer, "thy holy servant Jesus, whom thou didst *anoint*," and proceeds to the plot that ended Jesus' life. In Peter's speech to Cornelius' household, Acts 10:34 ff., the "message" (*logos*) of "good news of peace by Jesus Christ" is defined as the message "which was proclaimed throughout all Judea, beginning from Galilee after the baptism which John preached: how God *anointed* Jesus of Nazareth." It embraces the resurrection experiences, including the commission from the Risen Christ to preach. Other references to the baptism will be mentioned later, but here we see that what it has become the fashion to call "the kerygma" does not cover the whole life of Jesus, does not include his birth, but does concern the period that begins with John the Baptist and his movement.

It is with this and Jesus' connection with it that the Gospels begin their story. This is clearly so in Mark's Gospel (ch. 1:1–4), but it is also true of Matthew and Luke, each of whom makes a fresh start at this point (Matt. 3:1; Luke 3:1–3). It is even true of the very different Fourth Gospel where John the Baptist is suddenly intruded into a transcendental prologue on the Logos of God (John 1:6)—or, as J. A. T. Robinson has suggested, the transcendent poetry has been wrapped around a more primitive and matter-of-fact statement. "There was," says the author, "a man sent from God." While this was written of the Baptist it also applies to Jesus.

Jesus appeared on the public scene in the reign of the emperor Tiberius. He appeared among a people with whom nationalistic hopes and religious expectation ran at fever pitch. They did not much distinguish between the two, for nationalism and religion were at most points one and the same thing. National hopes were so infused with religious idealism and practice that the word "nationalism" in its modern connotations hardly conveys the right idea. Jesus can be understood, and the Gospels, only in this setting.

When the Evangelists compiled the Gospels, they worked as men for whom the Scriptures supplied the context in which religious thought must be carried on. For them the categories provided by their Bible determined what was possible. What is available to us in the Gospels is their interpretation of the events, not the events themselves. The interpretation exists at different levels of meaning and stages of development. We can only speculate as to what happened, but speculation does not lack something to work with because we know the kind of interpretation that was likely to be applied. We can see what they expected us to see and so can to some extent judge their evaluations. We must bear in mind also that they believed *something had happened* which controlled all their work.

THE PROBLEM OF THE BAPTISM OF JOHN

The traditions, then, agree that when Jesus appeared publicly, he came from Galilee to take part in the movement of John the Baptist (or Baptizer). This seemingly commonplace and brief statement constituted a difficulty for the Christians who recorded the gospel. That difficulty could only increase and become more apparent as the gospel assumed the characteristics of a faith to be proclaimed to a world which had a different set of presuppositions, whether the audience which received it was Jewish or not.

What we find when we penetrate the surface of the Gospels

is this process at work. Jesus is increasingly given stature and status over against John the Baptist. The process reaches a climax in the Fourth Gospel where the Baptist designates Jesus as "the Lamb of God" (John 1:29, 36) and "Son of God" (v. 34). When John says, "He must increase, but I must decrease" (ch. 3:30), he describes a process already at work in the literature itself. When we seek to get back as far as we can to the roots of the tradition we find this situation:

Mark has treated the baptism of Jesus as part of his "introduction to the Christian reader" (ch. 1:1–13). He states but does not describe the event (v. 9). He tells what happened to Jesus after his baptism: that Jesus saw the heavens split open, that Jesus saw the Spirit as a dove descend, and that Jesus heard the voice addressed to himself, "Thou art my beloved Son; with thee I am well pleased" (vs. 10–11).

Luke emphasizes the popular movement of which this was a part (ch. 3:21), that Jesus was praying, that heaven was opened (he does not say to whom), that the Spirit appeared in "the bodily form" of a dove, and a voice addressed Jesus alone, "Thou art . . ." (in some early texts, as we shall see below, in the words of Ps. 2:7).

Matthew makes two changes. The voice is now addressed not to Jesus but either to John or to the people watching the scene, "This is . . ." (ch. 3:17). More significantly, Matthew inserts a discussion between Jesus and John in which the Baptist states his reluctance to baptize Jesus on the grounds that Jesus should instead baptize him (ch. 3:14–15). Here the paradox is making itself felt and Jesus' reply can be understood only after further examination.

At this point we can see the issue which is involved. Jesus has now become the Christ worshiped by the early Christian church, accepted as in some sense the "Son of God," already beginning to occupy a place apart from all other men. How can it then be explained that this Christ submitted himself to baptism, especially the baptism described in Mark, the earliest of the Gospels (Mark 1:4–5), as "a baptism of repentance for the forgiveness of sins"? The passage which is found only in Matthew (ch. 3:14–15) is the only attempt to deal with this developing problem explicitly, but the other three Gospels have had to deal with it implicitly.

THE DIFFICULTY OF THE EXPECTATION

Jesus' apparent subordination to John the Baptist is a problem because we are looking at the incident from this side of the resurrection, from the point of view of the postresurrection follower of Christ. Another difficulty appears when we try to look at it from a point prior to the coming of Jesus. Here we are helped by the existence of material common to Matthew and Luke and not found in Mark. The Marcan account of John's message and activity is colored throughout by the preaching and practice of the Christian church. There remains, however, in Mark 1:7–8 a reference to the coming of "the One Stronger than I." To those who have been baptized John says, "I have baptized you with water; but he will baptize you with the Holy Spirit." (There are, of course, no capitals in the Greek text.) This is clearly a Christian version of the message, especially when the last two words are capitalized. In the later literature it is clear that the gift of the Holy Spirit comes through Christ and, in the Gospel of John, is sent by Christ. Mark has made John the Baptist a preacher of the Christian message. The question is whether he was in fact such.

It may be convenient for the purpose of comparison to set out in parallel columns the phrases used by the Synoptic Evangelists.

MATTHEW, CH. *3* v. *11*	MARK, CH. *1* vs. *7–8*	LUKE, CH. *3* v. *16*
But the one who comes after me is mightier than I . . .; he will baptize you with holy spirit and with fire (*en pneumati hagiōi kai pyri*).	There comes the one mightier than I after me. . . . He will baptize you with holy spirit (*pneumati hagiōi*).	But there comes the one mightier than I . . .; he will baptize you with holy spirit and with fire (*en pneumati hagiōi kai pyri*).

There has been a tendency to assume that since Mark's Gospel was written first, it represents the early stage of the tradition. In many places this is true but it does not always hold and it does not hold here. It does not follow, for instance, that because "Holy Spirit" occurs in Mark and the additional expression "with fire" occurs in Matthew and Luke we have to conclude that Matthew and Luke have conflated Mark's "Holy Spirit" with "fire" from the common source of Matthew and Luke (Q). As we shall see, to think so has led students of the matter astray by causing them to place a baptism by Spirit over against a baptism by fire and sometimes to seek for the origin of the fire metaphor in outside sources. The clue is not conflation by Matthew and Luke but compression by Mark. We may follow R. H. Lightfoot (see "Notes to Chapter Two," par. 4) and take Mark 1:1–13 to be the introduction. We notice that it consists of a formalized Christian version of the events it rapidly summarizes. To get behind this and discover its nature we need to examine the Q material in Matt. 3:11b–12 with its parallel in Luke 3:16b–17. Here it is significant that the prophecy of a baptism by "the Mightier One" is to be "by holy spirit and by fire." This may well be an earlier version than Mark's "Holy Spirit" which, as later, should be read with the capitals, while the Q version should be read in lowercase. Further, we may ask whether the Q version as it stands is the earliest or has also been modified, though not as drastically as Mark has modified his source.

THE NATURE OF THE BAPTISM TO COME

The reason for the addition of "and fire" (on the assumption that Mark is earlier) has been sought in apocalyptic literature in which the figure of a river of fire occurs. It seems hardly necessary to turn to this figure, because the Q material has all the marks of having existed in a more primitive form which would better fit its own context. Taken in context, it fits the conditions of the time and could with ease be heard with the ears of the supposed listeners (a good test of primitive material). If we ask in what sense "the Mightier One" is to baptize with (to use the literal terms) holy wind and fire, we find an immediate answer in the metaphor from primitive agriculture which follows. One need only recall the process of threshing and winnowing carried on in Palestine in Jesus' time and in primitive areas ever since. The mixture of kernels and husks that resulted from crude methods of threshing was, when a steady breeze prevailed, tossed into the air. The result was *separation*. The lighter husks were carried farther away while the heavier grain fell nearby. It was then possible to gather the grain into the granary and to burn the useless chaff without danger to the product.

The image, then, is one of separation, resulting in preservation and destruction. The function of the fire is as clear as that of the wind. It is "unquenchable" (*asbestos*) because it burns until its purpose is accomplished, the burning up of all the "trash." The function of the wind is clearly to separate what is to be burned from what is to be preserved. The two go together in a perfectly natural combination, vivid and clear to the kind of audience supposed to be gathered by the Jordan. (We shall return to the other uses of the figure of fire, including the "river" of fire, later.) We can credit John the Baptist with this kind of preaching unless we are overanxious to make his message conform to the work of Christ, and we can very properly ask whether the text did not originally depend upon the expression "with wind and fire."

Theologically, the metaphor speaks of judgment and salvation. The coming of the expected "Mightier One" will result in a discrimination. By it those who are to be saved and those who are to be destroyed are separated from one another. The one is of use, the other useless. It is to be no partial or halfhearted operation. As the winnower "clears" (*diakatharai*) the threshing floor, dealing with all that is there, so will no one be exempt from the separation and the resulting preservation or destruction when the "Mightier One" appears. The salvation and judgment described are apocalyptic in their sudden intensity. The agency is personal ("his winnowing fork is in his hand"); see also, "The axe is laid to the root of the trees" (Matt. 3:10; Luke 3:9). The function of the one who is to come and the result of his coming could not be clearer. This is why he is "stronger," "the Mightier One," not because he is greater than John the Baptist—the phrases "after me" and "than I" are probably Christian modifications—but because the power to distinguish and to carry through the judgment belongs to him. The same metaphor probably lies behind the similitud> found at Mark 3:27‖Matt. 12:29, especially in the form given by Luke 11:21–22 where the "strong one" (*ho ischuros*) is overcome by a "stronger one" (*ischuroteros*). "When a strong man, fully armed, guards his own palace, his goods are in peace; but when one stronger than he assails him, and overcomes him . . ." Apart from this the concept does not appear in the Gospels.

So there arises the possibility that the words behind the terms common to Matt. 3:11 and Luke 3:16 were originally "he will baptize you with wind and fire," that is, he will come to exercise *judgment*. The word "baptize" occasions no surprise in this connection as it is common to this kind of discourse. There is no difficulty in assuming that "wind and fire" could become, in the Christian preaching and tradition, "holy spirit and fire," since Greek and Hebrew each contain a word that can be used for either "wind" or "spirit." In Mark 1:8, as we see from the parallels above, the fire has dropped out and John the Baptist is allowed to predict only that the one who is to come will baptize, now in a favorable sense, with (the Holy) Spirit. Thus it comes about that Mark is made to express not what John the Baptist taught about "the Mightier One" but what the church was teaching about Jesus who has become the Christ and to whom John now serves as forerunner. Still less is it true, as some writers in an unguarded moment say, that John foretold that *Jesus* would baptize with the Holy Spirit. The texts nowhere make this assertion. It is read into them by the Christian reader who identifies Jesus with the Coming One.

THE NATURE OF JOHN'S WORK

It now becomes possible to look at the passage again in relation to the work of John the Baptist. If we conceive his preaching to have been a warning about the advent of a "Mightier One," what preparation did he intend the people to make? This must take the form of understanding the people to ask, "What must we do to be sure, when the separation takes place, that we shall be 'saved'?" That is, "What is to prevent our being burned? How are we to be preserved?" To this, John had what we should call, in liturgical language, a "sacramental" answer. He invited the people to *turn* and to be baptized, to take a new attitude to their position and to mark their having done so by accepting baptism. They would, in effect, accept one baptism to avoid another. They would accept John's baptism in water to avoid the necessity of having to face the baptism of "the Mightier One"; to express their repentance rather than to undergo the judgment referred to in Matt. 3:7||Luke 3:7 as the "coming (or imminent) wrath."

The word "repentance" has come with us to have a moralistic sense. In Hebrew it is associated with a verb which means "to turn (around)." In Greek the verb translated is *metanoeō* which is, literally, "a change of mind." In the Q passage it is clear that action is involved, not merely a subjective attitude. The change of direction asked for is to be known by a changed set of actions called "fruit consistent with a change of mind" (Matt. 3:8||Luke 3:8). For John, then, a change of attitude was necessary and the mark of this new intention, the beginning of a new activity, was to submit to baptism. (The attempts by Matthew to equate John's teaching with that of Jesus, or by Luke to distinguish between John's and Jesus' preaching, are another story and need not concern us here.)

Such a call hardly creates in our mind a sensational impression, yet it might well have done so if proclaimed to what we must assume to have been the Baptist's immediate audience. They for the most part, if not entirely, were Jews (Matt. 3:5||Mark 1:5). They had, in the persons of their ancestors, already passed through the Red Sea and crossed the Jordan (as they were used to asserting at every Passover Seder). They had, therefore, already been "baptized." By virtue of their birth as Jews and by entering the covenant of circumcision they were already securely set among God's people. This reaction is spelled out in the Q account of John's preaching: "Do not presume to say to yourselves, 'We have Abraham as our father'" (Matt. 3:7–10‖Luke 3:7–9). We may ignore the editorial work that leads Matthew to direct this to the Pharisees and Sadducees (where Luke has "the multitudes"), because the warning itself is obviously applicable to *Jews as such*. They, John anticipates, will reject his baptism because they consider themselves children of Abraham. His answer is that they are sons to Abraham only by the initiative and grace of God (as Paul says in another way in Gal. 3:6 ff.; Rom., ch. 4). The same God could, if he chose, raise up sons out of the stones. He was not dependent upon them or helpless without them.

If this version of John's preaching is to be accepted as his, it says, in effect: "A new Israel is necessary; the present Israel is about to be judged. To be an Israelite by blood alone will be no protection; only by becoming anew a member of God's people, by taking a fresh direction and marking this by being baptized—as though you were not even Israelites to begin with —can you be saved." The very paradoxical nature of this demand, its startling character, argues for rather than against its genuineness as an account of John's work as Baptizer. How radical a demand it was can be seen when we consider that baptism was reserved in normal Jewish practice for proselytes, persons who needed to be circumcised and then to wash away their pagan defilements. It was paradoxical to hear that an Israelite, to face the coming judgment, must face it initially by treating himself as having no claim to God's favor simply by virtue of his birth. He must in a sense be reborn (though that is a later Christian mode of expression). He must start an entirely new life.

So paradoxical a demand would help us to understand several

things that follow. It would explain why Mark (followed in various ways by Matthew and Luke) has changed the message of John to make him virtually a Christian administering a "baptism of repentance for the remission of sins" and preaching a Coming One who would baptize with the Holy Spirit. From this have been largely removed the apocalyptic warnings (though the Spirit can be a feature of the *eschaton*) and the nature of John's baptism as essentially an "eschatological sacrament." It would explain, historically, why Jesus was attracted to John. This was a difficulty for the church with which it dealt in various ways, for example, by making John and Jesus relatives and having John, who was conceived earlier, respond even in the womb to Jesus, who was conceived later (Luke 1:41 f.). The relation of this to the inheritance of the promise in Genesis by Jacob, then by Joseph, neither of them the older sons or natural heirs, is obvious; see the oracle in Gen. 25:22–26 where the term "the stronger" is used. The possibility that a sect of followers of the Baptist existed in the early days of the church would explain the urgency of the need to subordinate John to Jesus. Finally, it would help us understand why it is that Josephus explains the action of Herod Antipas in arresting John on the ground that Herod feared an uprising—a natural reaction in those times and on the part of Herod in particular. These are Josephus' words in *Antiquities* XVIII.v.2:

> Some of the Jews thought that Herod's army had been destroyed by God as a just punishment for his treatment of John called the Baptist. . . . [Here Josephus describes John's work as a teaching of virtue and his baptism as a purification] Now when the rest crowded together to him (for they were greatly moved by hearing his words) Herod was afraid lest John's great influence over the people might lead to a revolt, for they seemed to be ready to do anything he advised. He therefore thought it much the better course to anticipate any rebellion that might arise from him by destroying him than be involved in difficulties through an actual revolution and then regret it. So John, a victim of Herod's suspicion, was sent to Machaerus . . . and there killed.

On historical grounds this explanation is much more acceptable than the bazaar (and bizarre) story retailed in Mark 6:17–29, so beloved of dramatists and moviemakers. It shows that there was something about John's movement which, from where Herod sat, looked incendiary in the inflammable situation of the times. We shall have occasion to refer to Herod's suspicions again in connection with Jesus (see Chapter Five, below). At the same time, Josephus does not bring to the surface the essentially corporate and Messianic nature of John's movement but compares it to that of the Essenes. As C. K. Barrett has said, "Josephus has taken away the keystone of the arch, the clue to the puzzle" (see "Notes to Chapter Two," par. 6).

It is quite possible that John had formerly had some connection with the Qumran community but whether that is so or not, the baptism of John and the practices of the sect by the Dead Sea may be compared in one respect which makes the "proselyte baptism" theory reasonable if none the less paradoxical. A new initiation by water into a newly constituted people of God is by no means impossible to conceive, since this was the means by which a probationer entered into the company of "the sons of light." The difference lay in the fact that at Qumran the initial immersion was followed by repeated ablutions as confirmation of their status among the purified. In the case of John and his followers the initial immersion seems to have been once for all and there is no evidence of successive washings.

The existence of the Qumran sect, with its representatives in the villages, adds to the likelihood that the hearers of John in the historical situation would hear his call as an invitation to treat themselves as newcomers to Israel. The populace was unlikely to be acquainted with the literature of baptism as such and there is good reason to think that at this time the connection in their minds would be with the reception of a proselyte. To "hear" John's message in this way would indeed be startling. For this very reason, it may well have served to create a sharp division between those who were not willing to un-people themselves and those who were willing to accept so grave a view of the situation that they were prepared, by a symbolic act, to do even that.

THE UNFULFILLED EXPECTATION

While this approach takes us behind the "Christianizing" factors in the accounts of John the Baptist, it brings into the open other difficulties. If the picture we have given of John's expectation of a Coming One is true, then we can only judge that promise to have fallen far short of fulfillment. It is an interesting testimony to a basic "integrity" in the groundwork of the Gospels that this unrealized expectation should still be apparent in the records. We shall notice this feature in other places. The Gospels present in large measure a deposit of the preaching of the gospel. This is indeed their purpose, but they have not so completely obscured traces of the original situation that we can no longer see on what their interpretative work is based. Even when (actually, *because*) the original material needed to be transposed its marks can often be discerned. The further difficulties have to do with Jesus rather than with John the Baptist and will be the subject of the next chapter.

We can still see from the Gospels that in fact the judgment by division and destruction did not come to Israel at that time in anything like the way the prophecy attributed to John would lead us to expect. There was no "Mightier One" who fulfilled this drastic function, and the Evangelists do not pretend otherwise. The story told by the Synoptic Gospels does not present the fulfillment in terms of John's expectation. The story bears upon it the clear marks of a reinterpretation of this hope—or dread—even to the extent of changing John into a preacher of the Christian gospel and a precursor (even an anticipator) of the One who did come. Whether the Gospels also present Jesus' own reinterpretation is another matter and one that cannot be answered on the basis of this section alone. The Synoptics do, however, take account of the assumption of a problem posed for John. Of this the parallel passages Matt. 11:2–6 and Luke 7:18–23 are singular examples.

There has been much debate whether this is a passage designed originally to provide a witness to Jesus, whether it is meant to imply that the Baptist had begun to see in Jesus what (ignoring John 1:29, 32, 36) he had not expected to see, or whether he was beginning to lose an original hope that Jesus was in some sense "the Mightier One." These three options do not make a decision possible because the question would have to be asked about several stages of the tradition at one time. It is worth noting the concern of both Matthew and Luke with "the works" of Christ. Matthew (ch. 11:2) says that it was because John had heard of this activity that he sent his inquiry. In both forms of the answer John is directed to look at the works. Without question this is the answer of the early church to questions about Jesus (however slightly it may be covered in the kerygma isolated from Paul or from summary passages in Acts) and it is crucial for Mark's picture of the Christ. Jesus is known to be the Christ by the resurrection from the dead, but this is made real and given content by the works he accomplished among men (Acts 10:39, "We are witnesses to all that he did"). In this pericope, then, the imprisoned John (and the hearer or reader of the Gospel) is expected to be able to frame his own answer on the basis of the reports about Jesus as these are understood in the light of Scripture. We note that Luke represents a continuing modification of the story ("the Lord" in Luke 7:19 and the demonstration of actual fulfillment of the prophecy "in that hour" in v. 21). Each version ends with the striking beatitude, "Blessed is he who takes no offense at me," a clear pointer to the problem that existed in the discrepancy between Jesus, treated as the fulfillment of John's expectation, and the actual facts.

If we put this against what we have suggested was most likely John's own preaching, the story has to be read to mean that from John's point of view Jesus had not manifested the strength to divide, to destroy, and to save which would qualify him to be "the Mightier One"—clearly a problem for the church. In short, it was not clear to John, and this must to some extent include the first Christians, what Jesus' relation was to the Coming One, if any relation existed at all. Neither could the question be answered by the church simply on the basis of Jesus' preresurrection activity. The story points to Jesus' works of power which are at the same time works of mercy and relates them to the Messianic passages of Isa. 29:18–19; 35:5–6; 61:1. This can only mean that the power was at work but that to be understood it must be seen as working itself out in terms of a different kind of expectation. (It is probably intentional on the part of the tradition that the quotation from Isa. 61:1 here in Matt. 11:5 and in Luke 4:18 f. stops short of the words, "and the day of vengeance of our God"). This reevaluation or element of "discontinuity" would account for the beatitude of Matt. 11:6 and Luke 7:23, for not only disappointment but repudiation is involved and has to be dealt with in early Christian apologetic. An expectation is being so radically modified that to accept the modification without rejecting the Modifier might be very difficult indeed. Yet the Synoptic Gospels make quite clear the consistent refusal of the Evangelists to treat Jesus' works of power as in any sense "signs," that is, as inescapable proofs of his authoritative relation to the *eschaton* or to the Final Judgment of God. Only against the demonic world was Jesus' power and authority exercised as power, naked and direct, and then by a word (e.g., Mark 1:25–27).

JESUS' FULFILLMENT OF ANOTHER EXPECTATION

In the present connection we can say that the early church, aware of an expectation which was represented by the Baptist's preaching (perhaps preserved among a sect of followers), was at pains to point out that Jesus had fulfilled another kind of expectation. To put it another way, Jesus was to be explained in terms of works of mercy and evangelism ("The poor have good news preached to them"). The preaching to the "poor" suggests that those who were not in a state of expectation could receive the works of mercy while those who were in expectation (which is certainly one meaning of "the poor") have the proclamation that their expectation is indeed in the process of fulfillment. It was in these ways that Jesus' "power" (and/or "authority") was manifested, not in apocalyptic judgment. For the church, Jesus was truly "the Mighty One," but his might, it was now seen, was exercised in a particular—one might say a peculiar—way *and it could not be pretended that it was exercised in any other way*. This exercise of power required for its antecedent hopes not those of John the Baptist but those which found expression in one strand of Isaiah. If Jesus was ever to exercise the other type of power (or use the same power in another way), he would do so at the Last Day when he appeared as the heavenly Son of Man or the Christ. It is not in the canonical but in the apocryphal gospels that we see the power used in his earthly life in a destructive and vengeful manner.

THE GOSPELS AND THE PARADOX

Here it is left unanswered whether this was also Jesus' own interpretation of his place in the scheme of things. We cannot suggest an answer before we have considered other passages in the Gospels. Part of the question had to be what Jesus thought of John the Baptist, and we can anticipate here two ways in which this was dealt with. The importance of the question for some is suggested by the comment in Mark 11:32|| Matt. 21:26||Luke 20:6, "For all held that John was a real prophet." This intends to explain that it was fear of the people which kept Jesus' opponents from denying that John's baptism was from heaven. Jesus is here represented as having placed them in a dilemma arising out of the whole situation. The nature of Jesus' authority posed the same kind of question as was posed by the baptism of John. Jesus' *exousia* (authority) was always the problem rather than his *dynamis* (power), for such power could be admitted, since it was not absolutely unique—a point the modern mind fails to grasp. If they could make no effective decision about John, it was not likely they would about Jesus, yet the decision must be their own, in no wise compelled.

Here again is reflected the problem of which we have been speaking. As well as in the passage Mark 11:27-33 and parallels just referred to, it is evident in another shape in Matt. 11:16-19||Luke 7:31-35, where the reluctance to come to a decision is depicted by the parable of the children at play. The parable discourse is connected with the answer to John's question by Matt. 11:7-15||Luke 7:24-28 (to which is added Luke's note of vs. 29-30). Here, without going into the difficult problems of Matt. 11:12||Luke 16:16, is one of the passages in which John is likened to the Elijah of Mal. 3:1; 4:5 who ushers in the terrible Day of the Lord. Of Elijah we shall have more to say later, but here it is to be noted that this equation of Elijah and John the Baptist has been read so that John becomes the forerunner of Jesus as Messiah rather than of the Day of the Lord. The process by which this came about can be seen at work in the passage which follows the story of the transfiguration, Mark 9:9-13||Matt. 17:9-13. If Elijah, according to Jesus' words here, has already come, this does not mean in the first instance that therefore Jesus is the Messiah whom the Baptist has come to announce. It means, rather, that nothing remains to be expected except the Day of the Lord itself. It has become, in these passages, tied up with the theory of the suffering of "the Son of Man," and it is Matthew who has added, by v. 13, the explicit identification with Elijah. We are here in the realm of Christian transposition, but enough has been said to indicate that the basic problem is the discrepancy between the tradition of John's preaching and the actuality of Jesus' work.

We may note, however, another way of dealing with the matter of unfulfilled expectation. Although Q, in the passage concerning John's question, presented a new way of thinking of the uses of Messianic power, the author of the Fourth Gospel seems to have found it necessary still to deal with John's type of expectation (showing that his concern with the Baptist problem is not really confined to those passages which speak directly of John the Baptist). The Gospel of John asserts that the expectation was fulfilled in Jesus but in the form of a "realized" and spiritualized eschatology or, in a term of Goguel's, "actualized." As C. F. D. Moule has pointed out, there is also a tendency to individualize (see "Notes to Chapter Two," par. 7). The expectation that the Baptist had both hoped for and dreaded had been fulfilled; the division had taken place by virtue of Christ's very presence on the plane of history. The destruction and salvation that were to result from that division would come to pass because, in fact, they were already in effect (e.g., John 3:18 f.; 5:22 ff.; 8:16, 47; 9:39). Jesus, in the Fourth Gospel, actually causes division (chs. 7:43; 9:16; 10:19). The difference is that this had happened (and would continue to happen through the Risen Lord) on the spiritual level. The hope had been fulfilled, but the letter of the hope was of little profit; the spirit was what gave it life (John 6:63).

So it came about that the difficulty involved was handled by the discovery that the paradox itself must be confronted. The Coming One who was to have judged by wind and fire was himself judged by worldly power and condemned to death. To that aspect we must finally come. In observing this we learn how truly the message of the early church arises out of the actual situation. Christians found and proclaimed that in Christ the power of the Coming One had been exercised, not for judgment but for cleansing, not for destruction but for healing, not for breaking up but for making whole. If it was sometimes inevitable that it should divide men, that was their choice; it was offered as a means of making them at one.

NOTES TO CHAPTER TWO

1. On the disturbing factor in Jesus, see treatment of the parable of the leaven in my *Jesus of the Parables*, pp. 70–75.

2. On the paradox, see Martin Dibelius, *Gospel Criticism and Christology* (London: Nicholson & Watson, Ltd., 1935, limited edition), pp. 24, 11. It is a term that has found increasing use in writings about the Gospels and Christology.

3. For the structural relation of the mention of John the Baptist in the Fourth Gospel Prologue, see J. A. T. Robinson, "The Relation of the Prologue to the Gospel of John," in *New Testament*

Studies, Vol. 9, No. 2 (1963), though the Bishop's conclusions are open to question.

4. The treatment of Mark 1:1–13 as introduction is well set out by R. H. Lightfoot, *The Gospel Message of St. Mark* (Oxford University Press, 1952).

5. In Mark 1:8 the use of the aorist, "I baptized," is not of great moment. Mark's term may be addressed to those already baptized, Matthew and Luke's present tense to those not yet baptized as well. (See Rudolf Bultmann, *Die Geschichte der synoptischen Tradition* [3. Auflage mit Ergänzungsheft, Göttingen, 1957], p. 111; English translation by John Marsh, *The History of the Synoptic Tradition* [Oxford: Basil Blackwell & Mott, Ltd., 1963], p. 111.)

6. For a treatment of the Spirit, see Eduard Schweizer, "*pneuma*" in Gerhard Kittel, ed., *Theologisches Wörterbuch zum Neuen Testament* (Stuttgart, 1933 ff.), hereafter referred to as "Kittel's *Wörterbuch*." An English translation in four volumes has reached the letter *N*, viz.: *Theological Dictionary of the New Testament*, tr. and ed. by G. W. Bromiley (Wm. B. Eerdmans Publishing Company, 1964–1967); hereafter referred to as "E.T." The "Spirit" article is translated in *Bible Key Words*, tr. and ed. by J. R. Coates and H. P. Kingdon (Harper & Brothers, 1961), Vol. III, pp. 28 f. A fuller treatment of the topic and the quotation may be found in C. K. Barrett, *The Holy Spirit and the Gospel Tradition* (London: S.P.C.K., 1954), p. 28.

7. On the individualizing tendency of John, see C. F. D. Moule, "The Individualism of the Fourth Gospel," in *Novum Testamentum*, 5, 1962.

Three

The Baptizer
Who Was Baptized
II. The Baptism of Jesus

The promise of John the Baptist was that a "Mightier One" would come and would baptize. The ensuing difficulty could not be handled quite so easily. The inescapable fact presented itself that Jesus did not baptize, whether with wind and fire or with Spirit, or in any other way. The Synoptists, at all events, do not represent him as having done so, another example of their special kind of integrity. The Fourth Gospel does seem to attribute to Jesus, before the arrest of John, a ministry of baptism in water (John 3:22, 26; 4:1 f.) but a note has been added to deny that Jesus himself baptized; his disciples alone did so (ch. 4:1–2). This is the testimony of the tradition in a double sense. Jesus did not baptize—during his lifetime. His followers did baptize—after his resurrection. No attempt is made to produce a fulfillment of John's announcement, and there can be, therefore, only interpretation. Even if, as some scholars suppose, Jesus and John worked together for a while (which is dependent on the Fourth Gospel and doubtful) this would not be strictly a fulfillment. It would be simply an extension and repetition of John's baptism.

THE PROBLEM IN THE NEW TESTAMENT

To find out how the difficulty was handled we have to go outside the Synoptic Gospels to the author of Acts, for the Evangelist Luke did not include the resolution of the problem in his Gospel. The intrusion of wind and fire marks the Day of Pentecost as described in Acts 2:1–4. We are not told of anything accomplished by the wind or by the fire. It is probably intended to be an allusion. The best explanation seems to be that wind and fire and Spirit are all needed to round out the fulfillment of the prophecy, the wind and fire to supply John's promise which stands behind Q, the Spirit to answer the promise taken over by Luke from Mark. This in itself would be a testimony to the preservation of the early tradition of John's preaching. That it was necessary to include it here may be a further if indirect piece of evidence that there were those, whether forming a sect or not, to whom this Baptist promise was still important.

There are many references in the Old Testament to wind and fire but none of them seem to be exactly relevant here. As Eduard Schweizer has said, "The Baptist's saying about one who would baptize with storm and fire could have been turned into history, and so could have determined the formulation of Acts ii, 2–3" (article, "*pneuma*," Kittel's *Wörterbuch;* E.T., p. 47). Now at last the expectation is realized, but it is the Jesus who has died and risen, the Christ who has ascended to the right hand of God, who baptizes with Holy Spirit. The initial instance of this new baptism is, for Luke alone and in this one passage, accomplished by a mighty wind and tongues of fire. They act as pointers to the fulfillment implied. The version of John's promise in Mark 1:8 has been made to conform to the postresurrection fact. This was the experience of the early Christians. They had indeed been baptized by Christ with the Holy Spirit, but by the glorified Christ from whom this gift now had come. The wind had become the gift of inspiration (as in John 20:22). The fire had become the flame of power (though not in these terms) which, in Acts, produced from "cloven tongues" charismatic gifts of speech and of power used, as in the passages from Isaiah, for speaking the message and for works of mercy. Like the wind of Ezek. 37:9 ff., the Spirit had brought life to a new Israel. The tragedy of Babel (Gen. 11:6 ff.) could be redeemed.

Here, then, is another example of development and of reinterpretation of the tradition within the New Testament itself. Out of the paradox of the One who was to come and who was to baptize, discovered in One who had come and had himself been baptized, statements of the Christian truth were created. It is from the Risen Lord that the baptism by Holy Spirit is given. After accepting the role of recipient, of the baptized, Jesus had been exalted to the role of Baptizer with the Holy Spirit by the resurrection from the dead (cf. Rom 1:4).

The later Christian fathers were aware of the paradox involved. We find, for example, in a *Prophetic Eclogue* attributed (perhaps dubiously) to Clement of Alexandria, a quotation of John's prophecy in which the word "holy" is not attached to *pneuma*. Whether the author intended "wind" or "spirit" is insignificant compared with the firmness of his next remark: "But with fire he baptized no-one." There follows a tradition from Heracleon which seems to indicate that the tradition of Pentecost was in some places followed at baptism by touching the ears of the baptized with fire. The author proceeds to connect the wind very clearly with its agricultural function as we have done above. (See *Propheticae Eclogae* xxv.)

Accompanying the paradox and its resolution, however, is a difficulty acutely felt by the early church which has left its mark on the gospel records. If we do not try to understand it, we miss some points that have a great deal to do with understanding the incipient Christology of the Gospels. It is part of the same question and must be stated, How could he who was sent to baptize be himself baptized? It might occur in the form of scruples about so telling the story of Jesus' baptism that he would appear to be made subordinate to John the Baptist. So told, it would provide aid to anything like a sect of Baptist followers. They would use the story to justify the following of John rather than that of Jesus. We notice in fact that there is a progressive tendency to avoid any real description of Jesus' immersion or even (apart from Mark) to state the fact. Luke does not state that John baptized Jesus and, in fact, has introduced a note about John's imprisonment before he describes Jesus' baptism—as if to imply that even though it was John's baptism that Jesus underwent, John himself was soon to disappear from the scene. Here, as so often in Luke, we find a transition to the Fourth Gospel made possible. The Fourth Gospel does not recount the baptism at all, only the testimony of John to the descent of the Spirit; the only purpose of John's baptizing was to reveal Jesus to Israel (John 1:31 f.).

THE PROBLEM OUTSIDE THE NEW TESTAMENT

After the New Testament tradition had been formed the Christian apocryphal literature and the fathers wrestled with the problem. The fact that the Synoptic Gospels testified to Jesus' submission to John's baptism was inescapable. The fathers accepted this as something to be justified; it could not be ignored or explained away. The problem became the more urgent with the development of movements that tended to deny the reality of Jesus' human life. The gospel accounts could not be ignored because they were used by Gnostics and others who, from a dualistic basis, opposed the gospel as the church and the Gospels proclaimed it.

Jerome has preserved from The Gospel According to the Hebrews the following piece of apologetic:

> Behold, the mother of the Lord and his brethren said unto him: John the Baptist is baptizing for the remission of sins; let us go and be baptized by him. He said to them: In what have I sinned that I should go and be baptized by him? Unless indeed this very word that I have spoken be in ignorance. (*Contra Pelagius* III.2; see M. R. James, *The Apocryphal New Testament* [London: Oxford University Press, 1924], p. 6.)

Clearly the problem met here is not anything that the writer knew of John's baptism other than what he found in the text of the Gospels. From the reference to "remission of sins" he is clearly acquainted with Mark 1:4 f., and parallels. It is Mark's view of John's baptism that occasions the trouble. Matthew's apologetic, in ch. 3:14 f., is easily understood as an attempt to explain the fact that Jesus was baptized, because it deals with Jesus' act in relation to John's message to the people rather than to an inner and personal sense of sin as the Gospel of the Hebrews does. In The Gospel of the Ebionites (quoted by Epiphanius) the approach is curiously distorted, since the words with which Jesus replies to John, "Let it be so now," occur not before his baptism but after it, as a response to John's request that Jesus baptize him (John) because John has seen a great light shining and heard a voice designating Jesus as Son. If there had been no authoritative tradition in the Gospels to control the development, there might have been more along this line.

The Gospels did not attempt to deny that Jesus was baptized and that is another mark of their integrity. Instead, the attempt was made to put the record in perspective. The method was to explain that John's real relationship to Jesus was that of forerunner. Once John was cast in this role his message could be reexpressed to announce the Christian message. To do so involved the change in the pronouns of the Old Testament testimony so that Jesus himself becomes "the Lord" whose way John (as Elijah) is to prepare (cf. Mark 1:2–4, "thy way . . . the way of the Lord," with Mal. 3:1, "the way before me"). Jesus is later made to testify on his own account, as we have seen, that John's place is subordinate to his own, and not to his alone, for John is subordinate to everyone who belongs to the new age (Matt. 11:10 f.‖Luke 7:27 f.). It will be necessary to deal with the issue of John as the Elijah who was to come and its connection with Jesus in another place (see Chapter Five, below).

At Matt. 3:14–15, John is made to demur at the prospect of baptizing Jesus and Jesus reassures him with the words, "Thus it is fitting for us to fulfill all righteousness." It is hard to tell what this meant to the Evangelist or to his readers. There are clear marks in the beginning of the Gospel that Jesus is cast in the role of Israel (called out of Egypt, passing through the waters, tempted to put God to the test in the wilderness, giving the law from a mountain: see Matt. 1:1; 2:15; 3:16; 4:1–10; 5:1 ff.). Passing through the waters of baptism to hear himself designated "Son" makes sense in this connection. The baptism is necessary to carry forward the recapitulation of Israel's experience in that of the Christ.

To say this, however, would leave untouched the actual fact that Jesus had been baptized (or had baptized himself under John's direction). The fathers were vividly aware of the implications. They were sensitive to the problem of individual sin arising from Jesus' own will. To them he was more and more thought of as having come, in the most literal sense, from God. Matthew's phrase suggests another possibility. "To fulfill all righteousness" may mean to share to the full the experience of the people. Corporate guilt may be a modern concept but it existed in the form of the prophetic projection of a nation guilty before God. In the nation as church, as covenant people, existed a "corporate personality." Without raising any question of Jesus' consciousness of sin or lack of it, the passage may here intend to show that Jesus placed himself among his people, aligning himself with John's view of the critical state of affairs, accepting the necessity that the people of Israel turn and be renewed. He himself, as a man of Israel, must share in this experience.

In following this line it is easy to introduce theological implications which are not stated. The purpose of Matt. 3:14 f., in the situation of the early church is clear enough. It offers a means of explaining Jesus' baptism which bypasses the problem of sin. At the same time it opens the way for the theological interpreter to speak of the identification of Jesus with his people. That identification once made must, if pursued to the end, lead to the final self-surrender of the cross. Whether the Gospels explicitly develop this thought is another question, yet it is a valid interpretation. The introduction of the theme of the "Suffering Servant of Yahweh" at this point is justified only by treating the received text of the baptism itself as the (only) original text. Whether it was in fact so is the next question.

THE MEANING OF JESUS' BAPTISM

The actual description of the baptism of Jesus is lacking in favor of events that took place as Jesus emerged from the water. Each of the Synoptists says that as Jesus came up from the Jordan the heavens were opened (some texts add to Matt. 3:16, "to him"). The Holy Spirit (Luke) or the Spirit of God (Matthew) as a dove descended upon Jesus. Mark uses more vivid language when he says that Jesus "saw the heavens split open." The eschatological overtones are clear. (The imagery may be found in The Testament of Judah 24:2: "And the heavens shall be opened to him, To pour out the spirit," or, in another text, "And the blessing of the Holy Father shall be poured down upon him.") A new stage in the relations of God with man is implied, though, at this stage, with one man only, with Jesus. With it we must eventually relate Mark 15:38 where, at the death of Jesus, the veil of the Temple is split in two (the same verb, *schizō*). What at the baptism was true for Jesus became, at the cross, true for all men through his life and death; there was no longer a barrier to access to God. The eschatological nature of the baptism is also implied in the descent of the Spirit, the gift of which is one of the marks in Jewish eschatology of the *eschaton* or of the Messianic Age (cf. Joel 2:28–32). The narratives, then, have an eschatological intention. The baptism becomes in a new sense an "eschatological sacrament."

The Evangelists intend to depict the baptism as the designation of Jesus to be in some sense the inaugurator of the new age. This becomes clear in the Voice from heaven addressed to and heard by Jesus in Mark and Luke (in the third person in Matthew). The accepted text of Matt. 3:17‖Mark 1:11‖ Luke 3:22 reads, "Thou art my Son, the Beloved; with thee I am well pleased." It suggests a combination of Ps. 2:7, in which the king is designated by the term "Son," and Isa. 42:1, the election of Yahweh's Servant: "Behold my servant, whom I uphold, my chosen, in whom my soul delights; I have put my Spirit upon him." Attempts have been made to show from this that Jesus from the first thought of himself as Messiah in terms of the Servant of Yahweh. This is an extremely precarious deduction, though it may be true of the intent of the Evangelists. Bultmann calls the narrative a "faith-legend" (*Die Geschichte*, p. 264; E.T., p. 248). The Marcan tradition, with which Matthew and Luke are here dealing, at least means to suggest more than one role for Jesus, or more than one way of thinking of Messiahship. It is not necessarily a clue to Jesus' own thinking which would involve, in any case, unnecessary "psychologizing" (cf. Bultmann). A better approach arises from the following considerations.

THE PROBLEM OF THE TEXT

In the Western text represented by Codex Bezae (D) and the Old Latin version (*it*), Luke 3:22 reads: "Thou art my Son; today have I begotten thee." This of course is a transcription of Ps. 2:7 without the modification introduced from Isa., ch. 42. Attempts have been made to explain this variant as assimilation, a sort of inevitable following of the quotation from the psalm once it was started. As the "more difficult" reading, however, it may require another explanation. While it is found in the Western text only of Luke it is a form frequently referred to in the baptism story by early Christian commentators and apologists, and they often do so without any indication that it is Luke they are quoting rather than the other Gospels.

It is desirable to examine some instances where this is the case because at this point the paradoxical nature of the Gospels confronts the writers in an instance which seems to have been more crucial than almost any other. In many other cases they find an allegorical treatment more readily possible and they are able to read the gospel accounts in a later sense without apparent difficulty. Here, however, the fact of the baptism was crucial, since it was, as said above, vulnerable to Gnostic

attack and it had to be dealt with most carefully. More clearly
here than anywhere except with the passion are we able to
illustrate from the early fathers examples of the theological
and apologetical problems that arose. Thus we are able to see
why the Western text of Luke was the more difficult text and
also to surmise that if it did not actually exist in texts other
than Luke it once, in that form, had a place in the tradition.
(The passages which illustrate this are listed in "Notes to
Chapter Three," par. 2.)

We note that in the fathers there is no special mention of
Luke as the source of the use of Ps. 2:7 in full and it is possible
that the writers are quoting from memory and automatically
turn to the words of the psalm. If this were so, it might also
mean that the Evangelists originally did the same. This is not
impossible, but it is surely difficult to explain the words of
Ps. 2:7 in the Gospel text as the revision of the reading found
in our present text: "Thou art my Son, the Beloved, in thee I
am well pleased." It would be much easier to assume that Ps.
2:7 had originally been in use in the gospel tradition (if not
in the Gospel texts) and that it was eventually modified to
avoid the difficulties that were bound to arise. When Christological debate began to develop, the verse from Ps. 2 was vulnerable to the arguments of Adoptionists, Gnostics, and anyone else who wished to assert that the man Jesus had been
raised to the status of Sonship. It was already beginning to
become, as we see from the fathers referred to in the notes, an
embarrassment to churchmen who were asserting the pre-
existence of Christ and were eventually to hold his eternal
generation.

It is likely that the earlier Christian writers, however, did
not find the assertion, "Thou art my Son; this day have I begotten thee," a difficulty. They would not if they understood
it to speak, not of Christ's nature, but only of his role, his
function. It was, we might say, a "predogmatic" statement
and hence "preheretical." A reference to Ps. 2 would, to Jewish
ears, be far from unexpected here. It is Messianic in the old
sense that it is an Enthronement Psalm, celebrating the appointment of the king and the inauguration of his reign. Ac-

cession is marked by his acceptance as God's "Son," that is, as the representative both of Israel and of God. It is Israel which, in the Old Testament, is predominantly referred to as God's "Son." If the king is sometimes so designated, it is because he stands before God as the embodiment of Israel, *the* Israelite, so to speak, and therefore, *the* Son.

Understood in this more original and more Jewish sense, the Voice at the baptism once marked for the tradition behind the Evangelists the appointment of Jesus as the representative Israelite, the chosen and designated bearer before God of Israel's function, like the king, the contact point through whom God exercises his rule among his chosen people. The heavens therefore are opened to the king's approach to God and, as king, he is anointed with Holy Spirit for his task. The same idea is expressed in The Testament of Judah xxiv.2, quoted above. In Ps. 2 the king is described as Yahweh's "anointed" (v. 2) and in v. 12 the nations are urged to come to terms with "the Son" in order that they may avoid his wrath.

Before comparing this with the expectation attributed to John the Baptist we might note that this interpretation is consistent and does not depend on later Christology. The quotations from the fathers move more and more in another world of thought. My colleague, Prof. Lloyd Patterson, has pointed out to me that there was not only a Christological interest in the text from Ps. 2 and in its change but an involvement from Justin on with the problem of the creation of the Logos. In the case of Methodius, for example, who is not very exact in his use of Scripture, the text used is determined by the form of Clement's exegesis which he is here refuting on a particular point. That Ps. 2 was not at first thought to be dangerous, in view of its Jewish application, is shown by its use elsewhere in the New Testament.

THE USE OF Ps. 2:7 ELSEWHERE IN THE NEW TESTAMENT

The distortion which first presents itself as a danger is that to assert Jesus' anointing as king at his baptism involves a view of his role which is not supported by the records of his life as interpreted by the canonical Evangelists. We would expect, therefore, that the use of Ps. 2 would become attached to Jesus' ascension and glorification at or after his crucifixion. This is exactly what we find elsewhere in the New Testament. The records of Jesus' life have not been conformed to this because they could not have been and still be true to the facts. There seem to be limits set to the extent to which the Evangelists are prepared to allow Jesus' life to become an "epiphany." As we shall see later in the case of the transfiguration, but not only there, such preresurrection epiphanies tend to be confined to Jesus' own experience or to a strictly closed circle of intimates; for the rest, the disclosure is implicit, to be seen only by the eyes of faith.

In Heb. 1:3, 5, the author is speaking of the Son sitting "at the right hand of the Majesty on high" and asks, "To what angel did God ever say, 'Thou art my Son, today I have begotten thee'?" In ch. 5:5 the author argues that Christ's heavenly high-priesthood comes from God, since he was "appointed by him who said to him, 'Thou art my Son, today I have begotten thee.'" With this he combines Ps. 110:4, an Old Testament passage that will come to our attention in a later chapter. An allusion back to his use of the quotation is made in Heb. 7:28.

The use of Ps. 2 in The Acts of the Apostles holds a similar interest. In Acts 13:16 ff. the author is giving what he conceives to have been Paul's sermon in the synagogue at Antioch of Pisidia. Paul describes Jesus as of David's posterity, and then tells of John's baptism and the death and resurrection of Jesus, to which he applies the words of Ps. 2:7 in vs. 32 f., "And we bring you the good news that what God promised to the fathers, this he has fulfilled to us their children in raising Jesus; as also it is written in the Second Psalm, 'Thou art my Son, today I have begotten thee.'" Here the recapitulation theme, embracing the Davidic role, comes to a climax in the resurrection to which the psalm is directly related, but it also summarizes the whole. In two other places Ps. 2 has a more direct application to the baptism. Acts, ch. 4, may embody a quite primitive Christology based either on a source or on the author's able reconstruction. In any case, in ch. 4:24 ff., a thanksgiving for the release of the apostles, the first two verses of the psalm are quoted ending with the words "against the Lord and against his Anointed." The prayer proceeds (v. 27), "For truly in this city there were gathered together against thy holy servant Jesus, whom thou didst anoint," which seems clearly an early reference to the use of this testimony in connection with the baptism. The same impression is gleaned from the speech attributed to Peter in Acts 10:37 f., "The word which was proclaimed throughout all Judea, beginning from Galilee after the baptism which John preached: how God anointed Jesus of Nazareth with the Holy Spirit and with power; how he went about doing good."

We see hints that it may be considered another aspect of that mode of presenting Jesus as the recapitulation of Israel's story to which we have already referred (particularly since Acts 13:22 brings the story down to David, though another tradition seems to be represented in Acts 7:45 and Heb. 4:8 which ends with Joshua). Matthew makes use of Scripture to underline his point and the first two chapters of Luke can be understood as modeled on Genesis. Yet it is not only in the beginning of the Gospels that the Evangelists took the Pentateuch as a model. Matthew's division of Jesus' ministry of teaching falls into five "books," and Luke's central section (chs. 9:51 to 18:14) has plausibly been shown to be patterned on Deuteronomy. If these structures were once more apparent to the early readers of the Gospels than they are to us, it may well have been because there was an ecclesiastical calendar interest involved. By way of the synagogue such an interest associated Old Testament readings with certain seasons and these afforded a background to the Christian tradition taught and preached in the primitive Christian gatherings (see "Notes to Chapter Three," par. 6).

As with Israel, so with Jesus. The Israel of old was delivered from Egypt, passed through the waters and, by this act of God's grace, was constituted God's Chosen Son, the Elect One, the Beloved. But in the wilderness Israel endured in its hardships the temptation to put God to the test by questioning his intentions and thereby questioning its own election or sonship (see the warning in Deut. 6:16). The brief Marcan reference to the wilderness testing of Jesus (1:12, 13) is expanded along the lines of Israel's testing in the desert by Matthew and Luke (though we shall see that even Mark's account is not without its Scriptural allusion). It is not easy thereafter in the Gospels to follow the theme with any clarity, probably for the reason that the recollected story of Jesus' career imposed its own patterns on the artificial scheme or to a large extent penetrated the patterns of the Evangelists, each of whom adopted his own peculiar approach.

Enough has been said to indicate that it is into this general pattern of recapitulation that the story of Jesus' baptism falls as it is presented in the Gospels. The fact that Jesus was baptized by John the Baptist is made to say (in Matthew) that Jesus willingly shared in this eschatological sacrament as one of the people of Israel, identifying himself with the nation. Most probably the tradition soon, for reasons we have suggested, made out of this a designation of Jesus as the Servant of Yahweh by application of words from Second Isaiah in order to modify Jesus' designation as King in the words of Ps. 2. The work of the primitive tradition is the designation of Jesus as the elect and anointed King, the inaugurator of God's reign, since, as for no other king, to him the heavens are opened and the Spirit of God has been given.

Bultmann, E. Schweizer, Lampe, Barrett, and others have observed the relative absence of the Holy Spirit in the Synoptic Gospels. It is only Luke who follows the thread of the gift of the Spirit in any explicit way. He speaks of Jesus' being "full of the Holy Spirit" (ch. 4:1) when he returned from his baptism, of his being "led by the Spirit for forty days" (vs. 1–2) when he is tempted (where Mark 1:12 has "drove him" and Matt. 4:1 "led up"), and in ch. 4:14 Luke speaks of Jesus' returning "in the power of the Spirit." Luke has also, quite deliberately, moved the story of Jesus' rejection at Nazareth from its place in Mark (and, in logic, from its reference to Jesus' previous works) to the forefront of Jesus' ministry. Thus, in Luke 4:16–21, Jesus presents himself and his work to his townsfolk as the fulfillment of Isa. 61:1–2 where the word "anointed" also occurs: "The Spirit of the Lord is upon me, because he has *anointed me* . . . to proclaim the acceptable year of the Lord."

To return to the story of the baptism, we notice two things. Jesus receives the Spirit, but it comes upon him in the form of a dove. The only impressive references to this rather odd form of objectification of the Spirit show that once again we are in the circle of thought which centers about the people of God. If the baptism was a designation of Jesus in his role in relation to the people, the dove would be the natural symbol. The other thing we notice is that though it is for his role that Jesus is anointed by the Spirit, neither here nor later in the Synoptic Gospels does the human Jesus dispense to others the Holy Spirit, nor does he baptize them with it. That is deferred until after the resurrection so that words almost similar to those of John the Baptist are put into the lips of the Risen Christ at Acts 1:5: "For John baptized with water, but before many days you shall be baptized with the Holy Spirit." This is referred to later by Peter in Acts 11:15 f.: "As I began to speak, the Holy Spirit fell on them just as on us at the beginning. And I remembered the word of the Lord, how he said, 'John baptized with water, but you shall be baptized with the Holy Spirit.'" It is necessary, as we see in Acts, ch. 1, to explain that the fulfillment of John's promise is to take place "before many days," and not, for instance, at a remote *eschaton*.

When we look for the meaning of the early tradition in its connection with Ps. 2 we find that this psalm threads its way through the literature of later Judaism, both canonical and extra-Biblical, and has left its mark on the writings of the Qumran sect. It has been clearly demonstrated also by Max-Alain Chevallier that in the great majority of places where

Ps. 2 is quoted or alluded to we also find Isa. 11:1–9 (see "Notes to Chapter Three," par. 8). This prophecy of "the Branch" describes the gifts which will result from the Spirit of God resting upon him and sets out his work as judgment. In addition to judging the poor with righteousness and the meek with equity, "he shall smite the earth with the rod of his mouth, and with the breath of his lips he shall slay the wicked" (Isa. 11:4). It was mentioned above that a baptism of fire might be related to the stream or river of fire of judgment such as is found, for instance, issuing from the throne of "the Ancient of Days" in Dan. 7:10. As we have also seen, the metaphor used by John the Baptist was an agricultural one in which wind and fire belong together. It seems necessary to associate the judgment by a stream of fire with the anointing of Jesus to be the Son-King for whom, in view of the close associations of Ps. 2 and Isa., ch. 11, this role would be natural.

This line of thought was not forgotten or ignored, but it was transformed. Its influence can be seen in the Johannine version of the giving of the Holy Spirit to the disciples by the Risen Christ. "And when he had said this, *he breathed on them* and said to them, 'Receive the Holy Spirit.'" (John 20:22.) There may be an echo here of Gen. 2:7 where God breathes into the man He has made of dust so that he becomes a living being; in that case the thought here would be associated with a new creation. Even so, this in itself is a transformation of the expectation that the Chosen and Anointed One on whom God's Spirit had come would judge the world, its empires and its peoples, with a fiery breath.

It is important to consider that not even in the Apocalypse (where the term "fire" occurs many more times than in any other book) is the now glorified Christ represented as sending forth a fiery breath or anything like a river of fire. Consider such passages as: eyes "like a flame of fire," (Rev. 1:13 f.; cf. chs. 2:18; 19:12); "lake of fire," (chs. 19:20; 20:10, 14 f.; 21:8); angels, (chs. 8:4; 10:1; 14:18; 16:8); the enemy (ch. 9:17; cf. ch. 13:13 with Luke 9:54 f.); fire from heaven (Rev. 11:5; 20:9). Also, Heb. 12:29 quoting Deut. 4:24; Heb. 10:26 f.;

II Peter 3:7. The nearest the New Testament ever comes to ascribing this judgment to Christ is in II Thess. 1:7 f., "When the Lord Jesus is revealed from heaven with his mighty angels in flaming fire, inflicting vengeance upon those who do not know God and upon those who do not obey the gospel of our Lord Jesus." Like the agricultural metaphor used by Matthew in his special material in ch. 13:40, 42, 50, concerning the tares, the judgment by fire is postponed to the end and is not in the hands of men, not even of the human Jesus (see "Notes to Chapter Three," par. 9). For the Christian, there is a trial by fire, testing either his works (I Cor. 3:13, 15) or his faith I Peter 1:7) but, as in Rev. 3:18, this metaphor is different, derived from the smelting operation which extracts pure metal from the ore in the fires of the goldsmiths and the silversmiths.

A further, often overlooked, connection with the Ps. 2 and Isa., ch. 11, line of thought is found in the brief reference in Mark to the temptation in the wilderness referred to above. Short as it is, its Scriptural nature is shown by its reference to Jesus having been "with the wild beasts" (Mark 1:12). In Isa. 11:6–9 the sign of the Messianic Kingdom is that the wild beasts have all become tame as the result of the work of "the Anointed One." In the echo of this in Mark the new Anointed One is caused by the Spirit to go into the wilds to battle with the beasts as, in this line of prophecy, would be necessary. The victory is implied by the words, "And the angels ministered to him." After this, Jesus can proclaim (Mark 1:14 f.): "The time is fulfilled, and the kingdom of God is at hand." Matthew and Luke have completely ignored this line of interpretation in favor, as suggested above, of a line more closely allied to the "recapitulation of Israel" theme.

We might here question Bultmann's comment, "For the connection of the Baptism with the Temptation is secondary; there is no inner connection between the consecration of the messianic king and the Temptation" (*Die Geschichte*, p. 270; E.T., p. 252). The baptism of Jesus is a "king-making saga" in brief, but it is such because of its inherently Old Testament connections. With the temptation story itself we shall deal later in its aspect as a retrospect of Jesus' career rather than an anticipation of it in psychological terms of a "call" (see Chapter Eight, below).

THE SON-KING PARADOX

We find again, then, in the case of the Synoptic accounts of the baptism, as with the accounts of the Baptist, a scarcely concealed paradox. The Son-King theme is, in itself, a modification of an earlier picture of judgment by "the Mightier One." It is also not literally fulfilled. This hope too had to be reinterpreted and the reinterpretation is again a clue to the process that produced the Gospels as we have them. As we shall see, to attribute to Jesus in his ministry anything like kingship was a project invariably of the wrong people and had to be treated as such (see Chapter Six). It was either ignored, rejected outright, or transformed. Neither does Jesus anywhere explicitly claim kingship for himself. Rather, "the new rule" inaugurated is expressed in what takes place when Jesus is present. The beholders are left, for the most part, to make their own deductions and are sometimes invited to do so. It ought to surprise us more than it does that the Evangelists so seldom use the theme of kingship. (It is, we might note, a theme increasingly difficult to interpret to a modern world from which kings have virtually disappeared.) The reality that the baptism expresses emerges only when the Risen Christ is exalted to the right hand of God and his kingship is bestowed or revealed in the heavenly sphere. This lies beyond suffering and death.

So that here again we have the paradox of a traditional usage applied by the tradition but quite significantly not carried through in what follows. If we return to the fact that Matthew and Luke have preserved clues to the original preaching of John the Baptist and they, with Mark, to a primitive way of understanding Jesus as the Son-King, we see also that they have found it necessary to reinterpret the expectations by making Jesus the fulfillment of other lines of hope. He does not come as Divider and Destroyer, nor as one searing the nations by the wrathful breath of his kingly mouth, but as himself baptized so that he is identified with the people (upon whom such wrath might fall) and thereupon is designated and anointed by God as his chosen representative. These words suggest the description found in the anonymous Epistle to Diognetus:

> But did He send him, as any man might suppose, for tyranny, fear, and terror? Indeed not. But in gentleness and meekness He sent him, as sending his son who is a king; He sent him as God, He sent him as man to men; as One who saves He sent, as using persuasion, not force; for force is not to be attributed to God. (Ch. 7:3–5, my translation.)

Here also we see the figure of kingship retained but denuded of its apocalyptic fury. In this early Christian writing a modification of the hope is set forth similar to the change of line which can be detected in the development of the gospel records.

JESUS AS THE ANOINTED ONE

As has been said, the early church in what is now called the kerygma (as this is reflected in later summary form in Acts 1:22; 4:25–27; 10:36–38) marked the work of John the Baptist and the baptism or "anointing" of Jesus (ch. 4:27) as the beginning of the gospel (which in fact are the words that stand at the head of Mark's Gospel). The term "the Anointed" might point to either a king or a priest, both of whom were anointed. It was possible to speak symbolically of prophets being anointed. There was no consistent and single demonstrable hope designated by the term. We have learned from the Dead Sea Scrolls that an anointed king and an anointed priest were both expected by the Qumran community. There is also a trace of an expected prophet which is dropped, perhaps because it was thought to have been fulfilled in their great leader. That movement was almost certainly at first a revolt against the merging of the offices of king and priest under the Hasmonaeans whose high priests too easily became kings with blood on their hands—and not the blood of the sacrifices. The term "Anointed One" is, at the outset of the Gospels, defined by the application of the words of Ps. 2 to Jesus. Quite apart from the Western text the words "This is my Son" would suggest this. The kind of anointing he is shown as receiving is that of the chosen King who, as King, is to be viewed as God's Son—not in any more "essential" sense as "Son."

The fact of baptism was preserved, paradoxical as it might appear, and the mode of interpretation was fluid. What the baptism scene unfolds is consonant only with certain lines of expectation. It becomes a forecast of the postresurrection or heavenly resolution, but it is not applied to the record of Jesus' life and work before his death—a point worth reiterating. It lies beneath the surface as a Christological presupposition, but on the surface the Gospels (and presumably Jesus) are concerned with the hope of the Kingdom of God rather than with its King; with God's lost sons rather than with his Chosen Son. Between the baptism and the resurrection-ascension lies a realm of "incognito," in itself a testimony that something besides dogma and cult has been at work and has exercised sufficient control to keep theological treatment within bounds.

In its turn this process has had its effect on the use of the Old Testament. It is true that the Old Testament is sometimes (notably in the passion story) drawn upon for the formation of incidents in the evangelical records. There appears also to have been a reverse action in which the facts of Jesus' life and the nature of his character, even as these were known in the context of the resurrection, along with the need to interpret these religiously, have enforced a selection among the available Old Testament figures and themes. Not everything was grist to the mills of the Evangelists, because their mills were of a particular kind.

So the fact of John's work and the fact of Jesus' having been baptized were preserved. As W. E. Bundy has said of this beginning, "The Synoptic writers show no reluctance in beginning with John. In fact they turn historical necessity into a dogmatic advantage" (see "Notes to Chapter Three," par. 10). The incident of the baptism is used to date that "kerygmatic" period, that piece of actual time in which the new revelation of God was found walking on two feet through a real countryside.

The paradox of "the Mightier One" who did not baptize with "wind and fire," and of the Son-King who did not breathe forth his wrath on the nations, but was himself baptized and became the victim of the wrath of men, compelled the Evangelists or the tradition they handled to find other means of expressing the work that Jesus actually did and the life he actually lived, not to speak of the death he actually died. In the end we can say that the event was not ignored because the need to deal with it produced a series of interpretations that became in themselves of more value than the record of the baptism itself. To contemplate this development is more fruitful than to concentrate on the process by which a desert prophet became the forerunner of the Christ. Actually, John's importance consists in his remaining what he was.

The process of interpreting the paradoxical event leads us ultimately to the Christian paradox that "the Mightier One" expresses his might in works of mercy, that the work of the Divider becomes instead the work of the Reconciler and, finally, that he who was to come to baptize came to be baptized first with water and then in his own blood. If the early church deferred the coming of the Messiah and of the Kingdom, it was basically because the Jesus they had known and then recollected, knew about and preached, did not fit the part required. The conceptions of Messiahship and Kingdom had to be revised but, more immediately to our purpose, Jesus could only fit the role required after he had been transfigured and could come, not from Galilee, but from heaven itself. The "scandal" and offense of the Christian faith was not faith in the Lord but the problem of a paradoxical human life which was only with difficulty fitted into the expectations and itself caused the expectations to be revised more than once.

It is out of a situation of fundamental paradox that the Christian gospel has emerged. The dynamic that produced the Gospels begins in the inescapable need to deal with a man in a certain situation, a series of events that had to be interpreted in the light of the experience which so soon issued from them. How this worked out in the Gospels will concern us as we see that this was not the only aspect of the paradox which needed interpretation.

NOTES TO CHAPTER THREE

1. On the opening of the heavens, J. W. Doeve has suggested that "this event took place before the throne of God" (*Jewish Hermeneutics in the Synoptic Gospels and Acts* [Assen: Royal Van Gorcum & Co., 1954], p. 160). If so, it would suggest that the Kingdom and the glory are here given to Jesus as to the "Son of Man" in Dan. 7:13 f. The cloud is missing but appears in the transfiguration story which anticipates the giving of glory to Christ after his death (see Chapter Five). To Jewish ears a reference to Ex. 4:22: "You shall say to Pharaoh, 'Thus says the LORD, Israel is my first-born son' " would not be unlikely. See, e.g., R. Eisler, *The Messiah Jesus and John the Baptist* (London: Krappe, 1931), p. 282, for the Rabbinic treatment of Ps. 2:7.

2. For the references in the fathers, see, for example: Justin Martyr, *Dialogue with Trypho* lxxxviii, and *Apology* lxvii; Irenaeus, *Adversus Haereses* I.xxi.2 (cf. I.vii.2), and for the view of Cerinthus and Irenaeus' refutation, *Adversus Haereses* I.xxvi.l, and III.ix.3 (cf. also xi.3; xvi.l; xvii.l); Epiphanius, in passages ascribed to The Gospel of the Ebionites, *Haereses* 30.13.7 f. (see translation by Edgar Hennecke, *New Testament Apocrypha*, ed. by Wilhelm Schneemelcher, English translation ed. by R. McL. Wilson [The Westminster Press, 1963], Vol. I, p. 157); Clement of Alexandria, *Paedagogue* I.vi.25.2; Lactantius, *The Divine Institutes* IV.xv; Methodius, *Symposium* VIII, Thecla, 9.

3. On Heb. 7:28, Fr. Barnabas Lindars very properly observes that the author has here appropriated to Jesus the dignities assigned in the Qumran texts to the two Messiahs, kingly and priestly. See his *New Testament Apologetic: The Doctrinal Significance of the Old Testament Quotations* (The Westminster Press, 1961), p. 142.

For C. S. C. Williams' views, see his *Alterations to the Text of the Synoptic Gospels and Acts* (London: Basil Blackwell & Mott, Ltd., 1952), p. 46. He, following LaGrange, thinks Justin may have been the first to combine the two texts. Fr. Lindars does not think either Ps. 2:7 or Isa. 42:1 were first applied to the baptism. The situation was probably fluid, varying in time and place. Note, however, Fr. Lindars' remark, p. 141, "There is also no hint here that our Lord is 'Son of God' in any other sense than the messianic psalm itself means by the expression."

4. B. S. Easton considered the textual and patristic evidence for the Western reading "an interesting array of testimony." He says, "The problem of the Western reading in v. 22 [Luke 3:22] is not settled by dismissing it from the text. It evidently had a wide circulation, and it must have had a very early origin to have held its ground so long. It may even represent the original (pre-Markan) form of the words, transmitted by oral or non-canonical written tradition" (*The Gospel According to St. Luke* [London: T. & T. Clark, 1926], pp. 42–43).

5. A study of Luke, chs. 1 to 2, as Genesis is found in M. D. Goulder and M. L. Sanderson, "St. Luke's Genesis" in *Journal of Theological Studies*, n.s., Vol. 8, No. 1 (1957), where, however, the points of connection become so many and detailed as to seem to call for an ingenuity beyond the ability of the ordinary hearer or reader of the Gospel. A recent study of the five major discourses in Matthew as Pentateuchal is found in W. D. Davies, *The Setting of the Sermon on the Mount* (London: Cambridge University Press, 1964), pp. 14 ff. For Luke's use of Deuteronomy, see the suggestions in C. F. Evans, "The Central Section of Luke's Gospel," in Nineham, ed., *Studies in the Gospels*.

6. For my article "Tabernacles in the Fourth Gospel and Mark," see *New Testament Studies*, Vol. 9, No. 2 (1963).

7. On the figure of the dove, see H. L. Strack and P. Billerbeck, *Kommentar zum Neuen Testament aus Talmud und Midrasch* (Munich: Beck, 1926), Vol. I, pp. 123–125.

8. For Chevallier's treatment, see Max-Alain Chevallier, *L'Esprit et le Messie dans le Bas-Judaisme et le Nouveau Testament* (Études d'histoire et de philosophie religieuses, No. 49; Paris, 1958).

9. On the "Wheat and Tares" and associated themes, see C. W. F. Smith, "The Mixed State of the Church in Matthew's Gospel," in *Journal of Biblical Literature*, Vol. 82, No. 2 (1963).

10. For W. E. Bundy's conclusions, see *Jesus and the First Three Gospels* (Harvard University Press, 1955), p. 41.

11. On the Christological development, consult O. Cullmann, *The Christology of the New Testament*, tr. by Shirley C. Guthrie and Charles A. M. Hall, rev. ed. (The New Testament Library, 1964), and more particularly R. H. Fuller, *The Foundations of New Testament Christology* (Charles Scribner's Sons, 1965). Difficulties exist both in using the titles extracted from their contexts and in the question of how far the distinctions between forms of Jewish and Hellenistic Christanity can be carried through.

Four

The Universal Savior
Who Was a
Provincial Preacher

Christianity is understood to be. a universal religion. This might be taken to mean that Christianity is to be found everywhere. In modern times that has become a fact to the extent that there is at least a bridgehead of the Christian cause in every part of the world. More properly it is taken to mean that Christianity is a religion designed for all people, capable of making its appeal to all men without distinction, and designed so to appeal. It is held that Jesus intended his work to be for all mankind and that he actually commissioned his disciples to "go into all the world and preach the gospel to the whole creation" (Mark 16:15; cf. Matt. 28:19). It is therefore something of a paradox to discover that, as far as an analysis of the Gospels goes, Jesus never conducted a mission outside of Israel and, far from encouraging his disciples to go to foreigners with his message, forbade them to go beyond Jewry. It is the paradox of the universal Christ who was a purely provincial preacher.

THE GENTILE MISSION AND THE GOSPELS

Here again we may find signs of that integrity in the Synoptic Gospels of which we spoke above. The Evangelists all wrote at a time when the Christian message had reached as far as Rome, the center of the civilized world of the West.

The Christian faith was established in the form of local churches in many centers around the Mediterranean. One might suppose there would be every temptation for the Gospels to show that Jesus himself initiated this movement and sought out converts from among the Gentiles. All of the Gospels reflect in language and point of view the life and work of the church in a Hellenistic culture, a testimony to the reality of the mission among the Gentiles as well as with the Jewish Diaspora.

Before Mark compiled his Gospel the struggle over the admission of Gentiles without their first having become Jews had been fought out. Paul in his letters has left a record of his part in the struggle. The Acts of the Apostles later suggests that although he was a pioneer, he was not alone in the cause of extension. Circumcision had become the New Testament symbol of the issue. By the time Matthew and Luke wrote, Christians had been excluded from the synagogue. Non-Jewish members of the church and predominantly Gentile Christian congregations were a fact. It would be surprising if this struggle had left no impress on the gospel tradition, and of course it has. Yet it is not a mark of the Gospels that stares one in the face. We have to be aware of the fact that the problem existed and needed its own apologetic before we detect clear signs of its influence. It is because we are so sure the effect is there that we can successfully look for it. Are the Gospels, then, in this case also true to the realities of Jesus' own time and situation? Are the elements in them that have to do with what is called "the Gentile mission" or with the universal propagation of the faith demonstrably developments and adaptations, a part of the kerygma rather than of the history of Jesus? In other words, is there here, as in the case of the baptism of Jesus, both continuity and discontinuity with what came before and what followed after?

GALILEE AND JERUSALEM

As we shall see (in Chapter Five, below) there lies behind the Gospel of Mark a shift from Galilee to Judea which seems to have been prompted in some way by a critical turn of events in the north. Was this crisis simply a critical point in the theological pattern of the Evangelist or did he see the possibilities of theological meaning in a turn of events that left their mark on the tradition?

Whether Jesus ever went to Jerusalem before the final journey, that is, went there as a prophet or preacher after his baptism by John, is irrelevant to Mark's plan. Visits to the capital before the baptism would be important only for Jesus' inner development which is not, in any case, a subject of the Evangelist. The single exception is in the Prologue to Luke (ch. 2:41–51) and this, like the rest of the first two chapters, has no noticeable effect on what follows.

Galilee was indeed the place where Jesus' mission was concentrated. The Gentile atmosphere of Galilee—made very explicit in Matt. 4:12–17—offered, we may suppose, more "openness" to the breakthrough in religious thinking and action which Jesus may have aimed at. But Galilee was not, any more than Jerusalem in the denouement, the place of triumph—not before the resurrection in any case. Galilee was, as we shall see, the place where Jesus was welcomed for the wrong reasons, followed in a direction he was not going, acclaimed in a role he did not propose to accept. For this reason, in the upshot, he must leave Galilee when the reaction there proved inevitable and irreversible (a fact disclosed by his dismissal of the crowds and by Peter's "confession"), and he must make clear in Judea his real intention. There alone the issue could come to a final resolution. Yet in the comparative openness of Galilee, free of the centripetal force of the cultic center of the Temple and the nationalistic pull of the Holy City, was offered a place where Israel could be called to be a witness to its true vocation. This, however, could not be achieved by a call to the nations, but only by winning Israel to exemplify and expand its own calling to stand before the world in its God-intended power to make him known.

It is upon this basis that the Evangelists have been understood to have erected a theological interpretation of Jesus' career and his relationship to various places and groups. We must understand that such theological interpretations are to a large extent the work of commentators and do not uniformly have a basis in the text or in a reasonable understanding of the text as it crystallized the tradition at the point when it was written down. We shall see that in this area the element of apologia involved in the *Sitz im Leben* of the early Christian fellowship may well be underestimated. In the case of the Gospel of Mark a great many consistent theological schemes have been attributed to the Evangelist, all of which have some basis in the text and so point to an aspect of the truth. They tend to present a logical theological (or explicitly Christological) objective. The weakness of each of them is the presence of the others, all equally consistent and logical, so that we may wonder whether the Evangelist was always that self-conscious or self-consistent, and whether he was not rather trying to preserve in the written Gospel a paradoxical feature present in the tradition in various, and not necessarily consistent, forms. This feature would arise from the necessity to be true in general to the original event while at the same time preserving the nature of its presentation as a Gospel, without which the event could, in his own time and for the church for which he wrote, have no significant meaning.

It becomes necessary, therefore, to review the tradition as Mark has shaped it in the form of Jesus' original mission, paying attention to the rather formal or sometimes casual editorial connecting links, but more to the inner form and content of the separate sections (pericopes) so linked and placed side by side and in sequence. In this way, Mark has at times deliberately introduced clues at one point which become useful at a later point (as we shall see farther on in this chapter).

Jesus' Mission in Mark

The Synoptic Gospels, then, assert that Jesus began his own mission in Galilee after John the Baptist had been put in prison by Herod. Mark 1:14 and Matt. 4:12 say this directly; Luke 3:19 f., by implication.

According to Mark, when Jesus returned to Galilee, he

proclaimed "the gospel of God" (ch. 1:14 f.), though Mark expresses this in Christian terms. If we ignore the formal Christian sense of "evangel" and read it in a more natural sense, it can be taken to say, "The time has come; the Kingdom of God is near; repent and believe this message." It was no less than the announcement of a new era in the dealings of God with men, the culmination of a long preparation, a new "dispensation" which required that men acknowledge the fact. They would respond by reorienting themselves ("repent," *metanoeō*), accept the new situation and act accordingly. How may such a message be authenticated? What evidence is there apart from the proclamation of the herald? To these questions Mark sets out to give an answer. One might further ask, By what means or to what audience was this message proclaimed?

For our present purpose, the last question is the important one. In editorial passages, Mark gives hints of Jesus' activity and they point to a method of working that underwent more than one change. It is Mark's view that the synagogue at Capernaum provided a strategic center because from there the report about Jesus spread all around Galilee (ch. 1:21–34). The remarkable story of Mark 1:32–38 shows that Jesus was not inclined to stay in one place no matter how successful his work there might be in attracting crowds. Summaries suggest the widening of the field and some interest from those outside of Galilee (vs. 39, 45; cf. ch. 3:7 f., 10). With this he associates the rise of opposition and thus early in his story it is made clear that Jesus' methods were responsible for his prompt fate (see chs. 2:1 to 3:6; 3:19–35). It was not Jesus' power (*dynamis*) to expel demons that aroused objection but his implied assumption of authority (*exousia*), since healings, exorcisms, message, and attitude to the common people were all of a piece.

JESUS' MISSION AND THE TWELVE

We come nearer our theme of the mission of the church when we note the action taken is to select ("call to him those he wished," Mark 3:13) and to "make a twelve." We shall understand this with less confusion about Mark's purpose and sources if we refrain from thinking of these twelve selected followers as the apostles of the Christian church—as Luke would have us think. It would be better if we did not think of them as "apostles" at all, since in only one case (ch. 6:30) does Mark use the noun and there it is of little significance for the later sense. He uses only the verb "to send" (*apostellō*). What the verb means when applied to the Twelve (ch. 3:14) is either that they represent Israel as the twelve tribes or that they are delegated to go to the twelve tribes, i.e., to all of Israel. The two senses do not necessarily exclude each other. *Shaliachim* was the official term in Judaism (though it may be later than the Gospels). They would be Jesus' "delegated agents" by virtue of being sent, representatives to Israel of (and from?) a new and differently constituted Israel. If this be so, we have to recall what was said above about the impact of John's baptism in relation to the nation. Before going on their delegated mission the Twelve are to be "with Jesus"; he is to be the source of their authority, instructions, and message. They are then sent to preach, to proclaim (the same word as in ch. 1:14) and, along with the proclamation, to offer proof of its validity by exorcising demons (ch. 3:14–15).

Jesus' Mission Extended by Opposition

In its original setting in Mark the creation of the Twelve and their mission to Israel can hardly be taken as anything but a response to the challenge to Jesus' work which Mark has so vividly represented as coming from all directions. The appointment may be taken as an affirmation of Jesus' purpose, marked by a great sense of urgency. Along with it goes a repudiation of family ties. Those who sit in a circle at his feet have now become his "brethren"—"those about him" (*tous peri auton*, ch. 3:34)—taking the place of "those who belong to him" (*hoi par' autou*, v. 21). The result is that here Mark has, with a few quick strokes, brought Jesus to the place where the appointment of the Twelve and his words about his brethren declare his independence from two of the most powerful of human ties and institutions—church and home. It is followed by an indication (picking up vs. 7, 9, where Jesus "withdraws" to the sea and a boat becomes his platform) that the tie with the local synagogue was broken. It is not Mark's purpose to make clear whether Jesus was in any sense expelled, whether he was no longer extended the privilege of speaking, or whether the move was prompted by his own initiative. The experience of the early church with the synagogue is here traced back to Jesus' own experience and reaction.

The "withdrawal" of ch. 3:7 becomes operative in ch. 4:1. We may speak now in Mark of a clearly independent mission of Jesus, existing without the endorsement of the religious authorities, with no support from his natural associates, divorced from the local religious institutions, and creating for itself a new method and new agents. There is little need to question this as a reasonable recollection rather than merely a reflection of the early church, since neither the use of parables nor, after a brief period (if we trust Luke), the existence of the Twelve played any controlling part in the church's situation.

The process is completed and rounded off in Mark by the climactic story of Jesus' rejection in his own town of Nazareth (ch. 6:1–6). The Nazareth story is so placed in Mark as to provide a climax to his theme. The fact that it was early taken to be a summary is shown by his using it at the end of the Galilean mission, whereas Luke uses it at the beginning. For Mark it serves as a "curtain scene" to complete one act before the next is introduced—the mission of the Twelve. For Luke, as we shall see, it serves as an opening scene to set the stage. In Mark, Jesus, unable to alert the people by working through the familiar and local institutions most ready to hand, widens his mission and it assumes a new urgency and intensity. But even so it is limited both as to space and time.

The Mission of the Twelve to Israel

At Mark 6:6 we turn from the mission of Jesus to the mission of the Twelve. While Jesus was going about in the surrounding townships he summoned the Twelve and began to send them out (*apostellein*) "two by two" (v. 7). Sending by twos suggests that they were sent as delegates of (a new) Israel rather than to Israel (see "Notes to Chapter Four," par. 6). For their mission he is said to have equipped them with power over "spirits of uncleanness" and given them a set of instructions or a charge (vs. 8 ff.).

At this point we find the mission of the Twelve of Jesus' time and the mission of the apostles of the primitive church—indeed of the church itself—sorely in need of disentangling if it can be done. Many commentators confuse their readers by not trying. Others criticize the text on the assumption that there was no historical mission of the Twelve to be disentangled. Insofar as it can be recovered we can find evidence of an original charge in the overriding sense of urgency that forms the basis for parts of the discourse. This controlling urgency is not to be found in the later instructions and is not appropriate to the situation of a postresurrection church aware of the probability that no cataclysmic event was likely at once to happen.

In Mark 6:8 ff. we find the Twelve sent on their mission stripped to the barest necessities (vs. 8–9). They are not to delay by "shopping around" for convenient lodgings but to stay at the first place willing to receive them (v. 10). They are, most significantly, sent to Israel. In fact, they are sent to mark out a new Israel, a new sacred territory. Where neither they themselves are received nor their message accepted they are to repudiate that place as part of the sacred soil by refusing to carry its dust to more potentially acceptable and sacred areas (v. 11). It is interesting that Epiphanius preserves these words from The Gospel of the Ebionites: "You, therefore, I will to be twelve apostles for a testimony unto [of] Israel."

The mission itself is briefly described in v. 12. The Twelve went out preaching to secure repentance. The original source may well have ended here. The exorcising of demons and the healing of the sick may perhaps have belonged to the charge but the same cannot be said for the phrase in v. 13, "anointed with oil many that were sick," since it ill comports with the equipment carried and with the urgency implied. It belongs to the more leisurely and settled methods of the primitive church (cf. James 5:13–16). Since Matthew concludes his discourse at ch. 11:1 without mention of this verse and Luke (ch. 9:6) omits this phrase, we detect here the possibility of more than one expansion. (We note that in Mark 6:12 there is no mention of baptism nor of the remission of sins.) In the other Evangelists, Mark has been conflated with Q and with material peculiar to each Evangelist. In the discrepancy about sandals and staff (Mark 6:9; cf. Matt. 10:10) we are also warned not to take Mark prima facie as the most primitive in its present form. Since the church's mission soon came to include a great deal beside a proclamation calling for a change of mind, it is likely that the original mission had a very limited character. A study of this much rewritten material indicates both that some account of Jesus' original charge existed in all the sources and that in them all it was early and progressively modified. An original mission of the Twelve would have been in purpose and planning a very different thing from the mission of the church and, notably, in the limited time available for it or allowed to it. The theory of Professor Munck that Paul was also pressed by a time limit, but of a somewhat different kind, suggests a carry-over of this original feature rather than otherwise (see "Notes to Chapter Four," par. 1).

We may note, by way of example, that Matt. 9:35, a summary of Jesus' preaching tour in Galilee, is a repetition of Matt. 4:23 but, unlike Mark 6:6, which drops the mention of synagogues in Mark 1:39, simply repeats the earlier note and is not fitted to a new situation. A possible change in the original situation is of less interest to Matthew than the interests dictated by his own time as the church faced a new synagogue. Matthew's next verse, "When he saw the crowds, he had compassion for them, because they were harassed and helpless, like sheep without a shepherd" (ch. 9:36), comes from another situation altogether, as we shall see when we discuss the "crisis" in Galilee (Chapter Five, below). As is apparent from Mark 6:34, the parallel to Matthew, the reference to sheep with no shepherd was originally connected with another development. The Q saying about the harvest in Matt. 9:37 f., used appropriately there, is used at Luke 10:2 in connection with another and peculiarly Lucan mission. It may or may not belong here and in its source apparently had no narrative connection—like most of the Q sayings. Matt. 10:1, however, is again parallel with Mark 6:7. Matthew has modified Mark by changing "the twelve" to "his twelve disciples" and then giving their names. Mark, more logically, has put the list of names in his account of the selection of the Twelve at ch. 3:13–19. Perhaps Matthew's interest in the names is less "historical" and more closely connected with the mission of the church than with the function of the Twelve in the critical days of Jesus. But, in a section not dependent on Mark, Matthew has an account much more compatible with the original situation in which the mission of the Twelve is clearly limited to Israel (Matt. 10:5): "Go nowhere among the Gentiles, and enter no town of the Samaritans, but go rather to the lost sheep of the house of Israel." This charge no doubt prompted the inclusion of the reference to shepherdless sheep here rather than in its Marcan position, a move that has given the image a more "Christian" meaning.

The terms of the charge as expressed in Matt. 10:5–7 conform to Jesus' proclamation as in Mark (but this cannot be said for Matt. 10:8). It is unlikely that these instructions so far were invented by the church. It is quite feasible to think of a charge limiting the mission of the Twelve to Israel as Jesus' own words—or words reflecting Jesus' own policy—preserved because at one stage for a brief time the mission of the church was confined to the Jews. It was preserved, presumably, in the Palestinian church. It does, however, belong to the primitive charge because it illuminates Mark 6:11 (which Matthew reproduces without the words "for a testimony against them" in ch 10:14) and testifies again to an urgent situation. The Twelve are to go only to Israel, not into

Samaritan cities nor into any of "the places frequented by Gentiles" (the Decapolis?). The delimitation of those to whom the Twelve are to go conforms to Mark's description of Jesus' situation and practice—directed not to the local religious leaders, not to the synagogue congregations, but to the outcasts, the untended, the "lost" sheep.

THE BASIS FOR A UNIVERSAL CLAIM

We shall see how this definite restriction by geography and religion paradoxically made it possible all the same to claim for Jesus a universal mission because upon his mission to the outcasts could be built that extension to all men without distinction, men of whom the common people of Israel were typical. Even so, it is likely that the term, "lost sheep of the house of Israel," intended to include all of Israel, Israel as a whole, rather than to narrow the mission by confining it to the outcasts any more than it was confined to "churchmen." The emphasis must be put on "the house of Israel" rather than upon "the lost sheep," even if it means that, from the point of view of Jesus' intention and the urgency involved, all Israelites alike were lost to the real cause (again we recall John the Baptist). The function of Israel in Jesus' view justified a mission to them alone, and upon this proper function of Israel could be built a universal claim.

The urgency and the inclusiveness, though a limited inclusiveness, permit me to refer to the suggestion I have made that this mission was prepared for by the original call of the first four disciples who are included in the list of the Twelve (cf. Mark 1:16, 19 and 3:16 f.). The term "fishers of men" is used in Mark 1:16 and on the basis of evidence from Qumran this could convey its original and Old Testament sense of bringing the people together for the eschatological day and its judgment. Here is reflected the urgency in the accounts of John the Baptist and an explanation of the urgency recoverable in traces of the original mission charge. For Jesus, the Kingdom is near and there is no time to spare; no time, for instance, to parley with the synagogue, but only to proclaim the message to all Israel, to send the Twelve for this purpose on a "crash program" of warning and invitation. Their commission as "apostles" would come to an end when they had accomplished this task.

THE MODIFICATION OF THE MISSION

The modifications of the mission charge which have progressively changed its nature can be seen to belong to quite another time and their admonitions to have quite another purpose. Yet the presence of the charge in all the sources and its modifications in them all is testimony to an original situation that passed away with Jesus, leaving the church a no less compelling but quite different work. Underlying the records is a consistency that has become obscured under the pressure of persecution and a wider conception of the task. Before there could be justification of a mission to Gentiles or men could be commissioned to preach a universal gospel there had to be adjustment. It is a further proof of the "integrity" of the Gospels in dealing with a paradox that the mission was erected on the basis of an undertaking of Jesus that was no longer relevant and that the commission to go to all the world is attributed only to the Risen Lord.

Matthew's long charge in ch. 10 is an adaptation designed to meet the situation of his own time and place—the conflict of the later church with the later synagogue. It is compiled by importing from the apocalyptic section of the gospel tradition (Mark 13:9 ff.; Luke 21:12 ff.) discourse elements that have to do with the mission and missionaries of the church in a time of persecution. We can see adaptation at work because there appears in Mark 13:10 the difficult expression, "And the gospel must first be preached to all nations." Here we have a trace of the problem that faced the church when the end had not come (for instance, with the fall of Jerusalem) and one of the reasons offered was the need to make the gospel known to all people. In the light of the mission charge given by the resurrected Christ the end could not come until that commission had in some way (perhaps not literally) been fulfilled. There is, however, a question of interpretation of the Mark passage involved, including its punctuation (see "Notes to Chapter Four," par. 8).

Matthew had used as a transition another passage from Q (ch. 9:37 f.; Luke 10:2) referred to above, "Then he said to his disciples, 'The harvest is plentiful, but the laborers are few; pray therefore the Lord of the harvest to send out laborers into his harvest.' " The harvest is a familiar eschatological metaphor. It is used in this sense in authentic parables of Jesus (Mark 4:8, 29) but in Matthew's special material (ch. 13:30, 39) it has been given a specifically apocalyptic development, so that the angels have become the wielders of the sickle (cf. Rev. 14:15 f., and see "Notes to Chapter Four," par. 9). In the Fourth Gospel we find the figure of the available harvest has retained its eschatological tone, though, characteristically, it is now a "realized echatology." The harvest is no longer future (as when men say "four months"; cf. Amos 4:7) but an immediate possibility because of Jesus' presence ("I tell you, . . . see how the fields are already white for harvest," John 4:35). Interest in the original mission has diminished sharply. Yet its traces have unmistakably survived.

THE MISSION AND THE APOSTLES

Some critics have been so engrossed by the overlay and read the Gospels so consistently from the postresurrection point of view that they reject the idea that there was such a mission, a viewpoint that is sometimes inconsistent, particularly so when the ground is taken that the Twelve are "the Apostles" of the later church, for example, that "the Twelve went out, the Apostles returned." Is this an accurate view? After the *office* of apostle developed we would expect any more temporary and functional view to disappear. As said above, in Mark the noun (in the plural, *apostoloi*) is used only once (Mark 6:30), at the return of the Twelve from their mission. They do not necessarily come back as a group. Mark says, literally, "the sent-ones gathered to Jesus," that is, they came together where Jesus was. The noun here may possibly be an assimilation to Luke 9:10, but in any case it means no more than that "those who were sent out returned." Thereafter they are absorbed again under the general term "disciples." In Mark they have no permanent office and in this respect, if in no other, are like the *shaliachim* of the Jewish synagogue commissioned as agents for a particular mission and discharged when the assignment is over. In part the rewriting of the mission charge must be attributed to the different nature of the apostolate in the primitive church and the prominence given to it by Luke. Within the New Testament the tendency for charismatic functions to become "offices" is already apparent.

Luke and Matthew have preserved, each in different form, a Q saying about the Twelve which again indicates their eschatological significance. In Luke 22:28–30 it is part of the discourse at the Last Supper (another transition to the Fourth Gospel). The Twelve are "those who have continued with me in my trials" and they are to share in the Kingdom "appointed" for Christ which is described in terms of the Messianic Banquet. The connection we have stressed between the Twelve and Israel here becomes clear, though it is eschatological rather than ecclesiastical, "that you may . . . sit on thrones judging the twelve tribes of Israel." In Matt. 19:28 it appears as an addition to the discussion in Mark 10:28 ff., as a compensation for those who have left all to follow Christ. The eschatological setting is emphasized by Matthew's, "in the new world" or, rather, in the "regeneration" (palingenesis). When "the Son of man" is seated on his throne, the Twelve will share his judgment and his rule over Israel. The words about the thrones and judging the twelve tribes are common to both Evangelists. The function of the Twelve here is not associated with the mission to the Gentiles, but, as with the call to the original four and with the charge to the Twelve on their mission, with Israel and the *eschaton*. The language used in Matthew's version points to attempts to rewrite it, but the content rather than the form suggests an early and soon superseded viewpoint.

Doubts about the number of the Twelve do not arise so readily as they do over their names during Jesus' time. After the resurrection, and more particularly after Luke's Pentecost, even the limitation in number is no longer certain and becomes less relevant, except that it has become a way of thinking. As a feature of Jesus' own mission a band of twelve has every reason to be considered authentic both in their correspondence to the twelve tribes and in their temporary and very urgent mission. After the one reference in Mark (see again ch. 6) we read no more of "apostles" and, indeed, they are never again sent out in Jesus' human lifetime. Here again we see an underlying discontinuity that has been worked over until it has become the basis for a continuity conformable to the new situation of the post-Pentecostal church (e.g., in Luke-Acts). The possible basis for continuity is that some of the original Twelve became also "apostles" in the church, notably those who figure prominently both in the Synoptics and elsewhere—Peter, James, and John (Andrew of the original four does not figure outside of Mark 1:16, 29 and ch. 13:3 until he acquires new prominence in the Fourth Gospel, John 1:40, 44; 6:8; 12:22).

There is no reason to think that on their original mission the Twelve encountered active opposition or persecution. Rather, there is reason, as we shall see, to think they encountered success of a kind. We might expect them to encounter disbelief and indifference. Both with regard to indifference and persecution Matt. 10:24 applies, "A disciple is not above his teacher, nor a servant above his master." What Jesus experienced his agents could hardly avoid, the more clearly if they were known to be his agents and to repeat his message. As active opposition from the (reconstituted) synagogue arose after A.D. 70, it became natural to offer encouragement and even to lay down rules, practical and spiritual, for those who were likely to suffer. The "witnesses" or missionaries of the church (cf. Luke 1:1–4) could not expect to be exempt from the enmity that had engulfed Jesus. In due time the state, as also in the case of Jesus, was involved and this is reflected in Mark. Jesus' crucifixion by the Romans became a source of courage for those who could expect to be like their Lord, and faith in his resurrection their hope and stay. They came to know that he was, indeed, "the first-born among many brethren."

THE EXTENSION OF THE MISSION

We can leave neither the mission nor the Twelve without noting that this number becomes inadequate to represent in the gospel the basis for a universal mission undertaken by the church. The mission of the Seventy again suggests an original feature that needed to be modified. Just as in Num. 11:16–25 Yahweh took of the spirit he had given Moses and put it upon seventy chosen elders, so in Luke 10:1, Jesus "appointed seventy others and sent them." The number seventy ("seventy-two" in some texts) represented not only the number of the Sanhedrin but was figurative of the "peoples" or nations of the non-Jewish world (see, e.g., the seventy bullocks offered at the Feast of Tabernacles for the nations in my article "No Time for Figs" ["Notes to Chapter Four," par. 12]). In addition, those scholars are probably right who see in the doublet of the feeding of the five thousand in Mark 8:1–10 a symbol of the Gentile mission. The feeding of the four thousand with its seven baskets left over, in contrast with the twelve baskets of the earlier account, suggests a claim that Jesus can provide for the Gentiles as well as for all of Israel.

To the introduction of the Seventy, Luke has added the passage from Q, referred to above, about the harvest. It forms another of those transitions to the Johannine understanding of a figure which is so characteristic of John's treatment of the sources. Here, then, is one quite conscious attempt on Luke's part to extend the mission from the original call to Israel to a universal call. He has used material associated in Mark with the mission of the Twelve, but we find in Luke 10:1 also his characteristic designation of Jesus as "Lord." The fact that the seventy disciples were sent ahead into the places where Jesus was to come does not really fit what follows and can be better associated with the journey motif which we shall note below.

One of the clearest testimonies to the change from the historic mission of Jesus to new conditions which followed the resurrection is given when Luke adds to the Last Supper tradition a brief discourse in ch. 22:35–38. Here Jesus is made in v. 35 to refer back to the mission during his ministry, in this case specifically to the charge to the Seventy (ch. 10:4), which was placed significantly on the road to Jerusalem, the way to the cross. Jesus asks whether, under those circumstances of speed which required restricted equipment, they then lacked anything? Then he says, "But now . . ." The "now" obviously refers to the time after the resurrection. It anticipates a time of persecution, when a sword will be of more importance than a mantle; a more prolonged undertaking, when a purse and bag will be necessary resources. The critical event that is to produce the change is the crucifixion (v. 37). The enigmatic saying about the two swords (v. 38) need not here concern us, except that it also points to a new situation in which the mission of the church will be conducted under severely changed conditions.

Before we proceed we must mention again that the scene in the synagogue at Nazareth has been used by Luke to introduce Jesus' Galilean ministry (ch. 4:16–30). Here we see Luke's wider interest entering. Since no prophet is acceptable in his own country, there is the implied warning or promise (depending on the hearer or reader) that there are others quite outside of Israel who will respond—as Elijah went to the widow of Zarephath and Elisha treated Naaman the Syrian (vs. 25–27). Thus at the very outset Luke introduces the theme of the wider mission.

Luke's tendency is to eliminate or at least to obscure any mention of Jesus' work outside of Galilee (he has omitted from Mark 7:24–30∥Matt. 15:21–28 the story about the woman of Syrophoenicia as well as the healing of the blind at Bethsaida, Mark 8:22–26). Is this because he knows that the Gentile mission was not a part of Jesus' original work and not only because he has other means of providing a basis for a theme so important to his purpose? One of his methods, and again it is a point of transition to the Fourth Gospel, is his emphasis on Samaria and Samaritans. In The Acts of the Apostles the same author's scheme of expansion of the faith from Jerusalem (Acts 1:8) names Samaria as the first place beyond Judea to which the witness is to be carried, and it is there that the gospel wins its first non-Jewish converts (ch. 8:4–8, 14–17, notably by one of "the Seven"). In Luke's Gospel we find three references.

Luke's "central section" is constructed formally on the basis of a journey from Galilee to Jerusalem (to the passion). It begins in ch. 9:51 ff. with an apparent intention to go through Samaria, but opposition is encountered when the messengers attempt to secure hospitality. Jesus' rebuke when the disciples wish to bring punishment on the villagers indicates mercy for Samaritans (see the addition in some ancient texts to v. 55, "You do not know what manner of spirit you are of").

Within the same section are two other references to Samaritans, neither of which needs to be located in Samaria. In ch. 17:11 ff. ten lepers are cleansed and one of them is a Samaritan, the only one who returned to give thanks to Jesus. Here is another indication of the responsiveness of a non-Israelite which perhaps takes the place of the Syrophoenician woman. The other Samaritan is well known, since he occurs in the parable of the good Samaritan. Here he is made an example, superior to priest or Levite, of those who though "without the law live by the law." He understands (in Luke's setting of the parable, ch. 10:25–37) that the command to love one's neighbor depends upon the recognition that one must be or act as a neighbor (see "Notes to Chapter Four," par. 13). Critics have suggested that Luke has introduced the Samaritan into the original parable as the third and responsive character where one would naturally expect, after priest and Levite, an Israelite, that is, a layman. This may well be so and if the Samaritan is Luke's variation, the point is strengthened.

We can detect throughout Luke his broadening of the base of the mission without doing violence to the actualities of Jesus' time. His overall interest in the outcasts of society, significantly including women, points in the same direction. A study of his construction of the three parables in ch. 15 is an indication. We can see from the more original form of the parable of the lost sheep in Matt. 18:12–14 (though there the setting and application are also secondary) that he has adapted this to the parable of the lost coin—which may also have a Lucan application—so that both speak of the joy over one sinner who repents, affording potentially a universal base for the Gospel. The mission of the church has also influenced Luke's treatment of the call of Peter (ch. 5:1–11). Here there remain traces of Mark's account but the structure and motivation are much more akin to the resurrection story of John 21:1–14. The theme is the mission of the church under the figure of fishing, an enterprise that can be carried on with success only in the presence of the Risen Christ. It leads to the recognition of Jesus' true status. We noted that the term "fishers of men" in Mark 1:16 has been changed to "henceforth you will be catching men" in Luke 5:10 with its much more generalized connotations (see "Notes to Chapter One," par. 5).

JESUS AND NON-JEWISH ENCOUNTERS

In two places in the Gospels, Jesus encounters non-Jewish individuals. In a story from Mark 7:24 ff., partly paralleled in Matt. 15:21 ff. (so perhaps from another source) Jesus goes outside Jewry and is met by a woman who is carefully and definitely described as non-Jewish. It is evident that Jesus has not come to preach to the inhabitants, and the initiative comes from the woman. Jesus asserts that it is not proper (to use the then current vernacular) to give the "children's bread" to "dogs." This test of the woman is met by her willingness to accept the healing of her daughter as an act of grace, as an overflow of God's mercy to Israel. Once again we have the emphasis on the responsiveness of a non-Jew with its implications for the extension of the gospel.

The same theme is even more striking in a passage in which the dialogue is from Q though both Matthew and Luke have supplied their own introductions and conclusions (Matt. 8:5 ff.; Luke 7:1 ff.). This tells of Jesus' contact with a "centurion" who, whether of the Roman army or of Herod's, is clearly a non-Jew. Again the initiative comes from the Gentile (according to Luke a "God-fearer"). His request for the healing of his son or slave is granted because he reveals an insight Jesus has not found among his own people—the comprehension that Jesus is not acting on his own authority any more than the centurion does. Just as the officer's power to command depends upon his obedience to those above him so, it is implied, is Jesus' power to heal based upon his responsiveness to Authority. The unsought response of the centurion (prompted by Jesus' willingness to go to his house), like that of the woman, is an indication of a field that waits only to be cultivated for there to be a harvest without limit.

Though Jesus nowhere goes on a mission outside of Israel and does not preach to other than his own people, the two stories have within them the basis for the extension of his work. In each case Jesus does not see the person who is to be treated. In each case he heals from a distance by his word alone, not by personal contact. This is a perfect symbol of the Gentile mission. The Gentiles, as Paul found, were open to the gospel, and Christ could extend his work to them through his word and at a distance not only of space but in time. Matthew has taken the occasion of the centurion's response to add another Q saying (Matt. 8:11–12), "I tell you, many will come from east and west and sit at table with Abraham, Isaac, and Jacob in the kingdom of heaven." Luke has used this Q statement in another connection in his "journey" section at ch. 13:28 f. The saying, which is both warning and promise, is further implemented in the parable of the banquet which makes it clear that when the originally invited guests defer attendance out of certainty of their secure right to come eventually, others will be invited to take their place (Matt. 22:1 ff., Luke 14:16 ff.; cf. Matt. 3:9 || Luke 3:8) The Lucan form of this (which I consider more original) offers the possibility of interpreting it as the extension of the gospel to the outside world (see "Notes to Chapter Four," par. 13, and to Chapter Five).

As we noted above, in Mark the presence of outsiders is mentioned but not until Jesus' "withdrawal" in ch. 3:7 f. This is not antecedently unlikely but may also be an intentional modification implying the extension to others after the virtual failure of official Galilee to respond. It is possible that Mark intended the story of the demoniac healed in Gerasa (Gedara in Matthew) to be an incursion into Gentile territory (Mark 5:1 ff.||Matt. 8:28 ff.||Luke 8:26 ff.). This bears little weight, since the story is often treated as an addition to Mark and in any case the uncertainty of the text from early times shows that the geographical references are obscure and unreliable.

We might add to this examination the legend of the coming of the Magi from the East to worship the infant Jesus in Matt. 2:1 ff., but this is a purely symbolical story which of itself reveals the need to assert the claim that Jesus was intended in God's purpose to receive the homage of the whole world. Another symbolical story is found in all the Gospels, though differently placed and differently treated by the Evangelists. The story of the anointing of Jesus will be more properly discussed in a later chapter except for the phrase, "I say to you, wherever the gospel is preached in the whole world, what she has done will be told in memory of her," in Mark 14:9; Matt. 26:13. In Luke 7:36 ff. and John 12:1 ff. the story has quite different emphases. It may well be questioned whether the sentence is germane to Mark's purpose. It is clearly a late stage in the development of a story that has been much worked over and can hardly be attributed to Jesus in its present form (see "Notes to Chapter Four," par. 14).

THE PARADOX OF THE MISSION

An examination of the Gospels, including an understanding of their internal contexts (which reveals the purpose of each Evangelist), would seem to indicate that interest in people beyond the Jews and a mission to all mankind is an interest of the postresurrection church without explicit basis in Jesus' work or teaching .The underlying tenor of the Gospel sources is that Jesus' work was originally occasioned by an eschatological expectation and was limited to Israel. It would seem that the universal appeal only gradually became a part of the proclamation itself and the Gospels show it in process of becoming this. The attempts to supply a basis for a wider mission underline that it is a development.

Are we, then, to say that there was no basis in Jesus' work for the extension of the gospel? A basis in the authentic recollections of Jesus is certainly to be found in the form of a prolongation by reflection on his own work and teaching. In the introduction to Luke's Gospel the emphasis is at first on the future relation of both Jesus and John to Israel, but in the Nunc Dimittis, or Song of Simeon, in Luke 2:32 we come across the words, "A light for revelation to the Gentiles," recalling Isa. 49:6 where it is an extension of the Servant of Yahweh's initial work with Israel.

The church, as it came to reflect upon Jesus' fate in the light of the resurrection and to interpret it in terms of the Old Testament, found inherent in his work and sayings that universalism which had marked one stream of Israel's tradition (see Luke 24:46–49). We have seen it introduced in the rejection of the claim to be "sons of Abraham" attributed to John the Baptist and reflected constantly in Jesus' teaching, particularly in the parables. There is an undoubted base for this interpretation implicit in the teaching of Jesus. It was possible to interpret Jesus' very concentration on Israel as a means of implementing God's intention to save all mankind through Christ. Israel was designed in more than one strand of Old Testament tradition to be "a light to the Gentiles" and through Israel "all the families of the earth will be blessed" (Gen. 12:3 from J, etc.). Many sayings of Jesus must be understood as addressed to the people of Israel as such before they became adapted to a more individual and universal application. Apart from its purpose to be the means of revelation to the world, Israel has within itself no claim on God's special care. The people of Nineveh to whom Jonah was so reluctant to go and the Queen of the South will, in the resurrection, rise up to testify against an Israel that will not believe without indubitable signs (Luke 11:30 f.; Matt. 12:39 ff., though Matthew has applied the sign of Jonah to the resurrection). Jesus' insistence on a higher duty for Israel is found, for example, in the contrast he makes between his hearers and the Gentiles in Matt. 5:47 and 6:32. Mark, as we shall see, has stressed even the function of the Temple to provide a place for Gentile worship by his completion of the quotation from Isa. 56:7, "My house shall be called a house of prayer," with the words, "for all the nations" (Mark 11:17).

It is possible to find the influence of the Gentile mission clearly marked on the Gospels, but perhaps it is also possible to explain too much of the text in its terms. Bultmann, for example, tends to attribute the obstacles to Jesus' work and the opposition in Mark to the missionary experience of the early church. This may indeed be the way in which the pericopes were read but it does not, it seems to me, necessarily exclude some glimpses of the difficulties Jesus encountered or the very real possibility of more than one change of plan (see Chapter Five, below). The problem for the Evangelists arose when they considered the mission of the church (whether successful or unsuccessful) in relation to the tradition of the actual work of Jesus. They knew he had not only not reached beyond Israel but had failed in many ways and many places to reach Israel. They knew that, in fact, the church owed to the Risen Christ its charge to seek out the Gentiles and was confronted with the necessity (both apologetic and hortatory) to show some basis for this in the ministry of Jesus.

The missionary motif is, as Bultmann says, an important one in the resurrection tradition of Matthew (and of John). The charge to carry the gospel to all mankind (Matt. 28:16–20; John 20:21–23, with the story in ch 21:1–11) is dependent on Jesus' elevation to power (Matt. 28:18) just as his exaltation, as we saw, has made possible the bestowal of the Holy Spirit (John 20:22). What is shown by the placing of these charges is that there was a paradoxical element of discontinuity between Jesus and the work of the church and that the underlying continuity revealed by the resurrection and the Living Christ had to be sought for. It was found (and not, perhaps, exclusively by the Hellenistic church) but it was not found on the surface. There is again an integrity about the Gospels that no such charge is attributed to Jesus, but only to the Risen Lord. There may be implied here, in the traces of Jesus' eschatological expectation as it is related to the mission of the Twelve, a change in Jesus' conception of the situation, but that change is best studied in connection with indications of a critical situation in Galilee from which emerges another paradox. The fact that the charge to evangelize the world arises from a revelation of the Risen Lord is far from diminishing the importance of this task for the church. The Great Commission, as the Evangelists in various ways have set about showing, is deeply rooted in the very nature of Jesus' work and the underlying implication of his teaching. I have shown in *The Jesus of the Parables*, pp. 140, 286–288, how this theme, while not baldly expressed, echoes through his parabolic teaching. It is the resurrection and our own experience of its compelling reality which lays upon us the solemn obligation to provide that missionary dedication which is completely essential to the nature of the people of God. Without its mission the church has, in God's sight, not only no purpose but no reality, no existence.

NOTES TO CHAPTER FOUR

1. The viewpoint arrived at in this chapter is shared, e.g., by J. Jeremias, *Jesus' Promise to the Nations* (Studies in Biblical Theology, No. 24; 1958); G. B. Caird, *Jesus and the Jewish Nation* (Ethel M. Wood Lectures, 1965; the Athlone Press of the University of London). To the bibliography in Jeremias should be added: F. Hahn, *Mission in the New Testament* (Studies in Biblical Theology, No. 47; 1965). On the motivation of Paul's mission, see J. Munck, *Paul and the Salvation of Mankind*, tr. by Frank Clarke (John Knox Press, 1959).

2. On Jesus at prayer, see my article "Prayer" in *The Interpreter's Dictionary of the Bible*, ed. by George A. Buttrick, *et al.* (Abingdon Press, 1962). For a suggestion about the chronology of

John, see my "Tabernacles in the Fourth Gospel and Mark," *New Testament Studies*, Vol. 9, No. 2 (1963).

3. The importance of the demonic warfare theme is recognized in J. Kallas, *The Significance of the Gospel Miracles* (The Seabury Press, Inc., 1961)—but see my review in *Journal of Biblical Literature*, Vol. 81 (1962), pp. 321 f. See also V. McCasland, *By the Finger of God* (The Macmillan Company, 1951).

4. For schematic theological patterns in Mark, see, e.g.: James M. Robinson, *The Problem of History in Mark* (Studies in Biblical Theology, No. 21, 1957; later modified); Austin Farrer, *A Study in St. Mark* (Alec R. Allenson, Inc., 1951); P. Carrington, *The Primitive Christian Calendar* (London: Cambridge University Press, 1952); and perhaps most engagingly, E. Schweizer, "Mark's Contribution to the Quest of the Historical Jesus" in *New Testament Studies*, Vol. 10, No. 4 (1964), pp. 421 ff.

5. On the question of the Twelve and the apostles, see, e.g.: K. H. Rengstorf, *"apostolos"* in Kittel's *Wörterbuch;* E.T., Vol. I, pp. 407 ff., and "Apostleship" in *Bible Key Words*, Vol. VI; also, M. H. Shepherd, "Apostles" in *The Interpreter's Dictionary of the Bible*, and the literature cited in both.

6. On the authoritative nature of sending in pairs, see J. Jeremias, "Paarweise Sendung im N.T." in A. J. B. Higgins, ed., *New Testament Essays* (Manchester: Manchester Univ. Press, 1959), which cites H. van Vliet, *No Single Testimony* (Utrecht, 1958) as bearing on witness, etc., but not on sending by pairs.

7. On the use of *paradidōmi*, "hand over," see Chapter Five and Notes, and under *"didōmi"* in Kittel's *Wörterbuch;* E.T., Vol. II, pp. 169 ff.

8. On the problem of Mark 13:10, see G. D. Kilpatrick, "The Gentile Mission in Mark and Mark 13:9–11," in Nineham, ed., *Studies in the Gospels.*

9. For the harvest, see books on the parables, "Notes to Chapter Five," and my articles "Fishers of Men," *Harvard Theological Review*, Vol. 52, No. 3 (1959), and "The Mixed State of the Church in Matthew's Gospel," *Journal of Biblical Literature*, Vol. 82, No. 2 (1963).

10. Bundy (*Jesus and the First Three Gospels*, pp. 153–159) highlights the eschatological nature of the mission and the anachronism of the bulk of Matthew's discourse; I would not speak, how-

ever (p. 157), of "open discrimination against non-Jews" but only of an immediate and temporary restriction of the mission.

11. For the "witnesses," see Hans Conzelmann, *The Theology of St. Luke*, tr. by Geoffrey Buswell (London: Faber & Faber, Ltd., 1960), pp. 14–17, 210 ff.

12. For the Tabernacles offering in relation to the nations and to Mark 11:1 to 12:12, see my article "No Time for Figs," in *Journal of Biblical Literature*, Vol. 79, No. 4 (1960).

13. On the parables mentioned, see my *Jesus of the Parables*, pp. 104–109, 145–156, 170–180, 218–227.

14. The exegesis of Mark 14:9 in Jeremias' *Jesus' Promise to the Nations*, p. 22, must, I think, be questioned (cf. also Hahn, *Mission in the New Testament*), but the monograph as a whole is a significant treatment of the Gentile mission.

Five

The Eternal Son
Who Must Die

Jesus' message was largely conveyed through parables and since the modern mode of exegesis has displaced the traditional allegorical method their place in determining the character of Jesus' teaching and, indeed, of his person has been given increasing recognition. When the parables are reduced as nearly as possible to their original form, one thing becomes apparent —their secularity. One parable has religious figures in it (the good Samaritan). Only one deals with a directly religious topic, the Pharisee and publican at prayer. This isolated exception, on examination, turns out to make the most "secular" point of them all. It appears that Jesus was able to discuss God and the ways of God, without resort to "religious" language.

We have, therefore, throughout the Synoptic Gospels and in all their sources the paradox of the religious prophet who taught by means of secular tales. This teaching, moreover, was thrown out with a sort of divine carelessness, the analogies being open-ended, leaving the hearer to make the application while, in many cases, confronting him with the necessity of making a judgment in which the need for commitment could not easily be escaped. Since I have dealt with this matter in another book and shown how the parables largely contributed to Jesus' fate, which was his victory, space will not be taken here (see "Notes to Chapter Four," par. 13). The parables do not, originally, contribute directly to the assertion of Messiahship, though their indirect bearing on the problem is inescapable in terms of their implied authority. We cannot avoid the issue, however, in terms of another paradox.

"Jesus is to be found *in* his word and *in* his actions, and . . . he does not make his own rank a special theme of his message prior to everything else." These words of Günther Bornkamm have been strongly reinforced by Gerhard Ebeling, who says, "The primitive Christian Christological kerygma did not come into being because Jesus had already taught Christology . . . for Christology is not grounded in Christ because he gave rise to the primitive Christology by himself teaching Christology" (see "Notes to Chapter Five," par. 6). The question of how Jesus thought of himself, his so-called "Messianic consciousness," is a question to which, by their very nature, the Gospels may decline a clear answer. They are in a real sense kerygma.

The Evangelists, as they set forth the gospel, assume that Jesus was in some sense Messiah and so spoke of himself. In the Synoptic Gospels the cases where he clearly so speaks are historically insecure except as testimonies of the church in response to the fact of Christ. Yet the position taken by the Evangelists in these reports arises out of a historical situation. Therefore the question is, What historical conditioning can we recover out of which—before and apart from the resurrection experience—Messianic claims might arise? Can we discern anything related to the situation or are we dependent upon interpretation based on the resurrection? Was there a historical situation that accounts for what can only be called "the Christological ambiguity" of the work of the Evangelists?

The Caesarea Philippi Story

It is naturally not enough to say that Peter's "confession" at Caesarea Philippi, "Thou art the Christ," is sufficient by itself (Mark 8:29 and ||s). Assuming that Peter, evidently speaking for the Twelve, did make such an assertion, it is by no means clear on the surface what was meant by it.

In Mark, ch. 8, the rebuke of Jesus by Peter (v. 32) and the rebuke of Peter by Jesus which follows (v. 33) indicate that more than one conception of Messiahship was an issue when Mark was written. It may be read to mean that Peter's answer is virtually dismissed by Jesus. If Jesus dismissed it, he did not do so with a complete disclaimer. Mark has supplied a modification that would make the question of the application of the term "Messiah" to Jesus an open one. In a sense it is quite possible to say that Mark's "Messianic secret" may be applied to Jesus himself; that is to say, not that Jesus kept his Messiahship secret, but that to Jesus just what such a claim might involve, if made, was a mystery, was hidden also from him. This naturally makes no sense unless we are prepared to accept Jesus as a man—not as a divinity masquerading as a human being. It is true that unless Jesus was in the fullest sense a man the paradox that lies at the heart of the Christian faith and at the heart of the Gospels too has lost its meaning and its edge. The national Messiah in Jewish thought must be a man and should be distinguished from "the Son of Man," who may be a good deal more. Much more important for our present purpose, the development of the Gospels as we have them is hardly intelligible unless we approach Jesus and Peter also as actual human beings.

The sequel in Mark to Peter's "confession" seems at first a *non sequitur* and has been explained in various ways as an intrusion. Jesus begins to speak of "the Son of Man." He asserts that the Son of Man must suffer, be rejected, be killed, and rise again (Mark 8:31). Here is the first of three "passion predictions" (others in chs. 9:31; 10:33; cf. ch. 9:12; 10:45). It is this "prediction" which produces Peter's objection (v. 32) and, in turn, the stern rebuke Jesus administers to Peter (v. 33). At the very least this shows that for the Evangelists the subject was vital to Jesus and deeply moving—as well as to the church. We can credit this, as Bultmann does, to the urgency of polemic; a creation of the Christian community. Before doing so we might take it as the Evangelist has presented it and see what we can make of it. We must leave aside the important apologetic element here involved and deal with it later when more evidence has been examined (see "Postscript").

Modern study of the form of the separated sections of the Gospels has been of tremendous value. The formal characteristics, however, are sometimes left behind and judgments are made on the basis of content. At this point it is necessary to ask whether, for the writer and readers of the Gospels, the *context* of a given pericope, both its immediate surroundings and the context at large, does not control or to some extent determine the internal meaning of the pericope where it stands. In the case before us, fresh study of the context at large into which Mark has set this occasion raises the question whether this setting suggests something in the nature of a historical reminiscence which it is necessary to recover before the purpose and meaning of Mark can be discerned as well as the modifications made by Matthew and Luke. The story is overlaid by a good deal of "theological" (or "kerygmatic") development, but it is again a phase of the integrity of the Gospels (as I have called it) that there are traces of the original problem. Was there a situation that needed considerable modification before it could become a part of the Christian proclamation?

The Passion Predictions

The question of the "passion predictions" is directly involved here. They need not, at every step, be treated in isolation as though it was certain that they are additions. The large majority of modern critics are content to treat them as formulations of the church, constructed after the resurrection out of the events which they predict. This is so obvious to most critics that little further discussion is offered. The ground for this opinion is that the form in which they occur (more especially in Mark 10:33 f.) indicates a knowledge of the actual series of events attending Jesus' death and a knowledge of the resurrection.

That conclusion is not actually as clear as it is assumed to be. The words used in the "predictions" in Mark 8:31; 9:31 and 10:33 f. are not conspicuously those used in the actual

Marcan passion story. An exception is the verb *paradidomai*, used in chs. 9:31 and 10:33, which occurs in Mark 14:10–11; 15:1, 6. It is a fairly common term meaning "handed over" or, as we might say, "turned in" (see "Notes to Chapter Five," par. 7). The same can be said for the order of events, quite vague in Mark 9:31, and only generally stated in chs. 8:31 and 10:33 f. We learn in one place that the Son of Man is to suffer much and be rejected by the elders, chief priests, and scribes, and be killed. In the third case he is to be delivered to the chief priests and scribes and condemned, and then be delivered to the "Gentiles" and be mocked, spat upon, scourged and killed. All these items occur in the Marcan passion story. Of the "predictions" the one in ch. 10 is most like the sequel. It would seem that the Evangelist is well aware of the movement of the passion story, as though he had the written account in front of him but has not been concerned to summarize it with great care (cf. the description of the Sanhedrin in chs. 8:31 and 10:33 with chs. 14:1, 10, 43, and 15:1). At the same time the form in which it is presented shows unmistakably a knowledge of the process by which Jesus came to his end, with the striking exception that there is no mention of the means by which he was put to death, crucifixion—a feature prominent in the kerygmatic passages of Acts. It is worth noting that in none of the "predictions" is any mention made of the Christ, that is, the Messiah. Only when "Son of Man" is taken to be one equivalent for "the Christ" does the question of a "suffering Messiah" arise. To take it in this way, however, is to miss the force of the construction Mark offers.

Attempts have been made to defend the "predictions" as authentic, but with no pronounced success (see "Notes to Chapter Five," par. 8). A decision about their authenticity does not depend on the conclusion that the Son of Man is here presented as Suffering Servant, since this is a question initially about their form rather than about their historicity. The form they take can be explained only as a postresurrection production. The question is whether this decision disposes of the matter.

THE FEARS AROUSED BY JESUS

To make a preliminary brief sketch of the controlling factors in the Marcan context we shall assume that the Twelve did go out on a mission of great urgency and that on this mission Jesus had staked a great deal. We must, without any doubt, accept Schweitzer's emphasis on the eschatological nature of Jesus' ministry to be the core of any real historical groundwork of the Gospels. It is only as an eschatological enterprise that the mission of the Twelve, with its possible original charge, makes sense. For this the Twelve were selected. The call of the first four (in Mark 1:16 ff.) as "fishers of men" is clearly an eschatological call.

If we assume such a "crash program" as historical fact, we have also to assume that in addition to the attention caused by Jesus himself, the mission of his agents would only serve to add to that interest. It would in fact aggravate any element of disturbance or feeling of alarm about Jesus' activities. This is exactly what we find beneath the Marcan account, but so little beneath it that it shows through on the surface like rocks in a New Hampshire pasture. It serves no other purpose than to indicate that there were events which precipitated actions and words of Jesus and that these words and acts were, in turn, of immediate interest for the Christian gospel. The events appear, naturally, in a form suitable for their present purpose, held together by editorial sutures that are of no historical value in themselves. Our business is to ask what, if anything, lies behind the forms and the editorial links. Why, in effect, is this form or this setting the vehicle of the Christian proclamation? Why not something better suited, a little closer to hand, a little more "relevant"? That is to say, why not something less involved in critical events long since resolved and of no immediate interest to the postresurrection church?

The alarm caused by Jesus and his missionaries must naturally be viewed against the background of the times with its atmosphere of nervous tension, of, as it were, cold war. The local government, operating at the pleasure of Rome; the local church leaders, anxious to do nothing to precipitate a change in the situation; the increasing pressures from the left—those who were steadily moving toward violent action—with the occasional disturbances caused by self-designated messiahs: the whole delicately poised *modus vivendi* made responsible people all too anxious to avoid upheaval and to forestall any movement that threatened to get out of hand and tip the scales beyond recovery. This is precisely what is reflected in Mark by the passages which indicate the anxious concern of Herod Antipas, the local puppet ruler, who voices not only his own fears but the debate that is going on among the people (Mark 6:14–16). This makes it hard to understand, except as a consequence of rejecting any factual basis to the mission of the Twelve, why Bultmann says that the content of the question Jesus asks and his initiative in asking it are secondary. If the Twelve had indeed returned from a rapid excursion through Galilee, he would not be "every bit as well informed as were the disciples" (*Die Geschichte*, p. 276; E.T., p. 257).

The curious remark (in Mark 3:6) about a discussion or warning (rather than a plot) involving a combination of Pharisees and Herodians, a combination on the surface most unexpected, has often been asserted to be impossible or confused or, more likely, misplaced. It belongs, it is said, as a more immediate prelude to the passion. As a matter of fact the words are by no means out of place in the scheme as a whole when they are read (as the curious construction, *symboulion edidoun kat' autou*, makes possible) not as a plot but as a "tipping off" of the civil authorities by the ecclesiastical that there is a possible danger brewing. Mark has artificially but cogently combined in chs. 2:1 to 3:6 stories that set forth his view of the reasons for the opposition to Jesus. These are ecclesiastical on the surface, but we do not forget that there was then no such separation between religion and politics as we know or desire. The incidents brand Jesus as a danger because his words and acts imply a religious claim, though he is judged not to be in any usual sense an ecclesiastical figure. The response of the people to so ambiguous a character is disturbing. The counsel

given by the Pharisees to the civil authorities of Galilee is obviously that they should keep an eye on Jesus and his movement and take action before serious trouble develops.

We may observe here that this combination of civil and
ecclesiastical interest is far from uncommon. It has its climax
in the Gospel accounts as a charge against Jesus made by the
church leaders on religious grounds and carried out by the
civil power on political grounds—which we shall examine
below. A notable example of the tendency for the church to
condemn and the state to carry out the sentence is the case of
Joan of Arc, especially as it is commented on by G. B. Shaw
in his play *Saint Joan*, Scene IV (see "Notes to Chapter Five,"
par. 9), in the interview between the Bishop of Beauvais and
the Earl of Warwick. The Earl at the end says to the Bishop:
"If you will answer for the Church's part, I will answer for the
secular part."

It would not be improper to assume that the Galilean authorities were awake to the possibility that Jesus' activities might
stir the people to an extent embarrassing to the rulers of
church and state. According to Josephus (as we have seen
above), Herod had removed John the Baptist because he
feared a popular uprising might develop. Was Jesus another
source of danger or embarrassment?

This is exactly what Mark has suggested as a result of the
mission on which Jesus sent the Twelve. He introduces the
section about Herod (Mark 6:14–16) immediately following
Mark's account of the charge to the departing Twelve (modified, as we have seen, by later interests).

THE OPINIONS ABOUT JESUS

What we have in Mark 6:14–16 is a variety of opinions
which are rumored abroad. Some say that Jesus and his activities mean that John the Baptist has returned; others say that
Jesus is a prophet, "like one of the prophets of old." "When
Herod heard about it"—that is, both about the activity (which
might be a matter of indifference to him) and about the re-
actions (which would be of the most urgent concern) he said,

"John . . . has been raised." The people might not know for certain whether the rumors of John's death in an isolated fortress were true or not, but Herod knew. It has therefore, quite reasonably, been suggested that Herod may here be taken not to be guessing at John's resurrection but merely to be saying, "This is a case of John all over again!" that is, "Here is another 'John the Baptist'!" We would assume that he would then keep an eye on the movement and at the right moment stop it by arresting its leader.

It is against this background (removed from Mark 8:27 ff. by the "doublets" of ch. 8:1–26 which Luke has omitted and which have another purpose) that we should read the question of Jesus to his followers and their answers in Mark 8:27 f. Jesus is not here trying to find out how popular he is or how he has been accepted. He is asking whether they too have heard the rumors that have been disturbing the authorities or were likely to disturb them. The question is asked after Jesus and the Twelve have left Herod's territory.

The answers Jesus obtains are simply a confirmation of the rumors earlier mentioned and they represent three basic lines of surmise:

John the Baptist. The popular enthusiasm for John had apparently survived his death. The people, knowing Jesus had been associated with John, perhaps had even been designated as his successor, were ready to welcome Jesus as another John. If we are right in assuming that John's message had been eschatological, it would seem to lend weight to the view that the mission of the Twelve was an eschatological one, or that it gave that impression. It is not, I think, necessary to conclude that Jesus at first continued John's work along the same lines (see Chapters Two and Three, above).

Elijah. Others were inclined to think that in Jesus, Elijah had come. According to the Old Testament and a considerable development beyond it, Elijah was to "come again" as the precursor of the end, to inaugurate the Day of the Lord (see Mal. 4:5 and 3:1 ff.). About his figure a great deal of Jewish legend and even liturgical practice gathered, indicating that he was not only to return to usher in the end but that he was currently active in the life of the Jews as a sort of spiritual presence (see "Notes to Chapter Five," par. 10). We recall that Elijah had not died a natural death but, according to II Kings 2:11–12, had been carried up to heaven by a whirlwind or in a chariot of fire. He was, so to speak, "available." As the passage in praise of Elijah in Ecclesiasticus says, "You who are ready at the appointed time, it is written, to calm the wrath of God before it breaks out in fury, to turn the heart of the father to the son, and to restore the tribes of Jacob" (ch. 48:10; cf. Luke 1:17, Mal. 4:6). In some Gospel passages John the Baptist has been cast as Elijah, but as an Elijah who comes before the Messiah.

One of the Prophets.　This third line of rumor (in Mark, "one of the prophets of old") may indicate speculation along a number of lines and seems intended to be a summary. One set of Jewish expectations stemming from Deut. 18:15, 18, which has affected the New Testament, was that Moses himself would return. Moses is not here cast in the role of lawgiver but in the more Jewish one of prophet par excellence, *the* prophet. We note the question asked of John the Baptist in the Fourth Gospel, "Are you the prophet? And he answered, No." (John 1:21), and the application of the same to Jesus, "This is indeed the prophet who is to come into the world" (John 6:14). The tradition about Moses held that he had apparently died but that his death was a secret affair not witnessed by men (Deut. 32:48–53; cf. 34:5–6; see "Notes to Chapter Five," par. 11). We must also take account of the possibility that even more archaic and legendary figures were in mind.

The patriarch about whom most speculation centered and who became the standard figure of apocalyptic was Enoch, again one who had not met a natural end. A whole set of writings goes under his name and its influence on first-century Jewish thought seems to have been considerable. By way of the term "Son of Man" it has probably deeply influenced the Synoptic tradition, whether the actual Similitudes of Enoch were then extant or not (see "Notes to Chapter Five," par 13). It was reported that "Enoch walked with God; and he was not, for God took him" (Gen. 5:24). Just so God had "taken" Moses and Elijah. In the present form of The Book of Enoch the patriarch has been "named" and "hidden," reserved in heaven for his final role (see I Enoch 12:1; 48:2; 62:7; 69:26; 70; 71:1, 14). The figure of the "Son of Man," so closely associated with Enoch is here a supernatural figure who appears before the throne of God and is charged with judgment (cf. Dan. 7:13–14, 18, where, in contrast to the monsters that represent opposing nations, the term is applied to a human being who represents "the saints of the Most High").

The name of Melchizedek should probably be added. The Qumran literature suggests that similar speculation attached itself in some circles to this mysterious figure (see Gen. 14:18–20 and "Notes to Chapter Five," par. 11). As references in The Letter to the Hebrews indicate, Melchizedek had a sort of precedence over Abram, the very progenitor of the Jewish people (Heb. 7:10). He is described in the Genesis passage as "king of Salem" (that is, of Jerusalem) and "priest of God Most High" (*el elyon*). To Abram, who was at the time without an heir, Melchizedek gives his blessing and in return Abram gives a tithe, "a tenth of everything." We hear of him again in Ps. 110:4, a passage associated by the author of Hebrews with Ps. 2:7 in Heb. 5:5–6. It is into "the order of Melchizedek" that Jesus entered forever when he ascended to the heavenly throne (Heb. 6:19–20). Of Melchizedek the writer says he "has neither beginning of days nor end of life" (Heb. 7:3) and hence is also "available" as a "coming one," although there is no mention of him in the gospel tradition. The point of The Letter to the Hebrews is that since Christ has entered into heaven with the perfect sacrifice there is no need of another or a returned Melchizedek, any more than there would be of another Elijah, Moses, or Enoch.

THE AVAILABLE COMING ONES

In a sense the Son of Man gathers up the role of all these figures about whom there was apocalyptic speculation, the men who, as IV Ezra 6:26 says, "were taken up, who from their birth have not tasted death." Those who were expected to come as ushers of the end seem not to have died as other men do and this in some way equips them for their "Son of Man" role.

This, then, was one form in which the eschatological expectation was abroad. The reports of this opinion in Mark, widely held in various forms, indicate that it was a popular set of ideas without any universally accepted formulation and not confined to an esoteric literature. There may have been other sects like that at Qumran and their hopes and ideas a matter of public discussion. This, too, was what Jesus drew from the Twelve, the report that Jesus was currently thought of in an eschatological role. That role was conceived by various groups in different ways, but notably connected with figures of the past who were not past entirely but each one, as it were, waiting in the wings for the time to come when he should step again onto the stage of history and play his climactic part.

The idea that Jesus was thought of as one of the "coming ones" who had not died naturally but been transposed to heaven, may have been more clear in the tradition behind Mark than it is in his transcription of it. If this is so, then Jesus' question, "But who do *you* say that I am?" (Mark 8:29; in Greek the pronoun "you" is plural and the word order emphatic: "But you, who do you say I am?") is first designed to ask whether the Twelve shared these views in some form or another. The answer is given by their spokesman, Peter: "You are the Christ," literally, "the anointed one," the one elected and designated by God. What did they, or Peter, mean? Were they expressing an opinion at variance with that of the populace? Were they accepting it in general but giving it a particular application? Were they expressing an entirely different view, for example, that Jesus was the expected Messianic deliverer, a political and military fulfillment of the role? It would seem that, as far as Mark and his sources are concerned, we can answer this only by considering what follows, namely, Jesus' response to their answer. To treat it in isolation is seriously to miss Mark's point.

SECRECY AND PLAIN SPEAKING

First we are told in Mark 8:30 that Jesus sternly charged them not to spread this report, "to say this about him to no one." Why should he wish it kept secret? Is this only part of Mark's theory ("the Messianic secret") or did it mean originally that Jesus did not share the view of the Twelve (and of the populace) and wanted no one, including the Twelve, to think that he did? Or, as older commentators thought, was the claim loaded with dangerous implications? Was it capable of too many meanings and too readily given to a particular misapplication of a political nature?

I suggest we may approach an answer by noting another report in Mark which is often overlooked or fitted into theories about Mark only as a Christian proclamation. In Mark 8:32 we read, "He [Jesus] spoke this teaching openly." The words *ton logon* mean the teaching just mentioned in v. 31, the "passion prediction." The word *parrēsiai* here is very significant: it does not occur anywhere else in the Synoptic Gospels. It can mean "clearly" in the sense of "openly," or "outspoken," that is, "with confidence." It means, in contrast to the charge in v. 30: *this teaching was no secret.* Perhaps we can see why this remark has not been copied by the other Evangelists. In Mark it appears to be confined to the Twelve. Further, the teaching it refers to includes, or seems to foretell, the resurrection. It is the standard teaching of the New Testament that Jesus appeared only to his followers (see Acts 10:40 f.; cf. John 14:22 and Chapter Eight, below). Again, all the resurrection accounts imply that even the Twelve did not expect Jesus' "rising" in the sense of resurrection from death. We can see how the word *parrēsiai* was used by noting its meaning in John 10:24 where "the Jews" urge the Christ to tell them "plainly" (without ambiguity, straight from the shoulder) whether he is the Messiah or not. So here there was something Jesus had to say about the assertion of Peter and the Twelve, "Thou art the Christ," which he was willing should be made clear. On the other hand, that "confession" itself, without further explication, was not even to be spoken of. Here we meet for the first time the sharp transition from "Messiah" to "Son of Man" (Mark 8:31) which we shall find elsewhere.

The "teaching" of v. 31, the first of the "passion predictions," forms the crux of the problem, particularly so, since in its present form (along with similar passages) it is on the surface far from a clear or open doctrine. The detailed announcement of the series of events that constitute Jesus' condemnation and execution is almost inconceivable unless we take Jesus to have been an utterly abnormal figure—a "figure" rather than a real historical man. In its *form* it is part of a dogmatic structure, a literary device. There, as we have said, most critics are content to leave it, treating it as an isolated phenomenon apart from its context.

The study of that wider setting raises doubts about its isolated character. If Jesus forbids with extreme urgency the mention of Messiahship in connection with himself and then proceeds to teach openly or plainly another doctrine, we are bound to ask what is the connection between the two. It is easily explained as the substitution by the church of the teaching of Christ's death and resurrection for the Jewish idea of Messiahship. In that case we have to explain "the Christ" as pre-Christian, and we have not dealt with the real problem. The critics are right who see this section of Mark as the introduction to "the Way of the Cross." There follows a constant teaching that can be summed up in the counsel, "Take up your cross." This again is part of the Christian gospel. It is put in Mark in a form designed perhaps to encourage the Christians in Rome who, after Nero's attack, stood in danger of martyrdom and it may have had a more immediate polemical purpose. Having discounted all this, we ask why Mark has tied this passage, by Jesus' question to the Twelve, to the earlier account of Herod's fears and the public's speculations occasioned by their mission. Overlaid as it necessarily is by later interests, put in a form eminently suited to Christian preaching, is there, nonetheless, behind it the sign of a recollected historical crisis?

THE FORM OF THE "PREDICTIONS"

To say that Jesus may well, in some form, have anticipated trouble if he went to Jerusalem (a resolve which soon appears) and may even have foreseen his death by violence, would not account for the inclusion in the "passion predictions" of the phrase "rise again" (Mark 8:31; 9:31; 10:34). This is particularly difficult on any theory which finds that Mark is interpreting history, since when the resurrection appearances begin, the predominant initial response of the disciples is bewilderment, even skepticism. They show no signs of having been told in advance about the rising after three days; it is quite unexpected. This seems fatal to any attempt to claim the predictions as historical, since each of them, whatever else is omitted, mentions the "rising." Yet they are all of a piece. We cannot hold that Jesus foretold his execution and that the Evangelist added the resurrection. We can see the Evangelist, aware of the difficulty, more clearly at work in Mark 9:10, "So they kept the matter to themselves, questioning what the rising from the dead meant." That is a question we too must ask.

Let us assume, instead, that the *form* in which the "passion predictions" now appear is indeed a Christian construction, written with full knowledge of the passion and resurrection in hand. This is evidently true of Mark 8:30 and 10:34. We see also in Mark 9:12 and 10:45 interpretations of the topic which reveal at least three interests of the early church: the place of John the Baptist, the relation of the passion to the Scriptures, and a theological understanding that Jesus' death was a ransom "for many" (in which Isa., ch. 53, may be suggested to those prepared for the allusion). The introduction of Elijah into the context of Mark 9:12 by the disciples' question in v. 11 puts us back again into the matter we were discussing above, reinforced by the transfiguration to which we shall come below. The "second prediction" in Mark 9:31, however, is more general in form. It merely announces that the Son of Man will be "turned in" to men (not specifically to the Sanhedrin or "the Gentiles"), be killed, and (note the reiteration) "when he is

killed, after three days rise again." Except for the reference to
three days, this is much less specific.

Let us suppose, then (at the risk of being psychological),
that Jesus was confronted by the reports of the Twelve after
their rapid visitation of the countryside. The reports agreed
that eschatological interpretations of Jesus and his activity were
abroad. Further, that when Jesus asked them if they shared
these views about him he was confronted by a disposition on
their part to put him into the Messianic category. We then
read that Jesus was greatly disturbed and rebuked them, especially if they were tempted to share this opinion with anyone
else, that is, to adopt the popular view and spread their own.
His response can be read as a complete repudiation of the
Messianic idea and not necessarily simply in its "political"
form. If it was originally a repudiation, we are not surprised
that Mark has put it into indirect discourse rather than in
actual words of Jesus. What Jesus then does, according to
Mark, is not to make an immediate assertion and to drop the
subject, but to begin a process of "teaching" or, as we might
say, of reeducation (8:31; see ch. 9:31). This "teaching" we
find occurring most often in settings in which the Twelve are
confused and are supporting an attitude that Jesus opposes.
From here on, in Mark's Gospel, until the final desertion, the
gap between Jesus and the Twelve widens. They follow him
but with awe and fear (Mark 10:32), and Mark more than
once points up their failure to understand. The "teaching"
turns out to be largely a controversy in which Jesus is trying
to change the minds of the disciples to his own way of thinking; to "change the subject" as it were, from Messiahship to
the question of the Son of Man—or, we may better put it, to
his own trust in what God will do with the situation as it
develops.

BEHIND THE FORM

The suggestion is, therefore, that behind the form in which
the prediction of the passion now stands, and in part because
of the use in it of the term "Son of Man," Jesus is here dis-

associating himself from any conception of an apocalyptic figure from heaven. Moreover, he is *expressly* disassociating himself from any figure who was conceived to have avoided death in the ordinary sense and therefore to be "available" to appear or to be exalted, and in that sense "to rise."

The last term can be shown to be associated with the disclosures of the glory of the heavenly figure who is appointed to stand before God, or to stand at his right hand, or to be seated on the throne of glory and of judgment. This, in various ways, was thought of in connection with figures to whom the general term "Son of Man" could be applied. In effect, *there stands behind the predictions, not a prophecy of the passion, but a disclaimer by Jesus of any Messianic or apocalyptic role which involves the bypassing of death.* Beyond that it was noncommital. Enoch may be a candidate for Son-of-Manship because "God took him"; Elijah likewise might be expected to be available to come before the end by virtue of having been raised to heaven in a chariot; even Moses, alone with Yahweh on Mt. Nebo, might be a candidate, or Melchizedek, without "end of life." But, if Jesus were to be thought of in any such connection, if he were expected to be "Son of Man," or "Elijah," or "Moses," or "that prophet," it could only be after his death. It was not a claim even to be Son of Man, but a solemn warning that his own cause must end in death like any other man's, for he must be treated as a man and not as being from heaven, not a "heavenly figure."

This rather startling possibility arises out of the context in Mark and what most probably lies back of it. About it several things may be said. No form of the "passion predictions" can be considered to be original in which "to rise" is referring to the resurrection of Jesus. Yet no form is without this connection. Only by referring it to the widespread, popular, and deeply ingrained notion that some apocalyptic figure would appear who, by God's previous action, had been allowed to avoid the usual human end can it be seen to have some relation to the Messianic speculations of the times. J. A. T. Robinson and others have shown, with varying degrees of probability, that the resurrection itself, the "ascension," and the "coming" of Christ all originally belonged in the category of exaltation, enthronement, and vindication (see "Notes to Chapter Five," par. 14). The anointing of Jesus at his baptism (along with the theme of Ps. 2:7) would soon come to be thought of as his designation to be the elected one who is to be enthroned in heaven as king. The original subject, therefore, of the passion predictions was the apocalyptic exaltation, not the passion and resurrection of Jesus. It is this which Jesus here disclaims insofar as it requires that death be avoided. A great gulf exists between Jesus and any such figure for the very reason that Jesus must die. What might happen after that (that God might exalt one who has met a shameful death and has actually been buried) does not immediately come into view (see "Notes to Chapter Five," par. 15).

If Jesus had any thoughts on the subject, they are not explicitly expressed—for that matter, how could they be? They may be implicitly "read" or "heard" in the sayings if Jesus is understood to have said in some form: "If *this* 'Son of Man' is to be exalted, it must and can be only after his death" (see below). So to read it would mean that an identification is being made between the speaker and the apocalyptic figure, even if a future one. That does not seem to be the proper reading of such passages as Mark 8:38||Luke 9:26; Mark 13:26||Matt. 24:30||Luke 21:27; Luke 12:8 f. (see M's revision, Matt. 10:32 f.); Matt. 19:28 (see L's revision, Luke 22:30); Matt. 25:31; Luke 18:8; 21:36—all of which allow for a distinction between Jesus and a coming Son of Man of the future. In the case of Mark 14:62, Mark has more clearly made the identification than has Matt. 26:64 or even Luke 22:69, and it is Mark who has most consistently, if not exclusively, tied the Son of Man sayings to the passion.

That a suffering, crucified Son of Man would have been a difficult concept, likely to occur to hardly anyone, is interestingly enough remembered in the Fourth Gospel. There, in John 12:34, the question is asked, "Who is *this* Son of Man?"

It is a much more difficult idea than a suffering or crucified Messianic King with which it is so often confused or with a suffering righteous man of the Wisdom tradition. In John "the Jews" from whom the question comes do not represent the average Jews of Jesus' time but the synagogue of the time of the Evangelist. They have never heard of (and presumably could not accept) any such "Son of Man" as one who would be exalted by being crucified. Far from that, their assumption is that "the Christ remains for ever." That is the accepted view, that the figure who is to "come" or to "rise," whatever name he has, has not died and cannot die. How, then, can it be said that the Son of Man must be "lifted up"?—a phrase that has the typical Johannine double impact of being lifted up on a cross and of being, by that very means, lifted up to the throne of God. This is a later piece of Christian apologetic in John, though it may go back to a primitive way of thinking ante-dating emphasis on a separate resurrection and ascension. It is all the more important that at the beginning of the second century it was still known that what would be incomprehensible to the people of Jesus' time was that anyone who was to die could be a Son of Man. (The Christian use of the term "Son of Man" for the humanity of Christ is thus shown to be dubious in this earlier context and more than likely a later development.)

Since it is Mark who identifies the Son of Man with the passion, it seems much more likely that the "passion predictions" which lie at the core of this identification should have been worked up out of actual sayings of Jesus than that they should have been made up out of whole cloth. The kind of transition between the view which I suggest may have been expressed by Jesus and the view in the predictions *as they stand* is a transition with which we are familiar, produced by the experience of the cross and resurrection. It provides the Christian resolution of the paradox that he who was declared by resurrection to be Son of God was in his death the victim of men and circumstances.

THE AMBIGUOUS "SON OF MAN"

While it is recognized that the Fourth Gospel uses terms capable of two meanings, scholars are not always so ready to admit a deliberate ambiguity to words attributed in the Synoptic Gospels to Jesus. Yet one sometimes wonders why. In the recent past the suggestion that the term "Son of Man" not only had several possible meanings (which is readily enough admitted by most) but that Jesus might have used it *because* it was capable of more than one meaning is usually dismissed. G. Dalman, for instance, in *The Words of Jesus*, refers to the enigmatic aspects of the term. He says: "A complete understanding of his self-appelation [*sic*], Jesus could certainly not, in such cases, have looked for from his hearers. Yet one may hold that in using the title he purposely furnished them with a problem which stimulated reflection about his person, and gave such a tendency to this reflection that the solution of the problem fully revealed the mystery of the personality of Jesus" (E.T., p. 259). There are assumptions here that we would certainly not wish to make but there is the suggestion of an enigmatic possibility, if not intention, about Jesus' usage. More recently G. Bornkamm in his *Jesus of Nazareth*, speaking of an "ambiguous use" suggested earlier by P. Fiebig and later by E. Percy, says, "I find both these assumptions impossible to imagine and impossible to support with any text whatsoever" (E.T., p. 230). Bornkamm, with others, holds that Jesus never applied the term to himself. Yet it seems highly probable that in the Gospels "Son of Man" must sometimes be read with lowercase letters as well as sometimes with uppercase, that is, that sometimes it stands simply for "this fellow speaking," or "I" and may in some cases go back to an enigmatic use on Jesus' part.

The Evangelists sometimes substitute the first person pronoun for the term because it is possible to do this. They do it because they share the belief that Jesus was the Son of Man and therefore must have spoken of himself in this way. It is exceedingly unlikely that Jesus' contemporaries would have "heard" Jesus speak of himself in the uppercase manner. Yet, if Jesus used the expression (and it is never in the Synoptics attributed to anyone else), it was not only capable of being heard as a colloquialism but also of being understood in a far more awesome sense. It would take the experience of the resurrection and the rise of Christian faith for it to be "heard" in this last sense from his lips. I do not see, in spite of the lack of any text Bornkamm can rely on, and in view of the variety of uses in the Synoptics, how we can altogether exclude the possibility that Jesus left open more than one understanding (see "Notes to Chapter Five," par. 12). We must add the vitally important caution that it could be understood of himself only if it applied to some as yet undisclosed (even to himself) action of God beyond death and therefore beyond human foretelling. This would indicate a wholly committed trust in God which is characteristic of Jesus and one which he demanded of his followers.

So the suggestion lies open that behind the "passion predictions" there may well have been a saying strenuously repudiating the spreading of any Messianic claim and particularly of any apocalyptic claim for himself. This is what is needed in the context Mark gives us. It is not needed for Mark's self-consistent development of how Christian faith grows, in which the Caesarea Philippi scene is indeed a "watershed." It is needed to explain the material he has had (as I think) to use in order to do this even if it did not entirely fit his purpose and emerges as an outcropping rather than as the foundation of his scheme. When Peter in Mark 8:32 "rebukes" Jesus and when Jesus in v. 33 in turn "rebukes" Peter, Mark uses the same verb (*epitimaō*) which he had used in v. 30 for the "charge" to the disciples to make no such disclosure. That is, the "stern charge" was itself a rebuke. The atmosphere is charged with emotion. Peter, having heard Jesus' disclaimer of a role that involves no death, rather than the "passion prediction" as we have it, vehemently repudiates Jesus' attitude. It evidently means a great deal to the Twelve that Jesus should accept (or acknowledge) the role they wish to attribute to him and which, still more important for the Twelve, the crowds are evidently willing to accept.

Jesus, according to Mark, equally vehemently repudiates this presumption of Peter. At all events he restrains Peter to the extent of attributing this attitude of Peter's to human considerations of a demonic origin (see "Notes to Chapter Five," par. 16). It is, to use a term which appears elsewhere, to think *kata sarka*, "according to the flesh." There is no understanding of God's dealings in Peter's repudiation of Jesus' teaching. He is not thinking *kata pneuma*, "according to spirit."

The implementation of Jesus' desire to have this out in the open (v. 32) is found in v. 34 where Jesus begins to teach everyone ("multitude" as well as disciples) that anyone who wishes to follow him, thinking him to be Messiah or Son of Man, must be prepared to risk his life. The Christian form of this which appears is, of course, "Take up his cross." Life itself, in the verses that follow, is shown to be the final commitment; there can be no ultimate holding back. Whatever God intends to do with and through Jesus must somehow be possible in spite of his death, for Jesus himself is completely committed. This is what is meant if to "follow him" is taken to mean to follow his example or to learn his way. It also turns out to mean this even if taken to mean "Go where I am going" (see on Bartimaeus in Chapter Six, below).

We note that the theme of the Son of Man does not retreat into the background. It is still there. In Mark 8:38 we have the solemn assertion around which so much of the "Son of Man" discussion has centered. "For whoever is ashamed of me and of my words in this adulterous and sinful generation, of him will the Son of man also be ashamed, when he comes in the glory of his [Luke, "the"] Father with the holy angels." Again Jesus makes no explicit identification of himself with the Son of Man. The picture popularly held is here referred to, and the implication is that whoever—even Peter, or James and John— whoever seeks to claim the deathless way of the Son of Man and repudiates the human lot will himself be repudiated by the Son of Man when he is disclosed.

THE ATTITUDE OF THE TWELVE

In the underlying survival of signs of a Galilean crisis does the above point of view really fit? We have not settled what Peter and the eleven really meant by "the Christ," if, indeed, they had any clear idea. Or is it, too, a later version of their claim? Matthew and Luke were not content with its ambiguity. Matthew can be understood to take it as a full Christian affirmation not only of Messiahship but of divinity: "You are the Christ, the Son of the living God" (Matt. 16:16). In Matthew, Jesus accepts this as a divine revelation to Peter and delegates to him some aspects of his authority (vs. 18 ff.; see Chapter Eight, below). When Matthew at v. 20 picks up Mark again, he says nothing of the "Son of God" but records only the prohibition against mentioning "that he was the Christ"—a very different matter, even so, from Mark's ch. 8:30.

The question whether Peter and the eleven could have meant by "the Christ" ("the anointed one") that Jesus was the political Messiah, destined to be God's anointed King, or whether they echoed the reported apocalyptic opinion is not immediately clear. It is not clear even later. In the story about James and John in Mark 10:35 ff. they ask to share Jesus' "glory." It is difficult to imagine a request to share the heavenly glory of the Son of Man, yet, as many scholars think, it may for Mark have this intention. It reads more easily as a request for high position in the pomp of an earthly kingdom to be achieved in Jerusalem. It may possibly have both connotations, for the hoped-for triumph of the Messiah in Jerusalem had long been overlaid by the expectation that this triumph would have to come about by heavenly intervention. In any case, the point of the pericope is that such glory in Jesus' case, therefore in theirs, lies beyond the suffering depicted as drinking a cup and the death depicted as a baptism, without being more specific (see "Notes to Chapter Five," par. 15). It is a Christian interpretation, not supplied by Mark, which reads back into this a reference on the one hand to

Jesus' passion and on the other to the martyrdom of James and John. On the surface it says nothing more, in traditionally accepted figures of speech, than that all this lies beyond death for them as well as for himself because *they too* are human *as he is.*

THE "FEEDING" OF THE MULTITUDE

The return of the Twelve from their mission is, in Mark, immediately followed by and connected with the presence of a large crowd by the lake, by Jesus' meeting with them and his action in relation to them (Mark 6:30–45). The difficulties of the form in which this story has come to us are immense, probably because it has gone through several stages of development. At one level it can (and should) be taken to be a precursor of the institution of the Lord's Supper. The Fourth Gospel uses it in this way and it therefore becomes unnecessary to record the "institution" at the Last Supper (cf. John, chs. 6 and 13:1–12). At another level it can properly be treated as an epiphany story. Beyond this it may be read as a miracle story based on Old Testament motifs of feedings in the wilderness. This is the obvious level in Mark, a miracle of multiplication.

It has often been noted that Mark 6:45–46 is a curious ending in which Jesus "compels" the disciples to leave, himself dismisses the crowd, and finally retreats into the hills alone to pray. When, in Mark, Jesus goes off to pray, it always portends a critical situation with a decision to be faced. What was the crisis and need for a decision here? The "miracle" of feeding is recounted by all the Evangelists, by Mark twice, followed by Matthew. At whatever level, it was obviously an essential part of Christian preaching and worship. Was this perhaps because originally it was just as central to the story of Jesus?

John 6:15 comments on the story, as though seeking to explain Mark's statement; the reason for Jesus' withdrawal was that the people "were about to come and take him by force

to make him king." This suggests Messianic excitement in the
air, political and militant in character. There is no reason to
reject John's comment. It seems likely to be a historically
informed interpretation, as Goguel and others have suggested.

We may, therefore, welcome Hugh Montefiore's examination of the feeding story and his exposition of the underlying
Messianic disturbance (see "Notes to Chapter Five," par. 17).
In spite of the way it is written, permitting several equally
valid readings of value to the church, there persist indications
that Jesus here met and handled a crisis which determined his
future. This would go far to suggest why Jesus asked the
Twelve what the populace was saying about him, and that the
question was not, as some critics hold, "out of the blue."
Montefiore suggests that the phrase "sheep without a shepherd" (Mark 6:34, with no parallels here, but cf. Matt. 9:36
and the use of Micah 5:2 in Matt. 2:6, interpreted in Micah
5:4 as a shepherd-king) suggests an army without a leader as
in I Kings 22:17; II Chron. 18:16. "Shepherd" was a common
ancient designation for a king (e.g., Jer. 6:3 f.).

The people may well have been a throng looking for a
leader, as John suggests. This impression is strengthened by
the "many were coming and going" of Mark 6:31, which
aptly suggests a succession of delegates or a "gathering of the
clans"; by the fact that they readily fell into "companies"
(vs. 39 f.) of "hundreds" and "fifties" (cf. II Kings 1:9, 11, 13,
etc., and throughout IQM) and the fact that they were all
men (v. 44; Matthew adds the women and children). This
would explain the unprecedented number of people, a potential army prepared to live off the countryside, even, perhaps,
anticipating the finding of a leader who would in some Messianic fulfillment care for their needs. It would not be un-
reasonable to suppose that the original account, still revealed
by the connection in Mark, told of their gravitating to Jesus
because of the attention drawn to him far and wide in Galilee
by the Twelve on his mission. If, as we have seen reason to
believe, the missionaries made an eschatological proclamation,
it would not be unnatural for the people to gather and to

concentrate in the vicinity of Jesus. In that case, it would be fair to say that the mission had been an immediate and great success—*provided that was what Jesus wanted.*

The implication underlying the story as it proceeds, however, is that this was what Jesus neither expected nor desired. We must, as Schweitzer did, face the possibility that Jesus' expectation was not fulfilled—even if we cannot now actually define it—that God would in some way show his hand. Thus far Schweitzer may have been correct, especially in his diagnosis of the nature of the meal Jesus provided for the "five thousand." Schweitzer held that it was an eschatological sacrament, an anticipation of the Messianic Banquet, an act of "prophetic symbolism" (see "Notes to Chapter Five," par. 17). There is good reason to find in this the basis out of which the story has developed when we consider (Chapter Seven, below) the eschatological aspect of the Last Supper which lies even nearer the surface. In this case, Jesus, by a symbolical act for which very little bread was necessary, points the crowd toward a heavenly fulfillment, or at least to a future fulfillment when the Day of the Lord should come. By his actions as host he may indeed be suggesting, *for those with eyes to see,* that he would be the host at that heavenly banquet. This, again, is but an implicit claim which becomes explicit only to Christian eyes. In effect, Jesus, if our analysis is correct, faced by a crowd seeking in him a Messianic leader, met them with an acted-out message that the fulfillment of their wishes could find only a symbolical fulfillment at his hands. He then dismissed them, or "took leave of them" as Mark 6:46 puts it.

If, as said above, Jesus' withdrawal for prayer suggests a crisis and if we are correct, the suggested crisis is manifold. The mission of Jesus and of the Twelve has produced no real change in the situation; men still respond at the political level of force; there is no more that can be done in this direction, at least not in Galilee. It was at this point that Schweitzer turned to his suggestion that Jesus tried, in effect, to force God's hand by pressing forward to his own crucifixion. We may rightly reject this suggestion, along with his theory that Jesus did not expect the Twelve to return because the *eschaton* would have come, and yet not deny that Schweitzer had put his finger on the critical moment. We can also see that a gathering such as that described by the lake, even if Jesus disassociated himself from its avowed purpose, would do nothing to calm Herod's fears—far from it. When Mark comments about the Twelve, "They did not understand about the loaves, but their hearts were hardened" (ch. 6:52), we need not leap to "Eucharistic" conclusions. We may first accept it as stating that the minds of the disciples were closed, that they shared the attitudes of the people rather than the mind of Jesus, that they refused the implications of Jesus' sacramental meal. I fail to see why their failure to understand Jesus' action proves that Jesus did not so act, unless we must be committed to the idea that everything that Jesus did must have succeeded. I can see no such need, and I do not think Mark did.

THE TRANSFIGURATION

In Mark 8:27, Jesus' withdrawal from the area of upheaval and danger is taken up and with it the discussion about the attitude of the people. (Mark's Christian program has led him to insert other material here which would be of interest if we were at the moment studying Mark's message rather than seeking the underlying situation with which he has had to work to make it serve his purposes.) To resume the account at the point at which we left it above (Mark 8:38) we find that before Mark records the next visit of Jesus to Galilee (ch. 9:30) he has introduced the section concerning the transfiguration. It is held in place by the overall theme in this part of the Gospel of Jesus' suffering in Jerusalem (Mark 9:2–8 ‖).

A great deal of modern discussion has centered on this haunting and lovely scene. The transfiguration is most likely not a version of the resurrection moved back into the Gospels but a postresurrection story in which the heavenly glory of Jesus is disclosed by affording Jesus' inner circle a glimpse of the Parousia. A corner of the veil is for a moment lifted, and they see that it is indeed Jesus who is to be clothed in heavenly glory. The fact that this story is introduced here seems to confirm what we have been saying, that the knowledge of who the Son of Man is to be will be disclosed only from heaven and not, for instance, by Jesus, just as he can say nothing of who is to share the glory (Mark 10:40).

It can be shown that the rich threads of tradition out of which the transfiguration scene has been woven are basically eschatological rather than resurrection themes or mystical or spiritual themes, whereas the lake scene in Mark 6:47 ff. is clearly a resurrection appearance (see "Notes to Chapter Eight"). We note especially the appearance of Moses and Elijah, which shows we are still in the same context we have been discussing. Luke understands correctly that they appeared "in glory," that is, in their heavenly state. They are not there to represent, as has so often been asserted, the Law and the Prophets. They are there as the major examples of the expectation of the glorification and revelation of a "Son of Man"; they are the fulfillment of the popular hopes. We have met Moses and Elijah already in the speculations of the people. Luke makes an interesting comment on their "talking with Jesus." He says that their conversation was about Jesus' "exodus" which he was to "accomplish at Jerusalem" (Luke 9:30 f. in the Greek). They were talking about Jesus' passion and his *subsequent* exaltation.

So the story was originally designed as an underlining of Jesus' assertion that death must precede glorification, and the purpose of the scene is to assert the divine confirmation. The voice of God proclaims, "This is my Son, the Beloved; listen to him." This time it is addressed to others about Jesus not, as at the baptism, to Jesus himself. To what the three disciples present are to listen is at once obvious. They are to pay attention to the teaching on which Jesus is now (in Mark) embarked, that before he, at least, can be the Son of Man he must suffer death. Finally, when all is over, Moses and Elijah have disappeared and only Jesus is left—*to die*. There is to be no supernatural reappearance of anyone like Moses or Elijah, only Jesus in all his human susceptibility to suffering and death. Yet when the disciples see that suffering and death have come upon him, they are to know that beyond it lies the glory here proleptically (according to the Evangelist) disclosed. No such conception, of course, was possible until they had been changed by the resurrection experience.

Subsequent chapters in the Gospels show no signs of the three having received any such theophany or of having heard the announcement. Schweitzer's attempt to put this scene before Caesarea Philippi, as the prior disclosure to the three of Jesus' Messiahship which Peter then "lets out," fails to grasp the organic place of the scene in the Marcan context. It is not, in any case, history, but the illumination of history. It is the difficulty of the Twelve with Jesus and of Jesus with the Twelve seen in the light of the resurrection and the belief that by it Jesus has become all that was meant by the Son of Man. It is formed out of the faith that he had fulfilled all the expectations wont to center around those "prophets of old" who were attendant in heaven, Moses or Elijah or, for that matter, Enoch or Melchizedek. It is in this way that it fits and fits organically into the context at which we have been looking, the expectations of the populace shared in some way by the Twelve and Jesus' insistence that these things have no immediate relevance to him—unless it be beyond death. The Evangelist has demonstrated, by this story of the momentary lifting of the veil of the future, that the paradox of the Christian faith is indeed true; it is the crucified and rejected who is vindicated and glorified. Leaving Jesus alone to go to Jerusalem—estranged practically from even his disciples—leads on to the appearance of Jesus as the King who has come to his city and as the Lord come to his temple, as we shall see when we turn to a later chapter of Mark. So we read of Jesus' journey. The third, most explicit "passion prediction" is prefaced by the words, "Behold, we are going up to Jerusalem" (Mark 10:32–34).

THE EVANGELISTS AND THE PARADOX

To understand the nature of the Gospels, hence of the preaching of the Christian church, we have to keep constantly in mind that the real situation faced by the actual Jesus came

to its climax in the cross. The resurrection appearances, however we may think of them, marked the beginning of a completely new way of thinking about Jesus. The issues that
troubled his contemporaries and his own treatment of them
in teaching and action were now past. Jesus offered no nationalistic solution for the Jews, though their leaders well may
have intended their share in his removal to prevent the wrong
kind of solution and even to allay Roman fears of such. His
relationship with his own people in his own day provided later,
in the Gospels, the framework for the discussion between
church and synagogue, notably in the Fourth Gospel. Yet the
Jesus who was preached as risen was the Jesus who had been
forced to deal with the men of his time and expressly with his
own friends, the disciples including the Twelve, and their response to all the pressures of the time. When the Twelve (or
some of them) had become "apostles," and Peter and John, to
use Paul's term, "pillars" of the church, it began to be un-
thinkable that they at least had not seen in Jesus the Christ
whom God had sent or that he had not foreseen and spoken of
his own resurrection and, therefore, of his own exalted role.
The signs of this are evident in the very fact that the Evangelists had to modify the record to meet this expectation. What
is remarkable is that the signs that *this is a modification* are so
clear. It is a testimony to what I have called the "integrity" of
the Gospels and of the inescapable reality with which the
Evangelists had to deal and which the Christian preacher had
to proclaim. They were not dealing with a mythical figure
whom they could shape in any way they wished.

So, to return to the scene at Caesarea Philippi in its setting
of a crisis in Galilee, Luke and Matthew had to deal with the
ambiguities of Mark's account. Luke, typically, framed the
situation in prayer (ch. 9:18), has omitted all reference to a
controversy with Peter (after v. 22), and has modified "the
Christ" by adding "of God" (v. 20). Matthew is more interested in Peter. The church has always used Matthew's Gospel
before all the others, and when the early fathers deal with the
scene, it is normally from Matthew that they work. Far from

following Mark to deal with the "rebuke" of the disciples, Matthew inserts the "blessing of" Peter which has provided so fruitful a basis for appeal and controversy (ch. 16:17–19). We need not here discuss its terms. We need only note its intrusive nature. The interchange with Peter fits poorly the earlier blessing in which it now becomes necessary to emphasize the future tenses and to treat it as a prophecy of the situation after Peter's denial and restoration. Luke has safeguarded the position of Peter in advance in ch. 5:1–11 where Peter alone recognizes Jesus' real stature and alone is designated a "fisher of men." The resurrection aspect built into that story was mentioned in Chapter One and will be further discussed later along with other problems connected with Peter (see Chapter Eight, below).

After Mark has introduced the transfiguration scene he has, naturally, to extend Jesus' prohibition to the three—they are not to tell, not only that Jesus is the Christ, but also are not to tell that they have seen him in his glory (ch. 9:9 f.). Mark's v. 10 both Matthew and Luke omit. Mark is aware that "the rising" in the "passion predictions" presents a difficulty and he deals with it by asserting that the disciples did not know what a rising from the dead could mean. He is dealing with a paradox that first confronted the church, and his method of dealing with it as it affected the disciples in the presence of Jesus may seem to us almost clumsy and not always well coordinated. That very fact is itself a testimony that he was dealing with material which he could not, beyond a point, entirely ignore. Mark's disciples are often postresurrection Christians but the transformation is not entirely complete and some shadows of the real men and of the real Jesus still fall across his pages.

NOTES TO CHAPTER FIVE

1. The development of the modern critical approach to the parables begins with A. Jülicher, *Die Gleichnisreden Jesu* (Tübingen, 1888), and may be traced in the following:

A. T. Cadoux, *The Parables of Jesus: Their Art and Use* (The Macmillan Company, 1931).

B. T. D. Smith, *The Parables of the Synoptic Gospels* (London: Cambridge University Press, 1937).

C. H. Dodd, *The Parables of the Kingdom*, rev. ed. (Charles Scribner's Sons, 1961).

2. My *Jesus of the Parables* was published in 1948 before J. Jeremias' *Die Gleichnisse Jesu* (1947) became available, but both adopt the method of interpreting the parables against what may be known of the time of Jesus. The sixth German edition of Jeremias' work (1962) is the basis of the second English translation, by S. H. Hooke, *The Parables of Jesus* (Charles Scribner's Sons, 1962). This edition makes use of The Gospel of Thomas.

3. Eta Linnemann, *Jesus of the Parables*, tr. by John Sturdy (Harper & Row, Publishers, Inc., 1966) from the third edition of her *Gleichnisse Jesu, Einführung und Auslegung* (1961). For her theory of "interlocking," see E.T., pp. 27 f.; cf. pp. 80, 91, 144 n. 11.

4. Heinrich Kahlefeld, *Parables and Instructions in the Gospels*, tr. by Arlene Swidler (Herder & Herder, Inc., 1966). Linnemann and Kahlefeld are in the same tradition, though Miss Linnemann does not treat all the parables, but is important for refinement of method and bibliography; Fr. Kahlefeld's second volume has not yet become available.

5. Two books that attempt to go beyond the method to a more "existential" application are G. V. Jones, *The Art and Truth of the Parables* (S.P.C.K. 1964), which has a valuable survey of exegesis before Jülicher as well as after, and D. O. Via, Jr., *The Parables: Their Literary and Existential Dimension* (Fortress Press, 1967). Neither one mentions *The Jesus of the Parables*, in which it will be seen that the attempts to extend the application have worn less well than the discussion of original meaning.

6. For the quotations, see G. Bornkamm, *Jesus of Nazareth*, p. 169, and Gerhard Ebeling, *Theology and Proclamation* (Fortress Press, 1966), p. 74.

7. It is doubtful whether the passages in which the verb *paradidōmi* occurs can be treated initially as anything except reflections of the actual situation (see Chapter Seven) "predicted" in the passion sayings. See the cases where, especially with the Fourth Gospel, in the RSV the literal meaning is obscured by the transla-

tion "betray": John 6:64, 71; 12:4; 13:2, 11, 21; 18:2, 5; 21:20; "handed over" is the translation in chs. 18:30, 35 f.; 19:16. In ch. 19:11 "delivered" is used but is more appropriate where the verb is followed by *eis* (as in Mark 9:31, one of the "predictions"; ch. 13:9, 12, of followers; ch. 14:41 of the Son of Man; or by the dative in the ch. 10:33 "prediction"). The term comes to have deeper meaning, corresponding to the use of *dei* ("must") in Mark in the sense of the inevitability of the cross in the "foreknowledge" of God spelled out in Acts 2:23.

8. V. Taylor tried to argue the authenticity of the "predictions" in "The Origin of the Markan Passion Sayings," *New Testament Studies*, Vol. 1 (1955), pp. 159 ff. But see M. D. Hooker, *Jesus and the Servant* (S.P.C.K., 1959).

9. The quotation from *Saint Joan* may be found in context in *Selected Plays of Bernard Shaw* (Dodd, Mead & Company, Inc., n.d.), Vol. II, p. 363.

10. References to the "coming" Elijah may be found in J. Jeremias, "*Ēl(e)ias*" in Kittel's *Wörterbuch* (he tends, especially with reference to Mark 9:4 f., to pay too much attention to the Elijah who was precursor to the Messiah); Strack and Billerbeck, *Kommentar zum Neuen Testament aus Talmud und Midrasch*, Vol. IV, pp. 769 ff.; L. Ginzberg, *The Legends of the Jews* (the Jewish Publication Society of America, 1954), Vol. IV, pp. 195 ff.

11. On Moses and the possibility that he had been taken up to heaven, see, e.g.: H. M. Teeple, *The Mosaic Eschatological Prophet* (Journal of Biblical Literature Monograph Series, Vol. 10, Society of Biblical Literature & Exegesis, 1957); J. Jeremias, "*Mōusēs*" in Kittel's *Wörterbuch;* note from the Midrash on Deuteronomy: "Three went up alive into heaven: Enoch, Moses and Elijah." On the patriarchal prophet, see M. Black, "The Son of Man in the Teaching of Jesus," *Expository Times*, Vol. 60 (1948–1949), especially p. 34. For Melchizedek, see M. de Jonge, A. S. van der Woude, "11Q Melchizedek and the New Testament," *New Testament Studies*, Vol. 12 (1966), pp. 301 ff.

12. On the whole subject of the background and Gospel use of "Son of Man" the debate continues to extend itself without clear resolution. For summaries, discussions of varying points of view, and guides to the extensive literature in English, see especially:

M. Black, "The Son of Man Problem in Recent Research and

Debate," *Bulletin of the John Rylands Library*, Vol. 45 (1963), pp. 305 ff.

T. W. Manson, "The Son of Man in Daniel, Enoch and the Gospels," *Studies in the Gospels and Epistles*, edited by Matthew Black (The Westminster Press, 1962).

E. Schweizer, "The Son of Man," *Journal of Biblical Literature*, Vol. 79 (1960), pp. 119 ff.

_____ "The Son of Man Again," *New Testament Studies*, Vol. 9 (1963), pp. 256 ff.

A. J. B. Higgins, *Jesus and the Son of Man* (Lutterworth Press, 1964).

H. E. Tödt, *The Son of Man in the Synoptic Tradition*, tr. by Dorothea M. Barton (The New Testament Library, The Westminster Press, 1965).

R. H. Fuller, *The Foundations of New Testament Christology.*

M. D. Hooker, *The Son of Man in Mark* (Montreal: McGill Univ. Press, 1967).

13. For the absence of the Similitudes from the Enoch recensions at Qumran, see, e.g., J. T. Milik, *Ten Years of Discovery in the Wilderness of Judea* (Studies in Biblical Theology, No. 26; 1959), pp. 33 f.

14. For the resurrection-exaltation point of view, see J. A. T. Robinson, *Jesus and His Coming* (Abingdon Press, 1957).

15. The view of the vindication of the suffering wise man has been advocated by E. Schweizer, "The Son of Man." Mention of the deliberately ambiguous use of the title "Son of Man" begins to reappear, e.g., M. Black, "The Son of Man Problem in Recent Research and Debate," pp. 34 f., E. Schweizer in "The Son of Man Again," and S. E. Johnson, *The Theology of the Gospels* (London: Gerald Duckworth & Co., Ltd., 1966), p. 158—see his clear digest of the whole question, pp. 152–163.

16. The word *epitimaō* has been shown to have a distinctive background in exorcism in H. C. Kee, "The Terminology of Mark's Exorcism Stories," *New Testament Studies*, Vol. 14, No. 2 (1968).

17. On the "feeding," see H. W. Montefiore, "Revolt in the Desert?" *New Testament Studies*, Vol. 8 (1961–1962), pp. 135 ff.; cf. T. W. Manson, *The Servant Messiah* (London: Cambridge University Press, 1953), p. 70. The sacrament interpretation is found in A. Schweitzer, *The Mystery of the Kingdom of God*,

E.T. (Dodd, Mead & Company, Inc., 1914), pp. 168 ff., *The Quest of the Historical Jesus*, tr. by W. Montgomery, 2d ed. (London: A. & C. Black, Ltd., 1931), p. 374.

18. The transfiguration motifs are most completely explored in H. Riesenfeld, *Jésus Transfiguré* (Copenhagen, 1947); see a study in English, G. H. Boobyer, *St. Mark and the Transfiguration Story* (Edinburgh: T. & T. Clark, 1942).

Six

The King Without a Throne:
The Temple Without a Lord

We are aware how early Mark, as a Christian gospeller, has introduced the theme of the passion of Christ. It is forecast in the opposition complex of chs. 2:1 to 3:6 where the last verse intimates a sinister combination of church and state. Henceforward it is never far out of sight. For the Christian reader, it is anticipated in Jesus' identification with his people at his baptism. It comes to the surface like a great outcropping in the Caesarea and transfiguration scenes. It is strongly hinted in ch. 10 with the third passion prediction (vs. 33 f.) and the suggestion of the baptism in blood (vs. 38 f.). Of the fifteen chapters about Jesus' public life the last six are devoted to the events in Jerusalem. The story of Bartimaeus at Jericho in Mark 10:46 ff., however, is the real introduction. As far as Mark is concerned we must speak not of Jesus in Jerusalem but of Jesus in Judea.

THE WAY OF THE CROSS

The "way of the cross" is begun in Mark, ch. 8, and is announced in ch. 10:32: "They were on the road, going up to Jerusalem, and Jesus was walking ahead of them; and they were amazed, and those who followed were afraid." It becomes a reality when Jesus crosses the Jordan. It is hardly necessary to comment on the significance of Jericho as the historic point of entry into Judea for those aiming at Jerusalem from "the other side of Jordan," whether they went as pilgrims or had to subdue Jericho as invaders. A modern interest in the symbolical meaning of places and areas might easily ignore the historical background of the geography involved.

The story of the healing of blind Bartimaeus receives a good deal of discussion as a miracle story. It is sometimes misconstrued as a claim on Jesus' part to be "Son of David." The real significance of the pericope in Mark's scheme and for our subject lies in its connection with the "way of the cross."

Nothing is said in Mark of what happened in Jericho, though Luke has improved on this by putting the Bartimaeus story at the approach to Jericho and his own story of Zacchaeus at the leaving of the town. Mark's opening (ch. 10:46) reads: "And they came to Jericho; and as he was leaving Jericho with his disciples and a great multitude . . ." They all come to Jericho—Jesus, the Twelve, other travelers. But Jesus is singled out, as he is in ch. 10:17, "He was setting out on his journey," and once more in v. 32. So in v. 46 it is said, quite purposely, that the leaving of Jericho was on Jesus' initiative. It is his action that is emphasized, since to leave Jericho is to leave for no other place than Jerusalem, the place of the cross. With him went his disciples, but it was also, as we shall see, festival time and the pilgrim route was crowded. This is essential to the understanding of Mark's presentation.

The Greeting of Bartimaeus

The presence of a throng distinct from Jesus' followers is necessary to Mark's point. Matthew picks it up but puts a different emphasis on it when he says, "A great crowd followed him" and makes this festival throng into Jesus' retinue (Matt. 20:29). At this point in Mark, Bartimaeus appears. It is unusual for a person who is healed to receive a name, but whether it is a typical development in the course of tradition-building or original, it adds emphasis to the story. For Mark, it is not just another healing. At the same time, Bartimaeus is just there where he has long been, at his accustomed stand by the highway. The exit from Jericho, where the devout emerged on their way to the Holy City, was an obvious place for a beggar who was compelled to be a crowd pleaser if he was to succeed.

It is assumed that even a beggar has heard of Jesus of Nazareth. A blind person is quick to pick up the floating rumor and the mood of the populace, since he depends so largely on his ears. So Bartimaeus begins to chant the semiliturgical, royalistic phrase, "Son of David, have mercy on me!" We shall see the liturgical and festal significance of this but we must not miss the Messianic freight it carries. It would be convenient to know whether the blind man was joining in the cries of the crowd or whether he was, as it were, initiating a movement that took the people by surprise. The asking of this question is suggested by the quite unusual verses which follow, in which many object to his cries and try to silence him. Jesus stops his own progress to give Bartimaeus singular attention. We cannot here say what is fact and distinguish it from Mark's purpose, but there is more than one possibility.

We may note the important fact that this is the first place in Mark where Jesus is acclaimed as "Son of David." It is possible to understand the scene, including the rebuke to Bartimaeus in v. 48, in several ways. Bartimaeus, having heard that Messianic claims are associated with Jesus, joins in what he conceives to be the popular cry. On the other hand, Bartimaeus may be expressing a view of his own or formulating aloud a speculation the crowd had not yet openly voiced, or a rumor originating with Jesus' disciples. But it is not for a blind beggar to commit those who are free and have their sight.

We cannot and we need not speculate further. If Jesus' followers had secret hopes of a Messianic denouement (suggested earlier in Mark, ch. 10), this was not the time and place to make it public. If it was popular acclaim, a beggar incapacitated by the roadside had no place in it. If it was merely a festal chant sung by the pilgrims as they went up to the distant Temple, the significant thing is the addition of the word "Jesus" to the liturgical cry from Ps. 118:25 ("Hosanna," or "Lord, have mercy"). In whatever way we take it the addition of "Jesus" to the Messianic cry, heightened by the festival approach to Jerusalem, is of great importance, making public an identification which, if it existed at all, is at the moment secret, unspoken, the property of a closed group. We need not speculate because Jesus' action, not that of the bystanders, is crucial. Mark's plan is to make clear what Jesus' attitude is.

JESUS' APPROACH TO BARTIMAEUS

In the story, Jesus once again singles out a despised member of the community—if a beggar, any more than a leper, or a woman with an unclean malfunction, can be called a member of the community. We have to say "characteristically" Jesus singles out a virtual outcast for attention. (Is this why Luke, with more perception than some commentators, felt he could add here the story of Zacchaeus, another virtual outcast, whose unpopularity rather than his small stature kept him from seeing the scene?) Jesus orders the man brought to him. Some hint of Bartimaeus' lowly status is given by the encouragement now offered him: "Take courage; get up, he is calling you." The invitation makes a great day in a beggar's life. Jesus' question, in which undoubtedly the pronouns must be emphasized, "What do you want me to do for you?" gives to Bartimaeus a consideration as an individual to which he is hardly likely to have been accustomed.

We might say that Bartimaeus changes his tune. It must be intended to be significant that Bartimaeus addresses Jesus as "Rabbi." In Jesus' presence, singled out for attention, he no longer hails Jesus with an awesome title. He puts himself in the place, not of a camp follower or an aspirant to attention in the train of a king, but in the place of an ordinary Jew in the presence of a religious master-teacher. As far as a beggar might address a religious leader when invited to do so, he speaks as man to man. What he really wants is to be able to *see*—this more than alms, more than help for which one has to curry favor by being an echo, or has to demand attention by the utterance of an unspoken and secret intent.

Jesus' reply, "Your faith has made you well," is unexceptional. He has said it often before. It was both the response to faith and the evocation or discovery of faith. But his, "Go

your way," in this setting ought to carry weight. We note
that now, beyond Jericho, there is no command to silence.
"You are free now to go your own way," as he had not been
free when he was blind. It is a promise, since sight has not
yet been achieved. Then comes the climax. It is often said
that this is a miracle story without a pronouncement and with
no "choral ending." From a form-critical point of view this is
true. All the more significance then should be given to the last
words, especially in view of the subject of the story, its terms,
and its setting in this journey to Jerusalem. "He received his
sight"—this we expect. "And followed him on the way" is
exceptional. Just here in Mark it can mean only the way to
Jerusalem, and that means, with renewed emphasis, the way of
the cross. For we are leaving Jericho, the gateway to the Holy
City, the place of destiny.

MARK'S USE OF THE STORY

Mark's intention then may be summed up. It is a blind man
who cries out, "Jesus, Son of David." The "Have mercy on
me!" (on this road, at this time of year) is more acclaim than
petition. The blind man shouts, "Son of David"; the sighted
man follows Jesus on his way. Is it then true to Mark's intention
to say that Bartimaeus joined the throng of those who acclaimed Jesus as Messiah and was there, shouting, when the
days of "palms" and "Hosanna" came? I think not. That is to
read with presuppositions; to read Mark as if he were Matthew,
to take "Son of David" in too literal and physical a sense, and
to miss the organic place of this story in Mark's scheme.

We have to think of Mark's story as it stands, not as Matthew, for instance, has rearranged it. Here in Mark someone
cries out to Jesus, "Son of David," and the call is repeated
(vs. 47–48). Nowhere else in Mark does this occur with any
certainty. In Mark the term has not appeared before. This is
intended to be the first mention of it. What is the significance
of Mark's withholding "Son of David" until Jericho? From
an apologetic point of view it might be a dangerous point at
which to introduce it. It may be based on a real situation or a

deduction from actual circumstances. To Herod in Galilee and to the rulers in Jerusalem, Jesus might appear as the leader of the Galilean movement—or just another of them. So we read here that not until he set foot in Judea proper on his way to the capital was this leader hailed as "Son of David," that is, as a Messianic claimant as Jerusalem understood or feared Messiahship. Did Jesus' appearance at Jericho portend, to the apprehensive, a deliberate movement on the Holy City? In this sense the crossing of the Jordan and the departure from Jericho would be Jesus' "Rubicon," the point of inevitable commitment. From here on he must state his purpose. Or, is this another example of Mark's skill and artistic placing of an event and of enclosing a pregnant phrase within it? It may well be, since there is no real indication that the rulers feared any such move on the part of Jesus until the incident described as "the cleansing of the Temple." If it once existed, it has been suppressed.

In the Galilean section of the Gospel, Mark has made it evident that Jesus exercised unusual authority, that the powers of the Kingdom of God were at work in him. The "crisis" in Galilee had been caused in part by the mission of the Twelve and in part by the crowds gathered at the lakeside. Herod's anxious interest had been aroused. Yet Mark has no such explanation of why Jesus dismissed the crowd as John has (John 6:15). It may be that Mark could have added that elucidation of an otherwise unexplained move but preferred to keep the suggestion of the political or kingly motif of Messiahship until the Judean section. In this case it could come at no more appropriate place than Jericho. For Mark this *is* Jesus' "Rubicon." The acclamation "Son of David" by Bartimaeus prepares the way for the acclamation at Jerusalem, since the cry "Hosanna" is virtually the same. By this adroit story, located at Jericho, Mark has already safeguarded the later story and explained in advance Jesus' passive appearance in it and the absence of direct results from it.

The fact that Mark has put the Jericho acclamation on the lips of a blind man may be ironical. It may be intended to imply that the notion, applied to Jesus' advance on Jerusalem, is mistaken. It does not matter whether Bartimaeus' cry is the welcome Judea gives or the echo of a cry raised by the Galileans as they come. There can be no question where the road from Jericho (in the Gospel) leads—that "way" leads to the cross. The inference then would be that blindness to Jesus' real intention produces the Messianic acclamation in its traditional form. Sight, on the other hand, produces the understanding that it is necessary, rather, to take the way of the cross. This would seem to be Mark's purpose.

To understand the nature of Jesus' Messiahship one must hear and read Mark's "passion predictions" and his enigmatic declarations not only with "ears to hear" but also with "eyes to see." Though Jesus was acclaimed by Peter at Caesarea Philippi as "the Christ," there precedes it in the Gospel the story of the man whose sight came to him by stages. First, men appeared to his half-opened eyes as trees in motion and only later in their proper shape (Mark 8:22–26). Now there follows this other giving of sight to Bartimaeus which produces no such gradual vision nor does it produce any further cry of "Messiah," but only a following in the way. Jesus finds the same need here for the seeing eyes and the same faith.

For Jesus, the leaving of Jericho was indeed the casting of the die. It was so, however, because it meant he must meet with a people who in their blindness could cry out only, "Son of David," and this meeting must lead into the darkness. He offered them instead that opening of the eyes which leads a man to follow to the cross—and beyond. This would seem to be Mark's message.

THE "SON OF DAVID"

The title "Son of David" was to become important in Christian tradition increasingly for its emphasis on the descent from the royal house, as can be seen from the awkwardness of the genealogies in Matthew and Luke. Undoubtedly any claimant to Messiahship must be able to demonstrate lineage in the royal house of Judah and to say so is to emphasize the political and regal aspects of the office of Messiah. This should not lead us, however, to suppose that "Son of David" as an acclamation stressed the physical descent and so the inevitable destiny arising from it. Clearly, there must have been very many Jews who could trace their ancestry back to David, and it would be among them only that the Messiah could appear. But, from among that many, one must be chosen, elected, anointed, or otherwise singled out from the possible candidates. (Is not this, in fact, one of the purposes of the gathering of all the descendants of David at Bethlehem in Luke 2:4, so that it might be shown which of them was to be "in the city of David a Savior, who is Messiah the Lord," v. 11?) It is election that is significant, not ancestry.

It is easy in pursuing Christian theological developments to be distracted by the question of Jesus' birth and descent. That is the point on which the fathers settled in the story we are considering, partly because their opponents did so (see "Notes to Chapter Six," par. 1). In Mark this is not the issue and to make it so only confuses the exegesis. When Bartimaeus equates Jesus with the Son of David he cannot be supposed to have investigated Jesus' antecedents nor to have been advised about them. He is hailing Jesus as the promised King. If we keep our minds on this point, the significance of Mark's story is apparent. It is the virtual rejection of this aspect of the hope of Israel, the rejection of any claim to rule in and from an earthly Jerusalem, the putting aside of any claim to regal power or of any call to arms. It is the blind man who "sees" in Jesus a "Son of David." When his eyes are opened, he "follows in the way" without any such hope or assurance, willing just to go where Jesus goes, to share in whatever capacity Jesus serves. What that will be remains hidden. It is not, however, a royal progress with a political aim. In this, Bartimaeus provides, as he is no doubt intended to provide, a foil to the disciples of Jesus, while at the same time he is the true disciple.

We cannot tell at all, though the hints appear more than once, whether this emphasis is a reaction of the early church to the charge that Jesus was a political agitator, an apologetic against the fear of Messianism in the Roman world. Certainly,

Jesus was put to death as a "pretender," and here Mark is rejecting that charge as it is carefully rejected elsewhere in the four Gospels—most explicitly in John 18:33–38. We cannot tell for certain whether Jesus' activity gave any real grounds for such a charge. We must return to the problem later. Here we are concerned with Mark's Jesus who clears the sight of those who would see him in the role of "Son of David" or Messiah in the popular sense. Mark connects the issue with Jesus' entry into Judea before he connects it with his entry into Jerusalem. He has avoided the term "Son of David" in the account of the entry into the city, though the same interest is implied in the words: "Hosanna! Blessed is he who comes in the name of the Lord! Blessed is the kingdom of our father David that is coming!" (ch. 11:9 f.). The only place where the title occurs is in ch. 12:35 ff.

Before we look at that passage we notice that Matthew has ignored this carefully restricted use of the term in Mark. Jesus is already "Son of David" by Joseph's descent in the genealogy of Matt. 1:1–17 (especially v. 6). By the time he compiled his Gospel the church was concerned with Jesus as "descended from David according to the flesh" (Rom. 1:3). Matthew's parallel to the Bartimaeus story comes at ch. 20:29 ff. (the same context as Mark), though he has made Bartimaeus into two blind men. Mark's careful placing of the term is nullified in Matthew when an earlier doublet appears at Matt. 9:27–31 in a collection of ten miracles. "Son of David" appears there in v. 27, the cry of two blind men who follow Jesus. In response to their faith, Jesus restores their sight but sternly charges them that no one is to know of it—a charge they ignored. This differs from Mark, since in Matthew, Jesus seems to accept the term, although he wants it kept secret. It has, for him, a different meaning and Matthew has his own "Messianic secret." A Messianic use seems to be conveyed in ch. 12:23, where Matthew has the people speculating, after the healing of a man blind and dumb, "Can this be the Son of David?" It is rejected by the Pharisees, who attribute Jesus' powers to Beelzebul. Mark has no mention of this incident and

Luke, though he has the dumb demon, does not mention the speculation. Further, in Matt. 15:22 the Canaanite woman uses the term. This is an obvious difficulty, since she is not a Jewess and it belongs to the theme of wider recognition of Jesus discussed above in Chapter Four. Matthew did not find the term in Mark's parallel (see Mark 7:25 f.). Matthew alone in his version of the entry into Jerusalem has the crowd cry explicitly, "Hosanna to the Son of David!" (ch. 21:9).

Luke has followed Mark's caution, not using the term until the Bartimaeus story (ch. 18:38 f.) and, apart from the discussion of Ps. 110 (Luke 20:41 ff.), makes no use of it. It is like Luke to have understood the meaning of the cry of the crowds as they enter Jerusalem where he avoids the term but interprets it: "Blessed is the King who comes in the name of the Lord!" (ch. 19:38). If Luke were sensitive to the political Messianism implicit in the term, in view of his Gentile audience and his apologia to the Roman world, we should expect him to avoid it. We can only suppose that in so translating Mark he means to attribute the greeting of a King to the Jews—yet actually it is the "whole multitude of the disciples" who so cry out. This is one of the difficulties of taking Luke as an apologist pure and simple. Matthew with his need to justify Jesus to the Jews would be more likely to insist on the Messianic import of the term but also to use it in a growing "Christian" sense. The expression does not occur in Acts and the Fourth Gospel avoids it.

The place of the title in Christian thought, so important that it became in another form part of Jesus' name, is raised by Mark 12:35 ff. Mark gives three debates in Jerusalem in turn against the Pharisees, Herodians, Sadducees, and scribes. Then Jesus takes the initiative and poses the question: "How can the scribes say that the Christ is the Son of David?" We should take this to refer to the political understanding of the title, the kind of interpretation of Messiahship lauded in The Psalms of Solomon. In the quotation from Ps. 110, "my Lord" (by definition, David's Lord) is addressed by "the Lord" (God) and is seated in the place of power. From this it is argued that since

David here describes the Messiah as his "Lord," the Messiah cannot be David's "son"—or cannot in the accepted sense be his son. On the surface this is a refutation of the idea of "Son of David" in which Jesus seems to be rejecting the title as applied to any human figure. Does the "How . . . ?" leave open the possibility of taking the term in a non-Messianic sense? The church was prepared to reject the political Messianic application of the term but to accept it in one sense "according to the flesh." It would seem, in view of Mark's extreme reserve about this title, that we should take this rather ambiguous passage as intended to be Jesus' repudiation of the concept of "Son of David." The "Lord" who is to be enthroned over his enemies is not one to be conceived in the usual sense as "Son of David," whether as a political claimant to David's throne or as a lineal descendant of David (the former, of course, including the latter). Mark seems to have been perfectly aware of the danger that lay in the political messianism involved (as Luke and John seem to have been by their avoidance of it).

We see again the shadow of a paradox, that Jesus, who for the church has been enthroned, did not claim that throne as "Son of David." The enthronement has taken place in another realm where Jesus is addressed as "Lord," not as Messiah.

JESUS IN JERUSALEM

The same element of paradox leads to confusion in the reading by overeager commentators of the account of the so-called "triumphal entry," a reading which prompts them to assert that Jesus was here hailed as Messiah and that he not only accepted the acclaim but planned it. The nature of the accounts should make us extremely wary about such assertions. The entry into Jerusalem (Mark 11:1–10) cannot be treated in isolation. It has connections forward with the "cleansing of the Temple," the barren fig tree, the challenge to Jesus' authority, the parable of the tenants of the vineyard and the sayings which follow it down to Mark 12:12. This is the beginning of the passion story proper, no doubt itself the earliest continuous narrative in the Gospels, essentially a primitive feature of the kerygma. Yet the section Mark 11:1 to 12:12 has a unity of its own. When this is discerned, its connection backward also with the Bartimaeus story as we have discussed it becomes clear.

MARK'S ARRANGEMENT

Another feature in Mark of the passion story is the trace of the arrangement of the material under "six days." This may be the reflection of an early liturgical practice. As said above, it may suggest an original connection of the transfiguration (Mark 9:2) with the passion cycle, reinforcing the undoubted relevance it has for the topic of suffering death in Mark's Gospel. If "liturgical" in origin, it depends upon a stage of development in which the Christian Passover (the celebration of the passion and resurrection) has displaced Tabernacles in an earlier following of the Jewish festal calendar. Here I must refer to my articles for the details substantiating what follows (see "Notes to Chapter Six," par. 1).

A study of Mark's complex, chs. 11:1 to 12:12, reveals that the association of the entry into Jerusalem and the cleansing of the Temple with Passover, in the spring month of Nisan, is a later Christian development. At some more primitive stage the incidents were associated with the Feast of Tabernacles (or Booths; Sukkoth, "*the* feast") in the autumn month of Tishri. A curious relic of this recognition is found in Mark 11:13 in the words: "It was not the season for figs," a remark true of Nisan but not of Tishri, for Tishri was above all the time of fruit harvest and vintage. Whoever wrote the words was already reading the complex as a Passover story. In the setting of the Tabernacles festival all the details and themes fall into place. The coming of Jesus from the Mount of Olives, the chants of "Hosanna" from Ps. 118, the cleansing of the court of the Gentiles for the worship expected of them at that feast (Mark 11:17, "for all the nations"), the expectation of finding figs on a healthy tree, the vintage parable of the tenants, the "stone" testimony from Ps. 118:22, and even the moving of the mountain, all belong to the Tishri feast. Following the clue of Zech., ch. 14 (more important initially than Zech., ch. 9), which was read during the feast, we detect that all of this added together constitutes an eschatological claim.

When Jesus rides into the city from the Mount of Olives, he comes to the metropolis as its eschatological king (Zech. 14:4). When he enters the Temple precincts and reclaims an area of it for worship, he comes as the eschatological Lord in whose time the Gentiles are to worship there at the Feast of Booths (Zech. 14:16 f.) and "on that day" no trader will be permitted there (v. 21). The arrangement peculiar to Mark, whereby the cleansing is enclosed within the two parts of the story of the barren fig tree, is a significant confirmation of the original intent of this complex. The "day" has come and the Temple is revealed to be barren, as deficient in its purpose as a fig tree at vintage time which has a brave show of leaves but no fruit. "On that day" the rightful king has come to his city, the true Lord to his Temple—but he has come unrecognized. There has been no Armageddon and he has not exerted his wrath; there has been no "breaking with a rod of iron" (Ps. 2:9; Zech. 14:3, 12 ff.), no smiting "with the rod of his mouth, and with the breath of his lips" (Isa. 11:4; see Chapter Two, above). Even the so-called "cursing" of the fig tree did not appear to bear that meaning originally (Mark 11:14 is ambiguous in the Greek and Peter's words in v. 21 are necessary to make it miraculous). As far as what follows in the arraignment and trial of Jesus (at least as we have them), no evidence is offered from these scenes to condemn Jesus for a destructive role.

There lies within the groundwork of these passages deeply embedded the theme of "the Unrecognized," the Lord who came to city and Temple but whose coming was scarcely noted and certainly not accepted as such. A brief scurry in the outer court of the Temple raised only the baffled question, "By what authority?" (Mark 11:27 ff.), to be answered only by an unanswerable counterquestion (v. 30) and a parable that stresses the theme of responsibility and rejection. The unity of theme is either the work of the Evangelist or (perhaps more likely) of the tradition behind him. At that level the "three days" (vs. 11–12, 19, 20) are not part of a spring "holy week" but a device to separate the entry from the cleansing and to hold together the cleansing of the Temple with the pointers to its significance provided by the incident of the fruitless tree. No mention is made of Passover until Mark 14:1. The church's habit of associating Mark's complex with Palm Sunday is, however, probably incurable. Did the events actually happen at Tabernacles? The records no longer permit us to answer with more than a possibility.

When we grasp the Tabernacles nexus of Mark's passages, we see that the story of Bartimaeus is connected with them as a prelude and as an interpretative warning. He cries, "Son of David, have mercy!" and this is the Tabernacles' cry from the reiteration of Ps. 118:25 in Temple and synagogue liturgy (note also the reference in v. 24 to "This is the day" and in v. 27 to the "branches"). The throng passing through Jericho on its way to the Feast of Booths is the throng in which Jesus is involved in Mark 11:1–10. "Those who went before and those who followed" in v. 9 are obviously pilgrims filling the road on the way to the city (Luke in ch. 19:37 has made them into Jesus' disciples). The "leafy branches" of v. 8 are the *lulabim* (sprays of three kinds of greenery) the pilgrims carried at the festival. In John 12:13 they have become royal "palms." I have discussed John's treatment of Tabernacles in the article previously referred to, "Tabernacles in the Fourth Gospel and Mark."

We see no indication, however, that Jesus accepts the acclaim, at least to the extent of capitalizing on any support implied. In Mark he merely looks around in the Temple and returns forthwith to Bethany (ch. 11:11). It is Matthew who has felt the lack and has provided a citywide response and immediate action in the Temple (ch. 21:10 ff.), and both he and Luke have allowed for an immediate reaction of the authorities (Matt. 21:15 f.; Luke 19:34 ff.). This doubtless helps along the drama but completely misses the purpose of Mark's careful plan. It is probably deliberate that Mark has Jesus come twice from the Mount of Olives (his "Bethany," ch. 11:1, 11, 12). Once he comes as unrecognized King and again as unrecognized Lord. For Mark, or the tradition behind him, the "day of the Lord" has come—but how different a day it is! We should not minimize the difference between the underlying expectation and the described events. They are the essence of the paradox that was Jesus.

THE NATURE OF THE ENTRY

Is it implied that when Jesus came to Jerusalem he came with the hope, even the expectation, that God would in some way act to bring his Kingdom even more near? It is possible. If it were known to the tradition, we can understand why it would have been, if not suppressed, transposed. What follows seems to suggest that if there was any such expectation, it was not an event that Jesus intended to precipitate in any way (as Schweitzer, Eisler, and others have held) by any overt act of force or precipitate self-sacrifice, but one which he expected God to initiate in his own way. The Gospels no longer provide the answer to such speculations but the state in which we find them implies a transition of some sort.

We have so far left aside the feature so prominent in Christian imagination, art, and liturgy—the riding on the "colt." In view of the unity to be discerned underlying Mark's work we are compelled to think twice about the analysis of these passages offered by literary critics. The story of the ride into Jerusalem, in particular the sending for the colt, is widely accepted as secondary. It is often coupled with a similar sending to make arrangements, the preparation for eating the Passover in Mark 14:12–16. Bultmann is not alone in calling it "a manifestly legendary characteristic" and "a fairy-tale motif" (*Die Geschichte*, p. 281; E.T., p. 261). It has been described as a miraculous case of prevision on Jesus' part, since he knows about the colt and what will be said (Mark 11:2 f.), as also about the man carrying the pitcher and where he will go (ch. 14:13 f.). Obviously, a connection has been made with the "prophecy" of Zech. 9:9 f., though like so many of Mark's Old Testament allusions in the passion story, if it is an allusion, it is not expressed in so many words. In the case of the entry, actual quotation is the work of Matthew (ch. 21:4 f.) and John (ch 12:14 f.). Like the pervasive background of Zech., ch. 14, the allusion in Mark to Zech. 9:9–10 is, at the most, implicit.

In pursuing this analysis it would remove difficulties and make a simpler (also a more mundane) story if the section from the last part of Mark 11:1 to the end of v. 7 (the sending for the colt) could be treated as an intrusion. As an attempt to get at the original event this might serve but as an intrusion it does not help us follow Mark's purpose and perhaps it ignores a feature that may after all recollect something of the original circumstances.

If Jesus rode into the city on a colt "on which no one had ever sat," especially provided for the purpose, this would not be known to anyone except Jesus' intimates—unless indeed its dam accompanied it as Matthew has had it do. (This is not mere carelessness or literalism on Matthew's part. His "ass tied and a colt with her" is another way of indicating that the colt had not yet been used for riding.) To the populace Jesus would just be riding in a not uncommon manner, very likely not the only one seated on a donkey. Even today such riders can be seen. A study of the place of the horse and ass respectively in the Biblical literature shows that the ass was free of many connotations that in Israel were associated with the horse to its severe detriment. It appeared that an *unridden* ass colt was the mount of the ancient rulers in Israel before the dark days of Solomon's "power politics" in which the horse figured so largely as a means of oppression and confusion (see "Notes to Chapter Six," par. 6). The significance of the colt is not that Jesus is supposed here to be repudiating kingship or warfare by eschewing a horse. In Zechariah it is a king who comes, though he comes "humble and riding on an ass," yet also victorious. Rather, the claim to kingship in this symbolical ride is real but is a claim to a carefully guarded type of rule which antedated the introduction of the horse into Israel's economy with all its attendant miseries.

It would, obviously, take a knowledge of the ancient tradition to grasp this and, again, it would be obvious only to those who knew that the colt was suitable for the purpose (a knowledge available to the readers of the Gospel as well as to Jesus' companions). Such a choice would take careful planning, the kind of planning here described, where the colt is placed in a position to be picked up and a prearranged message is the means of its release (Mark 11:2 ff.). It suggests not publicity but the desire to avoid publicity—this more than any more "cloak and dagger" undertaking. One may well question whether it was originally intended to be a case of miraculous prevision.

Bultmann has said that the assumption necessary if the account is to be taken as history, namely, that Jesus "intended to fulfill the prophecy of Zech. 9:9 and that the crowd recognized the ass as the Messiah's riding-animal—is absurd" (*Die Geschichte*, p. 281; E.T., p. 262). Such recognition by the crowd is, as we have seen, obviously impossible. This does not prevent us from assuming that in Mark's tradition Jesus did arrange for such a ride and that it served as a veiled claim (perhaps to be described as "prophetic symbolism") accessible to the understanding of his followers. That such an "esoteric" undertaking actually took place we can neither affirm nor deny. That it was not and could not be a public manifesto is clear.

If we take seriously the original Tabernacles setting, the crowd would be chanting "Hosanna" in any case. Only disciples "in the know" would connect the cries with Jesus' journey amid the throng. If we are to accept the planning on Jesus' part as anything more than Mark's clue to the reader, the sign of riding on the ass may not be directed at the crowds at all but at the disciples. The "veiled claim" then becomes

virtually a rebuke, a warning to his followers that he has no
Messianic purpose which could not be covered by the "meek-
ness" of Zech. 9:9. We may say this is addressed to the disciples of the later church, which is of course true, but does
that necessarily exclude an act of "prophetic symbolism" on
Jesus' part characteristic of the Hebrew prophets? John, who
has made explicit the reference to Zechariah and turned the
green boughs into palms, says that the disciples did not understand until Jesus was glorified "that this had been written of
him and had been done to him" (John 12:16). This is probably an accurate account of the development that takes place
in the form of the story. If nothing at all lies behind Mark's
story, it is difficult to see why he had to engage himself in so
involved an account without benefit of quotation from Zechariah.

What is clear, amid the obscurities, is that Mark has again
carefully guarded against any open claim by Jesus or any
acceptance of Messianic dignity, and this conforms to the purpose we have found in the Bartimaeus story. Whatever claim
there is, is veiled and carefully guarded against the militant implications of current Messianism. There is nothing here re-
motely like an invasion of the city. For the Christian reader
with "eyes to see," the King comes with an archaic dignity
and, even for that very reason, is ignored by all except those
who do not need such a demonstration unless it is to cure their
own oversanguine expectations. The Day has come, but who
is to declare it? The Day has come, but it does not "burn like
an oven." Rather, to those who fear God's name the "sun of
righteousness" has arisen with healing in his wings (Mal.
4:1-2).

THE CLEANSING OF THE TEMPLE

The cleansing of the Temple is likewise an eschatological
drama. In its Tabernacles setting it too proclaims the Day, the
time when the Gentiles will enter into their rights as worshipers with Israel. In the haphtorah, (Zech., ch. 14), the

Gentiles are those who survive the eschatological war: "Then every one that survives of all the nations that have come against Jerusalem shall go up year after year to worship the King, the LORD of hosts, and to keep the feast of booths" (v. 16). Mark, however, consonant with the very different atmosphere of Jesus' presence in Jerusalem, has quoted from Isa. 56:7. In this instance the context must be recalled and the difference between Second Isaiah and the latter part of Zechariah. The passage reads: "And the foreigners who join themselves to the LORD, to minister to him, to love the name of the LORD, and to be his servants, every one who keeps the sabbath, and does not profane it, and holds fast my covenant— these I will bring to my holy mountain, and make them joyful in my house of prayer; their burnt offerings and their sacrifices will be accepted on my altar; for my house shall be called a house of prayer for all peoples" (Isa. 56:6 f.). By contrast to this expectation, the use of the court of the Gentiles in Jesus' time seems to have presented a picture of confusion.

Mark, followed by Matthew and Luke, has added the further reference to Jer. 7:11 which reads: "Has this house, which is called by my name, become a den of robbers in your eyes?" There follows it in Jeremiah the threat that the Temple will go the way of the former shrine at Shiloh. It may be significant in an allusive sense, that the word "robbers" is in Greek *lēistai*, a term which we shall see in the next chapter is a significant pointer to the charge on which Jesus is crucified and to the nature of his companions on the crosses. Whether the suggestion that the Temple itself has become a hideout or conspiracy place for the underground resistance has a historical reality it is difficult to say. It serves to remind us (and perhaps was intended to) that something more than a commercial exploitation of the rules about approved sacrifices was involved (see "Notes to Chapter Six," par. 7).

The early loss of the connection with Tabernacles meant the loss of an explicit reference to the Gentiles as we find it in Mark, since both Matthew and Luke have omitted the words, "for all the nations." In view of the original Tabernacles connection, the phrase is not an addition by Mark in the interests of the Gentile mission. Rather, its absence from the other Gospels is an omission brought about by the loss of the festal connection. The clearing out of the traders at least symbolically provides the place and opportunity for the Gentiles—since the Day has come without the apocalyptic upheaval—to fulfill their obligations. Apart from this clearing of the way there is no battle, the Mount of Olives is not reduced below the level of Mount Zion, and no stream gushes forth from the Temple precincts (see Zech., ch. 14). There is only a symbolical action to be read by those who can see its prophetic implications. The Fourth Gospel has caught this transposition by applying the figure of the stream of water to Jesus himself (John 7:37 f., though even there its fulfillment is deferred until after Jesus has been glorified and the Spirit can be given). Speculations that Jesus was trying to reform or even to do away with the Temple cult are beside the point; neither does the event assume the proportions of the greatest crisis in Jesus' ministry.

THE REACTION OF JERUSALEM

That Jesus' action for the moment at least disturbed the authorities is suggested by the Evangelists as it is not concerning the entry into the city. To them Jesus is an interloper who has no right, no authority (*exousia*). According to Mark, the incident and the reaction do not prevent Jesus from frequenting the Temple colonnades as a teacher and disputant (Mark 11:27 to 12:44). If the cleansing actually happened in the autumn at the Feast of Booths, there was plenty of time to elapse before any move was made against Jesus in the spring at the eve of Passover. The acute awareness of the danger that public agitation might be aroused by any such move to interfere with Jesus is noted by Mark at this earlier point (Mark 11:32 || Luke 20:6 f.), a note which by omission Matthew has deferred. Nothing is said of popular acceptance of Jesus as a Messianic agitator, only that he was taken to be a prophet—a significant enough estimate, since apart from John the Baptist prophets were unknown. The nature of Jesus' opposition to the authorities and their doubts about him are depicted by the parables and the controversies in the Temple which follow this incident and take the place in the Jerusalem section of the opposition stories of Mark 2:1 to 3:6 in the Galilean section.

It has sometimes been asserted that the cleansing played no part in the accusations brought against Jesus at his "trial." In the nature of the case (see the next chapter) we cannot tell. A threat to the Temple or its current operation, especially in an outer court, would not impress the Roman procurator unless it threatened a breach of the Roman peace. Traces show through the record of some concern about the Temple, whether from Jesus' action or from his teaching in general or from a report of some such discourse as that now embodied in the apocalypse of Mark, ch. 13. It appears in what is described as the evidence of "false witnesses" in Mark 14:57–59 || Matt. 26:60–61. It is ignored or dismissed by the priests, according to Mark, because of the lack of concurring testimony. It may reflect a historical recollection of (more than one?) disturbance in the Temple courts, though in Mark it leads back more immediately to the eschatological discourse (ch. 13:1 ff.), confusing forecast with revolutionary intention—or even further, to the implied warning of the parables of the tenants. It is an impression the Fourth Gospel has been careful to transmute in ch. 2:18–22, "He spoke of the temple of his body" (cf. ch. 4:23).

The "facts" cannot be recovered. Certainly, Mark's tradition took the circumstance to be a veiled claim or an act of "prophetic symbolism." Again, the Day had come. The Lord had come to his Temple (Mal. 3:1 ff.), though he came unrecognized. In that guise people were able "to endure the day of his coming," for he did not appear as "a refiner's fire" nor "sit as a refiner and purifier of silver" to purify the "sons of Levi" in any outward or apparent form (see Chapter Two, above). When the Temple had been destroyed in little more than a generation (which perhaps was the occasion for the publishing of Mark, at least in its present form) an apocalypse like that embodied in Mark, ch. 13, became possible. If anyone had such hopes before Jesus' death, he was doomed to be disappointed. The failure of Jesus to take any more definitive action is another step on his way to the cross.

THE PARADOX

We are confronted again with a paradox. Jesus is a simple pilgrim "keeping the feasts" who, if he claims any rights at all in the Holy City, can be said to have claimed them only inconspicuously and with discretion. Yet he is actually King of the city and Lord of the Temple, there to inaugurate "the day of his coming." But who was there to see this or to respond, except liturgically, "This is the day which the Lord has made; let us rejoice and be glad in it" (Ps. 118:24)? The people who chanted "Hosanna"—whether aware of the Pilgrim or not—had most likely nothing at all to do with those who later cried, "Let him be crucified." Only now, down through the years since, do we stand in his presence and face the choice. We have to decide whether we can see in what sense he is King and Lord or whether we spurn him because he will not now, as he would not then, lend himself to our schemes of power and of "take-over." Now we know that the Day is always his Day and the choice we make involves an eternal dimension of existence.

The expectations that went before can be seen to be fulfilled in the event only by Christian eyes. Paul has expressed the point in his own way by the use of the phrase "according to the flesh" (*kata sarka*), which sometimes is misinterpreted to support a lack of interest in Jesus as a man with a history of his own. In Rom. 1:3, Paul says of the gospel that it concerns God's Son, "who was descended from David according to the flesh (*kata sarka*)," but was "designated Son of God in power according to the Spirit of holiness (*kata pneuma*) by his resurrection from the dead." To debate the descent from David (embracing the Messianic claim) is to make an estimate of Jesus from a human point of view (*kata sarka*). The evaluation offered in the Christian gospel is determined by the resurrection through which the Jesus known to the Gospels is made known to be the Son of God—in function certainly, if not yet in another sense. By the resurrection, Jesus was enthroned, not in Jerusalem, but in heaven, "seated at the right hand" of God, to be King of all kings and Lord of all lords. In the gospel tradition there is again that "integrity" (here most notably in Mark) which places the fulfillment in another realm and at another time. As with "the Mightier One," as with the Son, as with the baptism with Spirit, as with the charge to go to all the world, as with the Son of Man, the tradition behind the Gospels puts this, too, after the resurrection.

Jesus had no throne and no city; neither was the Temple his in "historic fact." The city's "day" and the Temple's had come. So it was foretold it would come in Luke 13:34 f., and that it would be at Tabernacles, as the echo of Ps. 118 in v. 35 indicates: "You will not see me until you say, 'Blessed is he who comes in the name of the Lord!' " (and, differently placed, in Matt. 23:37-39). But no one could as yet see that it had. Human and mundane power could still work its will and seem to avert any danger. But the coming of Jesus to Jerusalem could open the eyes of those who expected of him either earthly weapons or apocalyptic miracles. The account of Jesus' "temptation" in the wilderness is a summing up of his whole career by one whose eyes have thus been opened (see Chapter Eight, below). Jesus' "secret weapon" was his own life, his own body; his ultimate strategy was his complete surrender to the way God would lead him as the situation developed. To the opened eyes of the Christian, paradoxically, his refusal to claim the city is his strongest claim of all, the revelation of a royalty not of this world, a power not "according to the flesh."

NOTES TO CHAPTER SIX

1. For an analysis of the relation of the Tabernacles festival and its liturgical aspects to the entry into Jerusalem, Mark's complex

in chs. 11:1 to 12:12, and the barren fig tree as it concerns the cleansing of the Temple, see my "No Time for Figs," *Journal of Biblical Literature*, Vol. 79, No. 4 (1960), the literature mentioned there, and "Notes to Chapter Four." Also, see "Tabernacles in the Fourth Gospel and Mark," *New Testament Studies*, Vol. 9, No. 2 (1963). Another study may be found in J. W. Doeve, "Purification du Temple et Desséchement du Figuer," *New Testament Studies*, Vol. 1, No. 4 (1955). For comments of the fathers, see, for example, Tertullian, *Against Marcion* IV.36; Origen, *On Matthew*, Tome XVI, 9.

2. On blindness and discipleship, see the further discussion in Chapter Eight.

3. For an analysis and viewpoint on Matthew's use, see J. M. Gibbs, "Purpose and Pattern in Matthew's Use of the Title 'Son of David,'" *New Testament Studies*, Vol. 10 (1964), pp. 446 ff.

4. On apologia concerning political claims, see Postscript.

5. On the liturgical use of the entry story, see my *Biblical Authority for Modern Preaching* (The Westminster Press, 1960), p. 160.

6. For a summary of the Biblical background of the use of the ass, see my "The Horse and the Ass in the Bible," *Anglican Theological Review*, Vol. 27, No. 2 (1945), pp. 86 ff. In this chapter I am modifying what I said there about the Gospels.

7. On the possible uses made of the Temple, see, e.g., G. W. Buchanan, "Mark 11:15–19, Brigands in the Temple," in *Hebrew Union College Annual*, Vol. XXX (1959), pp. 169 ff., and "An Additional Note," *ibid.*, Vol. XXXI (1960), pp. 103 ff. Also, N. Q. Hamilton, "Temple Cleansing and Temple Bank," *Journal of Biblical Literature*, Vol. 83 (1964), pp. 365 ff. For further on "brigands," see Chapter Seven and Notes.

Seven

The Final Paradox:

The Savior
Who Could Not Save

The essential paradox of Jesus, according to the Gospels, was stated by Jesus' enemies. Of the comments on his career, none contains a more profound compliment than the one expressed as derision directed toward Jesus while he hangs on the cross. Mark gives it emphatically in the Greek: "Others he saved; himself he cannot save" (ch. 15:31). This may be a construction of the Evangelist. If so, it is all the more interesting that he puts the greatest possible tribute to Jesus in terms of a derisive rejection on the lips of his detractors. We may hear in it an echo of the scorn of Jewish contemporaries for the early Christians. But it also represents the climax, the bringing to conclusive expression what gradually emerges from Mark's construction, that Jesus' opponents more acutely grasped that there was some kind of claim inherent in Jesus' work and message than did his followers. Hence, "He saved others; himself he cannot save," is the paradox of all the paradoxes of Jesus' life as it emerges from the Gospels. The one who could heal others and secure them from the demons, who could overcome the causes of terror and of whom it was even said that he could give life to the dead, could not save himself from suffering and death. It was to be and it remains the glory of the church that it found in this paradox the very clue to God's new action, his renewed revelation. In accepting this paradox, it was able to digest all the others—those we have examined and many others that might be expressed as the leader who followed, the restorer who disrupted, the strong man who was conquered, the glorified who was despised, the clarifier who was absurd. The church was able to record his challenge, "Blessed is he who takes no offense at me" (Matt. 11:6 || Luke 7:23).

The derisive challenge directed at Jesus in Mark 15:32 is, in Luke, carefully rephrased, "He saved others; let him save himself, if he is the Christ of God, his Chosen One!" (ch. 23:35). So is restored in full force the temptation to put God to the test which is the theme of the temptation story common to Matthew and Luke (Matt. 4:1–11; Luke 4:1–13; see next chapter). Those who congratulated each other (Mark 15:31) on their triumph in disposing of Jesus are not intended to be acknowledging Jesus' work. The fact that Jesus was unable to save himself meant to them that he had really failed to save anyone else, had only claimed to do so. This is what Luke has brought out. A conclusive demonstration of Jesus' claim could be accepted, indeed could be made explicit, only if he could himself avoid this shameful death. Recurring notions, such as appear in Hugh J. Schonfield's book *The Passover Plot* (see "Notes to Chapter Seven" par. 1), that Jesus somehow intended to, or in fact did, survive crucifixion seriously misjudge the Gospels (as we have seen particularly in Chapter Five, above).

THE ACCOUNTS OF THE PASSION

So the paradox stands, fully implemented in the passion, the account of which is full of paradoxes of its own. It is properly assumed that the passion story was the earliest continuous segment of the Gospels and of the kerygma. Even so, subjected to literary and linguistic analysis, there are indications that separate units have been brought together to produce its present form. At the literary stage, certainly, it was still fluid after Mark was compiled. Here, Luke, for instance, is less dependent on Mark than elsewhere and may have used another basis for his outline. We detect also a growing tendency to develop Old Testament allusions into actual quotations and testimonies, as can be seen when we put the Gospels side by side. Some aspects of the account of the crucifixion are made out of Old Testament material, notably Ps. 22. The meaning of this can be exaggerated, since the details of Roman executions may be presumed to have been common knowledge. Here the common features have been given allusive expression. In Matthew and John they happen *because* the Old Testament anticipated them. It is inevitable that Christian faith, preaching, and worship should have entered into the formation of the tradition as we have it.

THE DIFFICULTIES OF THE STORY

The underlying "plot" so preserved can hardly, however, be called coherent. The question is whether the difficulties are a confusion caused by oral and literary development or whether they reach down more deeply into the tradition itself, back to a course of events in which the paradoxical elements are firmly grounded. It is not to be expected that by successively removing layers we shall reach a firm historical set of facts, because in the process there would be discarded some of the very inconsistencies that were inherent in the situation. Notable difficulties concern the chronology, the nature of Jesus' last meal with his followers, the so-called trial before the high priest, the nature of the charges against Jesus, and the part the Romans had in the outcome. There are undoubted embellishments of a bare account, but that there was ever preached or taught a bare narrative, such as might be reached by radical elimination of every suspect element, is of course unlikely. Even as austere an account of the death of Jesus as that in Mark has elements in it which express its Christian purpose— and, one must add, it was intended for this purpose.

Perhaps hundreds of Jews were crucified in this period by Roman authority, but only one of them became the Savior of Christian faith. This, we say, was because he was "raised from the dead." We are still compelled to ask, Why this one? The gospel tradition set out to answer that question. The first point around which the answer must gather would be the crucifixion itself. How did Jesus come to be executed, and why? How did he take it, and how did it appear to others? Since, by general consent, hardly anyone was there to witness the event (conspicuously absent were the "apostolic" witnesses of the resurrection), the answer had to be largely in terms of how it appeared to Jesus' followers after his "raising." Basically, what the Evangelists had to work with was the commonly known course of Roman crucifixions, Old Testament passages that strikingly illuminated its normal features as predetermined, some knowledge of the temper of the times, and the character of the chief actors, especially the kind of person Jesus was.

A little imagination reveals the critical nature of the problem for the gospel tradition. Paul does not exaggerate when he says that the crucifixion of a Messiah ("Christ crucified") made nonsense to the cultured Greek world and, as for the Jewish church, it could be to its adherents only a "scandal" (I Cor. 1:23). What of the Romans? Are they assumed under the term "Greeks"? It almost staggers the mind to try to think of proclaiming to a sophisticated "power structure" that a provincial Jew, who had been condemned and executed by Roman authority in a subsection of a remote province as a pretender to some kind of rule in which religion and politics were confounded, was actually chosen and sent by God to redeem men from their troubles and someday to rule the world. Unless we try to visualize this, we miss the astounding nature of the passion tradition, especially when we come later to consider the atmosphere of Messianic suspicion at the time.

Naturally, mere recital of the facts would not be enough. They must be explained. Something in the nature of an apologia was necessary, a justification of the naming of Jesus (see Ebeling, *Theology and Proclamation*, Ch. X). We would expect, since the gospel had to be preached in a world dominated by Rome, an attempt to justify Pilate's decision, in view of the claims that Jesus was "Lord," to remove the blame

from the procurator's course of action. There are clear traces
of such an attempt, yet why is it not more thoroughgoing
or even more subtle? That Pilate was known to be ruthlessly
firm but inept is not ignored and seems to have a historical
basis. The blame is not entirely removed (though a radical
stage is reached in Matthew's recension in ch. 27:19 f., 24 f., for
purposes of polemic against the Jews rather than to clear
Rome). The titulus on the cross read, "The King of the Jews"
(Mark 15:26). There is, therefore, no attempt to conceal the
charge, although there is a good deal of attention to why and
how one who was innocent of the purpose implied came to be
executed for it. There is an ironical paradox here when an
innocent Jesus takes the place of a guilty Barabbas which we
must examine.

We perhaps underestimate less the problem of convincing
the Jews that a carpenter out of Galilee, without the support
of any recognized party, repudiated by synagogue and Sanhedrin, who was susceptible to being charged with a crime
accepted by the alien ruler, could be God's Anointed. We find
Paul dealing with it in his letters and in Luke's attempt in Acts
to show Paul at the task. We are told that the fact of crucifixion itself put such a claimant out of countenance as one
accursed (Gal. 3:13). A different technique was needed here.
It had to be shown that what happened and what was intended
was all foreshadowed in the Old Testament. This motive has
at least as deeply affected the telling of the story as has an
apologia to Rome.

THE ANTI-SEMITIC HAZARD

For the twentieth century, all too belatedly, a particular
problem arises that threatens the freedom to interpret the
passion story more than any other part of the Gospels. Anti-
Semitism is a shameful blot on the history of the Christian
church. It has been especially heinous when it has raised or
fostered the cry, "You Jews killed the Son of God." It is hard
to see how any Christian can feel free of the stain or how the

Christian community can atone for the horrors inflicted. Objective inquiry must nonetheless not be inhibited from seeking the truth, nor must exegesis of the Gospels be dominated by an overzealous effort to avoid the taint. It is one thing to deny the shameful distortion that made all Jews responsible for the death of the Lord but it will not do to determine in advance that the texts shall be read to find no involvement of any Jews, any more than it was right in the past to be controlled by a determination to fix the blame. Fixing the blame and avoiding taints are, neither of them, useful tools in the understanding of any historical record, much less so distinctive a piece of literature as the Gospels.

An Emergency Situation

We assume that we are dealing with the literary expression of a message intended to convict and convince, to instruct and explain. The problem that we have seen to exist in other parts of the Gospels is even more acute here. Why does such a message take the form it does? What we are asking is why was the record not made more self-consistent—by making the chronology clear, the Jewish hearings more conformable to rabbinical accounts of proper procedure, the intentions of all persons agreeable to their subsequent actions? The answer to be proposed is this: *They were not consistent nor particularly coherent when they happened.*

Many of the Christian features introduced do not so much confuse the story as try to give it a regularity it did not have to begin with (a tendency that increases in Luke and John). In the twentieth century we have all too unhappily become familiar with the same kind of irregular action, inconsistent with professed ideals or even with legal and constitutional provisions. In Asia and Africa and South America, even in our own country, not to speak of Fascist, Nazi, and Communist areas, there have been actions taken under the rubric of "a state of emergency." In some cases this has been done to deal with actual circumstances threatening the legitimate peace and order of the community. But sometimes the circumstances have first been created by those who wished to suspend the guarantees of a constitution for their own purposes and so have identified with their own interests the "peace and order" which was threatened. Resort to a declared "state of emergency" can be defended as essential or it can be condemned as nefarious. It depends upon who writes the history. In the urgencies of a crisis there is seldom time or opportunity to weigh all the facts, since the supreme fact is the violence exerted or threatened. A "state of emergency" can, by the suspension of the normal rules, give responsible authority a chance to reestablish the normal procedures and, in due course, reform them. Everything depends upon the character of the powers in charge and their intentions. In such situations it often happens that some innocent people suffer, but they suffer because they are trapped in a process that is intended to restore or achieve the common good.

It is not suggested here that there was at the time of Jesus' execution the pronouncement of "a state of emergency," but a good deal of what is described fits action in accord with such a situation. As the Fourth Gospel interprets Jesus' arrest we find a word of the high priest intended to express his policy. The question before the Sanhedrin is, What shall we do about Jesus? This is occasioned by the report of his "signs," by the following he seems to have, and by the approach of festivals in Jerusalem which were increasingly tense occasions. Caiaphas expresses the opinion that it might be "expedient" that one man should die for (instead of) the people, so that the whole nation should not "perish." The fear of the council is a reasonable one—that if Jesus is allowed to continue his course, "everyone will believe in him" and *the Romans will intervene.* The fear that everyone would follow Jesus might not have had any basis in a clear knowledge of Jesus' intentions but, whatever they were, the leaders could not risk anything that would lead to Roman suppression.

As far as we know the history, this is a sound presentation of the problem that would have confronted the Sanhedrin, and one we must not underestimate or attribute to base motives. The council had its responsibility to the people as a whole and to the Roman overlord, whose view of the situation they may well have reflected. We cannot assume that it did not do its best to carry out this responsibility, whatever private interests individual members may have had or whatever party pressures they may have been subjected to. John is not, of course, trying to recover the history, as he goes on to explain. He is trying to uncover the Christian paradox that a ruler's "secular" judgment becomes a prophecy of gospel truth. "He did not say this of his own accord, but being high priest that year he prophesied that Jesus should die for the nation, and not for the nation only, but to gather into one the children of God who are scattered abroad." (John 11:47–52, cf. ch. 18:14.)

Although the passage is interpretation, the reasoning seems soundly based. It is reasonable to assume that the Jewish leader would find it within his responsibility to see that the Romans moved against one agitator rather than allow a disturbance to take place. Such a disturbance would develop a magnitude certain to bring about Roman intervention with all the possible results of a loss of that local control under which the Jewish nation-church functioned with Roman consent. That the Romans were watchful and prepared to take an agitator into custody (even for his own protection, as Luke describes it) is suggested by Acts 22:22 ff., where Paul is extricated from a rioting mob. There is too the real possibility that the procurator had given instructions to this effect and made the Jewish leaders responsible as something more than informers. This is the conclusion Paul Winter arrived at (see "Notes to Chapter Seven," par. 5). It is foreshadowed by the warnings of the Pharisees to Herod and by Herod's surveillance of Jesus' activities, along with the precedent of his treatment of John the Baptist.

Just what grounds the Sanhedrin or Pilate had for judging the situation to be critical we can no longer tell. The texts to some extent reflect a messianism current among the followers of Jesus in the early days of the church which both the synagogue and the Roman state felt it necessary to suppress—with reason, since in one form or another it led to the disastrous upheavals of A.D. 66–70 and 132–135. The common denominator is that Jesus had a following and a capacity for stirring up the people which the rulers feared. Whether it was Jesus' intention to "stir them up" in their sense is to be doubted. The Gospels suggest that agitation, when it came, arose from a misconception of his role, even stimulated by his closest followers. It would appear to be a correct reading of the story that Jesus' arrival at Jerusalem and his at least occasional presence there alarmed them, especially just before the Passover when the city and its environs were filling with excitable pilgrims. The probability that Jesus' entrance into the city and his "cleansing" of the outer court of the Temple took place at Tabernacles but was followed by no serious upheaval makes reasonable a period of watchful debate, of attempts to find out his intentions, mounting to measures of particular vigilance as Passover approached with its influx of Galileans. The impact of his ride into the city and the scene in the Temple has been compressed and heightened in the tradition to express the claim discussed in Chapter Six, above. When we have made allowance for the Christian motifs, we must still give initial credence to the account of developments if they are conceivable under the circumstances. It is too easily assumed that the circumstances remained normal and could be dealt with dispassionately by rule. If we assume instead that a "state of emergency" is much more likely to have dictated rapid action, the story as a whole makes sense, difficult as it may have been to assimilate to the gospel message.

THE DANGER OF POPULAR SUPPORT

The picture of Jesus in Jerusalem is concerned more with his activity than his words. What happened to him there and why is paramount. He has come to face the city with his cause, which is bound up in himself, since only in the capital can the decision of destiny be made. It seems hardly open to question that there is a historical basis for this. No force is used, only the compulsion of his presence. The reaction it produces must be the evocation of a decision. It soon appears to the rulers that Jesus offers and is no solution, only a danger. Since the nature of the threat he represents involves the clearly estimated reaction of the populace and its festival augmentation, the danger to peace can be met only by dealing with Jesus apart from the crowd or any considerable following. It is clearly a conceivable situation and fits the time and conditions as far as we know them. The Gospel story emphasizes this necessary strategy even to the point of producing what appears to be an inconsistency.

In Mark 11:32 ("They were afraid of the people") and ch. 12:12 ("And they tried to arrest him, but feared the multitude"), the concern about Jesus' influence is clear. Mark 12:13 suggests, not unreasonably, attempts to discredit him, and what follows (down to v. 34) records their failure. So Passover approaches with its tense combination of religious zeal and nationalistic self-consciousness, the most inflammatory time of all. Mark's note of time in ch. 14:1, two days before the feast, indicates by the verb in the imperfect, *ezētoun*, that the search for a way to remove Jesus without causing an uproar was not new at this point, only that it had not yet produced any results. (John 7:32, 44 and 11:53, 57 are later readings of this impression that it was no last-minute decision, extending, in John, from Tabernacles.) The concern to eliminate Jesus before the festival began (Mark 14:2) is dictated not so much by religious scruples as by the realities of the case. Once the festival had begun, it was hard to see how Jesus could be found anywhere except among the excitable pilgrims, most likely among a concentration of Galileans. Even the procurator came to Jerusalem with reinforcements for the garrison, apprehensive of disturbances. We can quite properly assume that the authorities had no way of knowing what the function of Jesus' Twelve might be. They might be a bodyguard or a cadre for the formation of a militant expansion. Anyone planning an arrest would have to assess the chances of resistance and its aftermath. So far the story is quite reasonable.

Objections of scholars at this point (apart from the propriety of trying to reconstruct the facts in any case) take the ground that it appears from the Synoptics that the rulers do, after all, arrest Jesus on the feast day (for the day starts with its eve). Mark places Jesus' arrest after his supper with the Twelve on "the first day of unleavened bread when they sacrificed the passover lamb" (ch. 14:12). Mark's terminology may not be precise in a Jewish sense but his intention is clear —he intends, from a Roman reckoning, the day when the lambs were offered, the same day when the feast began in the evening. So the objection is that having looked for a way to take Jesus into custody *before* the feast they now do so *after* the feast has started, and his crucifixion is accomplished on the first full day of the festival itself. To suppose that they meant to defer his arrest until after the feast ignores the problem.

Yet the Gospels do not say that it is the feast they wish to avoid as such (this is deduced from Rabbinic prohibitions) but only an arrest amid the throngs. If the Romans had a hand in it from the start, cultic prohibitions would have less weight, and Pilate had not previously proved himself sensitive to Jewish scruples. Neither is it altogether clear that under certain circumstances the Jewish ordinances did not permit the authorities to proceed against offenders. In a state of emergency, in any case, rules are not the prime concern.

THE JUDAS SOLUTION

The gospel tradition provides its own answer in the crucial factor of the activity of Judas, which the obvious development of later tradition has overlaid but which remains as a thoroughly reasonable factor. Whatever Judas was in a position to disclose, it removed the problem of the presence of the festival crowds by enabling the authorities to take Jesus at night, in a quiet spot, with no confusion as to identity, and with assurance that there would be no riot. The treachery of Judas has been subjected to a reaction of horror expressed by a series of Old Testament motifs (Matt. 26:15; 27:9 f.; John 12:4–6; 13:2, 21–30; Acts 1:16–20). When allowance is made for this, an informer (rather than the loaded term "traitor") is still the missing link. What the authorities needed to know, a member of the Twelve would be in a position to supply—as Luke understands in ch. 22:6, "an opportunity to betray him to them *in the absence of the multitudes*." This readiness to inform (for reasons we can no longer recover) makes logical a sudden change of plans which simply carry out the original intention. Literary analysis of the tradition is unable to improve on the situation, unless a confession of complete ignorance be considered an improvement. Stages in the modification of the tradition are demonstrable but do not eliminate Judas' function in the story as it stands (see "Notes to Chapter Seven"). The Gospels are no longer interested in what he disclosed. The psychological reasons for his acting as informer are a modern concern.

THE THREE CROSSES

There is another factor in the Gospel narrative likely to be ignored which also lends support to the probability of an emergency procedure. It is concealed by the usual English translations within the account of Jesus' fellow sufferers and the Barabbas incident. These also have been modified by legendary development but there is no need, therefore, to dismiss them. The case of the two others crucified with Jesus is obscured by the words with which readers and hearers (and preachers) are familiar. That Jesus was crucified between two "thieves" (as the KJV has so long read at Mark 15:27 and Matt. 27:38) seems to occasion no surprise, but it is hard to find any discussion of why thieves were crucified with Jesus and Jesus with thieves. When we consult the Greek, we find the term *lēistai* in Mark and Matthew, a word that occurs also in the works of Josephus. It means literally "brigands" and in Josephus is by no means a simple description of common criminals (see, among many examples, *Wars* II.254; IV.504; *Antiquities* XIV.159 f.; XX.160 f., 167).

When militant Jewish resistance to Rome began, the underground had no means of support and had apparently to prey on the populace as outlaws (so, for a later period, the Bar-Cochba letters which were recovered have shown the resistance forces living "off the land"). Since Josephus was writing as a Roman supporter, he does not hesitate to use the derogatory term "brigands." Modern history has been full of the stories of those who led the opposition to occupying forces or to the "establishment" and for them such terms as "guerrillas," "resistance fighters," "militant underground," *maquis*, and the like, have been used (see "Notes to Chapter Seven," par. 8). The Zealot who did not hesitate to assassinate was indicated by the term *sikarios*, a person who carried a knife. It may even lie behind the term "Iscariot," indicating that Judas was a Zealot or insurrectionist. Simon among the Twelve is also described as a Zealot (by Luke in ch. 6:15; Acts 1:13). So it seems probable that there were members of the resistance among Jesus' followers. However that may be, the term *lēistēs* means something very different from what is conveyed by the word "thief," or even by the term "malefactor" in Luke 23:32 f. (*kakourgos*) or the translations "criminals" and "robbers" in the RSV. *The New English Bible* has the more literal term "bandits" in Mark and Matthew.

THE CASE OF BARABBAS

The meaning is clear when we read in Luke 23:40 f. that one of the sufferers admits that he and his fellow "are under the same sentence of condemnation" and "we indeed justly." What this condemnation was, which applied to all three on the cross, is found in the charge against Jesus as spelled out in Luke 23:2. Jesus, under the indictment and from the point of view of the Roman court, is certainly considered to be an equivalent of Barabbas, charged with the same crime even if he has not, like Barabbas, violently sought to implement it. It is again Luke who makes this plain and shows what is meant by a *lēistēs*. In ch. 23:19 he explains that Barabbas was "a man who had been thrown into prison for an insurrection started in the city, and for murder" (cf. Mark 15:7). He is obviously the leader of a resistance movement in which the two others crucified are followers. Luke has polemical reasons for making all this clear, while avoiding the term *lēistēs*. Barabbas may have been, as Matt. 27:16 says, "notorious," but we have no means of identifying "the" insurrection (Mark 15:7), any more than we can the ruthless action reported of Pilate on another occasion in Luke 13:1, though attempts have been made. John uses the ambiguous expression "two others" (ch. 19:18). That there was activity by and against such "resistance fighters" going on is suggested by the words of Jesus found in Mark 14:48||Matt. 26:55||Luke 22:52, where Jesus, as he is arrested, says, "Have you come out as against a *lēistēs*?" We noted in Chapter Six the use of the term in the Temple scene. It is clear that from the official point of view there were crucified together *three* rebels, members of the underground or resistance. One, Jesus, is distinguished for the extravagance of his claim by the charge hung over him on the cross, "King of the Jews" (see "Notes to Chapter Seven," par. 7).

The deeper irony is that Jesus is innocent of the charge (as Luke 23:40 f. has one criminal admit), whereas the others are guilty. Jesus hangs on the cross in place of Barabbas the chief offender. However this may have come about, the point in any case is clear. Students of the trial before Pilate are baffled, in the absence of external evidence, by the tradition that Pilate offered to release either Jesus or Barabbas according to custom (Mark 15:6||Matt. 27:15—found only in some readings of Luke, ch. 23, where v. 17 may be an assimilation). That no record of such a custom exists may not be so difficult to explain if it were merely a local peculiarity of Pilate's, perhaps an effort to atone for his past mishandling of this strange people. Certainly, down to the present, paroles and amnesties at festival times are not unknown (for example, the custom exists in Massachusetts as a prerogative of the governor at Christmas). In any case, the point is made clear that the mob present, whoever they were, wanted the genuine "freedom fighter" to be released and not Jesus who was reported to have made large claims but did not act. A textual variant of Matt. 27:17 even gives Barabbas the name "Jesus," so that what may have been the original reading made the antithesis of choice sharper with: "Whom do you want me to release for you, Jesus Barabbas or Jesus who is called the Anointed?"

The mob, which in Mark 15:8 takes the initiative in asking for Barabbas, is hard to explain as a crowd of citizens or pilgrims, especially on the morning of a festival. It is a group susceptible, so the Evangelists claim, to the incitement of the priests by whom they are encouraged to ask freedom for Barabbas and death for Jesus. Again there may be an element of polemic against the hierarchy in order to spare Pilate. One might ask how effective it is as an apologia, since it presents a Roman official susceptible to pressure. A collection of people gathered at the trial would best be accounted for if they were followers of Barabbas or fellow workers, supporters of the Zealot movement. They could hardly be the general populace, the "fickle crowd" of pulpit oratory who one day cry, "Hosanna!" and a few days later, "Crucify!" On any reckoning of the timetable given, it would have to be early in the morning by special arrangement and in an unpopular setting, and a gathering of citizens is highly inconsistent even with the account. With their removal, any responsibility of the people of Israel as such for Jesus' condemnation disappears; it rests with the hierarchy whose motives we are unable to judge and, most likely, with a prearranged gathering of Zealots who were willing to rescue their hero at whatever cost to anyone else. The irony is complete; Jesus had no such support.

It is possible to argue, then, that obscured by the tradition as we have it *is* a situation which is neither inconsistent nor incredible, irregular and paradoxical though it may be. Jesus, the friend of the outcast, the proclaimer of the Kingdom of God, who commanded no legions and counseled no resistance, is condemned as a treasonable agitator and dies as a substitute for the man who put revolt into practice, and dies between two of that man's fellow conspirators.

Does this make a reasonable conclusion to a possible series of events? Paul Winter, after careful study and with due appreciation of the Gospels as highly developed preaching forms, thinks it does. Of the narrative as a whole he says, "By disregarding their present position in the Gospels and concentrating upon the items themselves we may hope to arrive at an appreciation of the earliest form of the tradition. . . . The main themes remain stable and still give some indication of the nature and contents of an early pre-synoptic report" (see "Notes to Chapter Seven," par. 5). This hope is reasonable provided we do not expect to find or reconstruct a plain account of happenings untouched by dogma. On the other hand, what we may discern is dogmatic (evangelical, apologetical, polemical, and Christological) treatment not untouched by a tradition of historical events which has limited and to some extent determined the nature of the treatment.

TOWARD A CHRISTOLOGY

There have intruded into the passion narrative two matters. First, what seems to be a cycle about Peter, which has had its effect on the move from the city to Gethsemane (Mark 14:26–31 and parallels), on the Gethsemane scene itself (vs. 33, 37), and on Peter's relation to the hearing at the high priest's (vs. 54, 66–72). It is not enough to say that Peter's vacillation and self-concern are a foil to Jesus' dignified and unprotesting acceptance of his fate. The story of Peter we shall look at in the next chapter.

The second matter is the concern to bring out the Christian understanding of Jesus' crucifixion, a Christological interest in defining the meaning of his "Christhood." The high priest is made to ask Jesus directly whether he is "the Anointed." In Mark, the title is defined with a feeling for Jewish circumlocution, as "the Son of the Blessed" (ch. 14:61), equivalent to Matthew's "Son of God" (ch. 26:63). About this, Luke has been more cautious, as well as about Jesus' answer. We must not forget the original kingly Messianic background of the term "Son" (Chapters Two and Three, above). The Evangelists (and the variations in the texts which obscure what they wrote) are ambiguous about whether Jesus by his reply accepted the designation or not (see "Notes to Chapter Seven," par. 9). Mark's "I am" is progressively modified by Matthew and Luke, though we cannot always assume that Mark is the earlier and that the variants indicate that the present text may have been reduced to an affirmative.

What appears in each case, however, is that transposition of key which we have seen before in the transition from the term "Messiah" (or "Anointed") to the term "Son of Man." We shall look at the possible apologetic aspect of this later. What seems clear in the accounts is this transition from the royal to the eschatological and the reference to the "Son of Man" here (Mark 14:62||Matt. 26:64||Luke 22:69) is to the enthroned and triumphant figure. The variation among the Evangelists comes with the question when the revelation of the Son of Man in glory is to appear—in the unspecified future (Mark's "you will see"), after this present (Matthew's "hereafter"), or immediately (Luke's "from now on"). Luke omits the reference Mark and Matthew have to the "coming with the clouds," but in the immediacy of glorification provides another of his transitions to the Fourth Gospel where the crucifixion itself is Jesus' glorification. The identification between Jesus the speaker and the glorified Son of Man is not made, explicitly, but it is there to be recognized or accepted by those who are capable of doing so. In the account it represents a deliberate modification of the term "Anointed" in the priest's question and removes it to a different realm of discourse.

The purpose of the Jewish "trial" is to bring to a climax what we have seen lies not far below the surface of earlier sections of the Gospels, that Jesus' "claim," in whatever form it existed, could not be judged by history or by man's judgment. It could only be revealed by God's action after his death. It was the resurrection that disclosed the true meaning of Jesus' life, his deeds and his teaching, which those who opposed him increasingly felt constituted an inadmissible claim. It may be said that this element of suspicion, obstruction, and enmity in the earlier pages of the Gospels is but a preparation for the final move against Jesus. This, of course, is true as a literary judgment but it does not settle the question whether there was not an earlier and steadily more concerned reaction to Jesus. Mark, as we have seen, has the cross always in mind and this finds its climax in the Fourth Gospel where the cross is present from the beginning. It would be unwise to treat this as a purely literary device or a kerygmatic one. Once the crucifixion had happened, it became increasingly clear how previous incidents could be put together to show its inevitability.

For the church, Jesus was not crucified as Messiah in the proper sense, only in the sense of the shift of that term to include religious as opposed to political, eschatological as opposed to historical, claims. Thereby, "Messiah" as equivalent to "Son of God" came to be equivalent to "Son of Man" in its transcendent sense, and from "Son of God" as King to "Son of God" by birth. For Christians it was the *crucified* Jesus who was the "Messiah." The chief purpose of the passion narrative with its steady augmentation and embellishment is to make this clear, to proclaim it, by a variety of means the general nature of which is the use of contrast throughout. At the root of it all lies the question how "the Christ," "the Anointed," "the Messiah," is to be understood—according to the flesh or according to the Spirit? What the hierarchy, what Pilate, what the mockers of Jesus, what the crowd, Judas, and even Peter are doing is judging Jesus' Messiahship from the human point of view. They are submitting what it meant to the estimate of the flesh. They reflect the world's ambition for such a claimant—and its scorn for one who would not act upon it. Barabbas and his "resistance fighters" had acted on it and the world applauds them. To accept in the Spirit the truth of the resurrection was to effect a complete transvaluation of judgment, to estimate Jesus and all he had done and said from a different point of view.

Peter's place in the story (as we shall see below) is as one undergoing the agony of this transfer from "flesh" to "Spirit." This is Paul's point. Not, surely, in the context of II Cor., ch. 5, that we are no longer interested in Jesus as he lived and as he was (see the limitations of the flesh in vs. 1–9 with its emphasis on the Spirit and the courage of faith, the mention of the judgment of Christ on the bodily life in v. 10, and the scorn for human opinion in vs. 11–15). Rather, because of the "love of Christ" which now controls us, this new way of estimating the human situation must be applied to all men alike. The "human point of view" about our fellows will no longer serve. A new situation exists (v. 16, RSV) because "we" —Paul identifies himself with priests and people, with Peter and all who misjudged Jesus—once made this mistaken estimate of Jesus and now know that we can never do so again. We were all implicated in the distorted judgment about Jesus and, in our deliverance, must learn to free ourselves from distortions in our view of other men. We might add, even as Jesus in the Gospels could see outcasts, even enemies, as objects of God's love—a point brought out in some texts of Luke 23:34 where Jesus, as he is lifted up to die, prays for those who carry out the sentence.

It is probably a sign of how deeply ingrained historic issues were in the Christian movement and of its actual origin among Jews and Jewish traditions that the church clung, against all reason it would seem, to the term "Christ," so that it became irretrievably attached to Jesus as a name. Whatever the reason for it, the transmutation of it had to be accomplished (as with even the term *kyrios*, "Lord," in another way) and the developed passion narrative is part of the means of this shift from "flesh" to "Spirit."

THE WORDS FROM THE CROSS

There are two moments in the narrative which prepare the way. First, the words of Jesus from the cross and, second, his words and acts at the Last Supper. There is a long tradition of interpreting Jesus and his passion by means of the "Seven

Words from the Cross." To gather them together it becomes necessary to draw one from Mark (ch. 15:34), three from Luke (ch. 23:34, only in Sinaiticus Alexandrinus, the Lake miniscules, etc.; vs. 43 and 46), and three from John (ch. 19:26 f., 28, 30). Each of these "words" separately and all of them together are interpretative and, if they cannot be regarded as historical, are "historic" in the sense that they serve the purpose of explaining "that strange man upon his cross." They can be illustrated from the record of Jesus' ministry as well as from the passion. They are part of the "point of view of the Spirit" and have their own kind of truth.

With what words Jesus' died, if any, cannot in the nature of the case be known. Mark says he expired with "a loud cry" (ch. 15:37) and in this some have seen a cry of victory. Mark may be thought to give a clue in his quotation from Ps. 22:1 if it were clear what it meant: "My God, my God, why hast thou forsaken me?" All kinds of interpretations have been based on the remainder of the psalm (as though the whole were "filed by title") which is used to undergird the passion story (e.g., Mark 15:24, 29; Matt. 27:43). In the context of the Gospels as a whole, its place seems to be as a final draining of the cup of the human lot where, in a sense, Jesus too is forced to the extremity of "the human point of view." Efforts to adduce the incongruity of this verse as its proof of authenticity are convincing only in this sense. It seems clear that Mark had access to a tradition in which it was known that whatever Jesus had expected to happen to his cause (rather than to himself) had not happened and that his human death was accepted without any clear answer for himself. (We can say this, I think, without having to accept the speculations of Schweitzer, Eisler, Brandon, Schonfield, and others who have seen the problem even if they have not found the right answers.) Yet even human despair is expressed in words of worship which lead on to an answer from beyond. Dogmatically speaking, the paradoxical picture of Jesus would not be complete without this human experience of having been, as it were, abandoned to his fate (Phil. 2:5–8; Heb. 2:10–15; etc.).

THE LORD'S SUPPER

The second moment, the Last Supper, involves too many extraneous problems to discuss fully here. The actions taken by the hierarchy and Pilate in the emergency may well have been "irregular" enough to remove most of the difficulties of this having been a Passover meal. Many of the arguments against it depend upon an effort to establish John's chronology as original (rather than as a means of making Jesus the "Lamb of God") and on a failure to take Mark's account as an etiological cult narrative which, having assumed the Passover, proceeds to ignore features of the occasion that have not been retained in his time as part of the Lord's Supper (see "Notes to Chapter Seven," par. 11). Luke's longer text, probably a conflation, on the whole bears this out and properly emphasizes the eschatological aspects.

The highly suspected preparation for the occasion falls into place as a prearrangement to ensure that the meal could be taken without interference. It was a unique occasion, planned by Jesus, who counted a good deal on this last act with his Twelve (Luke 22:15 being less cultic than historical). It is with reference to the Passover haggada that Jesus' words over the bread and the (later) cup achieve their meaning. Whatever is to happen, by this act the participants are bound together by ties which have all the solemnity of an accepted death and all the potentiality of an anamnesis or reincorporation by something more than recollection. It is easy to say, in view of future developments, that this too is a cultic afterthought, but better than anything else it fits into the pattern of what we know about Jesus and the circumstances that he should have relied on his and their Jewish background in creating the basis for a renewal of their fellowship, in whatever way it became possible, after his death (see below on the Emmaus story). That they would remain Jews was to be expected and the transmutation of ideas associated with the exodus redemption of Israel at Passover brought about by his words over the bread and the cup do no more than justice to the occasion and the mind that could conceive them.

THE NEED FOR A RESPONSE

In both the words at the Last Supper and the cry from the cross (interpreted as each is by the scene in Gethsemane, as they are meant to be, since, like the temptation story, it is retrospective) there is that element of the final insecurity of human plans and life which can be redeemed only by the security of the faith that God's purpose will triumph in his way rather than in ours. Mark, however, in addition has dramatically supplied two comments on the crucifixion death of Jesus which bring out the meaning of the passion in the light of the outcome. From the Jewish point of view, the Temple veil is forever rent asunder (Mark 15:38). This may be a relic of the portents found in the unnatural darkness of v. 33 and elaborated in Matt. 27:51-53. It is more likely that its present function is to assert that the death of Jesus makes available to all men that access to God (and of God to man) which had come to Jesus himself by the rending of the heavens at his baptism. It is so interpreted, for example, in Heb., chs. 4:14 to 5:10; 6:19; 9:6-14, 24-25; 10:19-22. On the other hand, for the Gentiles, there is the response of the centurion (Mark 15:39) who, when he saw how Jesus died, said, "Truly, this man was a son of God"—an opinion which, like the use of the Hebrew term "son," might need Christian transformation but is the kind of response we met from Gentiles earlier in the Gospel (see Chapter Four, above).

As we examine, then, some of the senses in which the final paradox is expressed in the Gospels we approach more and more the matter of the response itself. That is what Christology, taken as more than a dogma, a way of life initiated by the response known as the resurrection, in essence is. There is no resolution of the paradox of Jesus in the Gospels which is not demanding and, in the deepest sense, a "following" of the paradox of Jesus who is taken to be, in our own transmutation of the term, "the Christ." The question of commitment, now as then, is an essential and an existential element in Christology, and to some aspects of it arising from what we have said, we must in conclusion turn.

Notes to Chapter Seven

1. For discussion of the topics of this chapter at variance with the usually accepted views, see:

R. Eisler, *Iesous Basileusou Basileusas*, E.T. *The Messiah Jesus and John the Baptist.*

S. G. F. Brandon, *Jesus and the Zealots* (Manchester: Manchester Univ. Press, 1967), with full bibliography. See also his *The Fall of Jerusalem and the Christian Church* (S.P.C.K. 1951).

H. J. Schonfield, *The Passover Plot* (Random House, Inc., 1966).

2. On the Zealot movement, see W. R. Farmer, *Maccabees, Zealots and Josephus* (Columbia University Press, 1956).

3. The critical literary analysis of the passion story that divides it into at least two main strands (see, e.g., V. Taylor, *The Gospel According to St. Mark* [The Macmillan Company, 1952]; additional Notes H and J, pp. 649 ff., 653 ff.) does not necessarily mean that a "secondary" strand, added to one judged to be more original to the Evangelist, contains no primitive or valid preservation of the course of events—even if not, as Taylor suggests, Petrine reminiscences.

4. The danger of anti-Semitic interpretation is well discussed in F. C. Grant, *Ancient Judaism and the New Testament* (The Macmillan Company, 1959). See also the pronouncements of the Second Vatican Council, October 28, 1965: "Declaration on the Relation of the Church to Non-Christian Religions," National Catholic Welfare Conference translation (St. Paul Editions), pp. 6–7.

5. On the problems connected with the arrest and sentencing of Jesus, see notably P. Winter, *On the Trial of Jesus* (Berlin, 1961), and the literature cited. The quotation is from p. 22. Participation of Romans in the arrest is based on John 18:12 and seems dubious.

6. On the matter of chronology and the Last Supper, consult J. Jeremias, *The Eucharistic Words of Jesus*, tr. by Norman Perrin from the 3d German edition (Charles Scribner's Sons, 1966).

7. On the term for "brigand," see K. H. Rengstorf, "*lēistēs*" in Kittel's *Wörterbuch*. Note, "The word does not unconditionally imply lack of honesty; hence it can be used for the regular soldier or mercenary, who in antiquity had the right to plunder. . . . But the bad sense has always been predominant" (E.T., Vol. IV, p.

257). "It should be noted, however, that the Romans themselves did not in fact treat as *lēistai* the Zealots whom they captured. Their punishment was crucifixion, and this alone was enough to show that they were regarded and treated as political offenders" (*ibid.*, p. 259). Barabbas might well have been an *archilēistēs*. Rengstorf points out that Celsus called Jesus a *lēistēs* (*ibid.*, p. 262).

8. For the Bar-Cochba letters, see Y. Yadin, "New Discoveries in the Judean Desert," *Biblical Archaeologist*, Vol. 24 (1961), pp. 34 ff., and "More on the Letters of Bar Kochba," pp. 86 ff.

9. On the problem of the reply of Jesus to the high priest, see, e.g., O. Cullmann, *The Christology of the New Testament*, pp. 117 ff.; cf. 161 f. On the use of psalms in the passion story, see B. Lindars, *New Testament Apologetic*, pp. 88–110. On Mark 14:62 see the extension of Lindars' theory by N. Perrin, "Mark xiv. 62: The End Product of a Christian Pesher Tradition?" in *New Testament Studies*, Vol. 12 (1966), pp. 150 ff.

10. "That strange man upon his cross" is a phrase from a letter of Fr. George Tyrrell to the Baron F. von Hügel in 1900, used as the title of a book by Richard Roberts (Abingdon Press, 1934).

11. On the Last Supper, see, in addition to Jeremias above, the summary in A. J. B. Higgins, *The Lord's Supper in the New Testament* (Studies in Biblical Theology, No. 6; 1952); cf. O. Cullmann, F. J. Leenhardt, tr. by J. G. Davies, *Essays on the Lord's Supper* (Ecumenical Studies in Worship, No. 1, Lutterworth Press, 1958), and another view, M. Black, "The Arrest and Trial of Jesus and the Date of the Last Supper," in A. J. B. Higgins, ed., *New Testament Essays*. (Much of the debate seems to me to ignore the "emergency" factor.)

Eight

The Paradox
in Resurrection and Retrospect

If we had been seeking to tell the story of Jesus' life, we should now have come to the end. The factor that makes it impossible to stop here is the experience of the resurrection of Christ. In Chapter One we have suggested instances where it has entered into the construction of the Gospels and we must explore this further if we are to understand the paradox of Jesus and the Gospels.

It is obvious that the Gospels throughout are informed by the resurrection as that experience was handed on and developed by the witnesses and those who followed them. Throughout the New Testament as a whole the resurrection and exaltation of Christ are assumed. By comparison it is far more pervasive than any other topic, more characteristic, for example, than the virgin birth which appears only in the introductions to the Gospels of Matthew and Luke. In the kerygmatic passages of Acts there is constant reference to the resurrection but none at all to the mode of Jesus' conception and birth (Acts 1:21 f.; 2:22–36; 3:12–26; 4:8–12, cf. 24–30; 5:29–32; 10:34–43). This means that for the major part of the New Testament and its sources it was possible to proclaim the gospel without reference to the birth of Jesus but impossible to do so without reference to the resurrection. Yet we are unable to describe it. In fact, descriptions of the resurrection as an event are characteristic of the apocryphal gospels, an element from which the canonical Gospels are free. Only in Matthew is there anything approaching it, and that only a description of the means by which the stone was rolled away from the tomb, tied to the apologia (or counterapologia) relating to the guard set over the tomb to prevent a "fraud" (Matt. 28:2–4; 27:62–66).

The attempt to display the inconsistencies in the accounts (classically undertaken by Schmiedel in the *Encyclopedia Biblica*) and to uncover the layers of tradition yields no positive results except the theory of a tendency to move from an original "spiritual" experience toward a "physical" manifestation. We cannot by this or any other means answer the question of objective historical fact. We can, however, reach solid ground when we discuss the testimony of the tradition to the effects, witnessed to by the words and by the changes in the witnesses themselves, as these have come down to us and are reproduced in the experience of myriads since then—and in ourselves. The resurrection is, in fact, the evocation of a response to Jesus, not simply to his death, but to his whole work, to his end, and to his person. So we shall inquire into the nature of that change, how it is described, and what are some of its effects on the Gospels.

THE TESTIMONY OF PAUL

The modern starting point is the assumption that the first testimony we have is that of Paul in I Cor. 15:1–9 which is assumed to describe a spiritual experience (perhaps also referred to in II Cor. 12:1–4 and Gal. 1:12–16). It is further assumed that the experiences of the earliest witnesses were on a par with Paul's and that anything which does not fit into this pattern is a later, tendentious, development. This theory may be accepted with reservations. It is true that Corinthians, like the rest of Paul's genuine letters, was written before the Gospels as we have them (though it is not clear that they had any widespread "publication" before at least Mark's Gospel). This is not to say that there are no more primitive accounts in the Gospels than there are in Paul. It is also germane that Paul's purpose in First Corinthians is not historical description but a recital of the *paradosis*, or what he had received by way of tradition and had handed on, with a view to correcting false ideas concerning the "resurrection of the body." This purpose is not unlike the function of some of the Gospel testimony.

The *paradosis* he gives in summary form is by way of a reminder. Only in The Acts of the Apostles is any attempt made, and that at a much later date, to recount what Paul actually preached to the unconverted. His letters are occasional pieces, addressed to Christians, dealing with particular situations. Having said this, we read the list of "appearances" in I Cor., ch. 15, with interest because it mentions some which the Gospels do not clearly record—to Peter (v. 5, as we shall see below, only indirectly in the Gospels), to five hundred brethren (v. 6), and to James (v. 7). Paul appears to distinguish between the Twelve and "all the apostles" (vs. 5, 7). It has been argued that at least two separate traditions are here combined (see "Notes to Chapter Eight"), but this is not certain and I have suggested above in Chapter Four that the distinction between Jesus' Twelve and the church's apostles may be a valid one.

The assumption that Paul's experience of the Risen Christ was on all fours with the others appears at first clear, but we ought to clarify in what ways this is so by a discussion of the Gospel evidence. In I Cor. 15:8 Paul says he was "the last of all" to whom Christ appeared (*ōphthē kamoi*) and that this was a special act of grace because he was an "abortion" (RSV, "one untimely born"), since he was a persecutor of the church. This is an important distinction, not because he was "last of all" but because he was no friend of Christ, an enemy. He did not oppose *Jesus*—he could not—but his "name" (Acts 26:9). All the others had been followers of Jesus or had known him before his death.

That Paul was understood to mean this, at least by the author of Acts, is shown by the fact that each of the three accounts of his conversion given, though they differ in detail, agree that Paul saw a bright light which blinded him and that he had to ask *who it was* who addressed him (Acts 9:3–9;

22:6–11; 26:13–18). In each case Paul asks, "Who are you, Lord?" (chs. 9:5; 22:8; 26:15) and the heavenly speaker replies, "I am Jesus" (in ch. 22:8, "of Nazareth"). It is not clear from these passages whether Paul was thought able to distinguish form or face. One would judge not. A light greater than the eastern midday sun and a Voice not of earth prompt him to say, "Lord." In Acts 26:19 he is said to have described this to Agrippa as a "heavenly vision," but in view of the words, "I was not disobedient to," it would be unwise to press this to mean what the stories by no means say, that Paul saw anything; he is made to refer to the Voice, to the charge. The accounts in Acts may well have their own purpose but they are the earliest commentary we have on Paul's own reference. Whether he "saw" Jesus or not, it is clear that he was distinguished from the others to whom Christ appeared in not having known Jesus before, but not necessarily by his inability to "see" Jesus. The measure of what he strongly felt to be a stupendous act of grace was that he, a persecutor of Christ's following, who had never known him, should have had this manifestation, and he alone.

THE FORM AND NATURE OF THE RESURRECTION NARRATIVE

One of the chief characteristics, then, of the resurrection tradition is that Jesus, with one exception, was made known as risen and exalted only to those who had been with him in his life. Indeed, the implication of the New Testament is that, apart from a supreme act of grace for Paul, the resurrection experience was not possible for anyone who had not known Jesus. The Acts also makes this clear in ch. 1:21–22, which describes what having known Jesus meant—Jesus in his public ministry, from his baptism by John until "he was taken up from us." This knowledge alone qualified a person to be a "witness to his resurrection."

In this is also an important guide to the form of the resurrection stories (as Dodd has seen; see "Notes to Chapter One"). Jesus appeared only to those who *could* recognize him and yet they did *not* at first know him (John 20:14; 21:4; Matt. 28:17, "some doubted"; Luke 24:37 f., 41). It is surprising that anyone should therefore claim that the gospel accounts speak of a *resuscitation*, that is, of the restoration to life of the human body of Jesus just as he was. The notion of a mortally wounded man staggering around on crippled feet is entirely excluded. Resuscitation is not the issue. Whatever the accounts intend, it is not that. Whatever is "seen" becomes recognizable only after some "word" is spoken or recalled.

Neither can the accounts be explained on the basis of expectation. We have mentioned this difficulty above in Chapter Five in connection with the "rising" in the "passion predictions." So little did the witnesses expect what happened that according to all the sources, they did not believe the reports when they heard them. They had difficulty seeing when they were given the opportunity (cf. Mark 16:8 and the appendix in vs. 11, 14; Matt. 28:17; Luke 24:11–12 [but not in D], 37; John 20:14, 20, 25; 21:4). We shall see later that one strand assumes that a revelation was necessary because the witnesses were not permitted to know simply by seeing for themselves. In other words, all the accounts assume that it was not a *discovery* of the witnesses but a *disclosure* made by a power or a manifestation from outside themselves.

The first intimation in the accounts as we have them comes from the message of an "angel" (or messenger, or young man or men at the tomb; see Mark 16:5–7||Matt. 28:5–7||Luke 24:4, but note the differences in Luke). Only in John 20:1–10 does the emptiness of the burial place stand alone, and only in Luke and John does the discovered absence of the body precede the message. Luke and John are also together (as we have had occasion to notice before) in referring to the relevance of the Scriptures (see discussion of Luke 24:13 ff. below, and John 20:9; cf. I Cor. 15:4). The only reference to the "passion predictions" is in Luke 24:6–8, reflected in John 20:9. The tendency to "objectify" the appearances, particularly in Luke (ch. 24:39–42; John 20:27; cf. Matt. 28:9, "feet") is probably to be ascribed to a double necessity—to refute the

belief that the appearances were a purely subjective experience, and to deny that they were, in the ordinary sense, physical (cf. Jesus' disappearance in Luke 24:31 and the locked
doors in John 20:19).

THE CONSISTENCIES IN THE NARRATIVES

What we have seen so far indicates that there are underlying
constants about the resurrection stories which may easily be
missed in discussions of the place of the empty tomb or
whether Jesus could be touched or could eat and drink, or just
who saw Jesus when or where. The debate about Galilee or
Jerusalem tells us more about the concerns of the Evangelists
but is not crucial for our discussion. The consistencies may be
found in the relation of message to story, in the difficulty of
seeing Jesus without some form of disclosure, in the stress on
factors which make it clear that no purely subjective experience is indicated, nor a bodily manifestation without change.
The stress on the marks of the crucifixion in Luke 24:39, followed by John 20:20, 27, indicating a continuity of the Risen
Christ with the crucified Jesus; the continuity with his teaching indicated by Acts 1:3, "speaking of the kingdom of God"
(cf. vs. 6–7); and the continuity of person in ch. 1:11, belong
to the emphasis on the fact that the witnesses were those "who
had been with Jesus" and, as Peter says in Acts 1:21, "who
have accompanied us." The absence of any appearance to opponents (apart from Paul) or to the public, is part of the
overall refusal of "signs" (in the Synoptic sense) which we
shall deal with later, making the last and greatest "sign" (in
the Johannine sense) the cross itself. Furthermore, there are
the references to Scripture and, in Luke and the appendix to
John, references to meals.

THE EMMAUS STORY

Luke 24:13–35, which comes to a climax in a meal, is the
key passage for study of the relation of the resurrection experience to the Gospels. It is placed on the first day of the

week when two disciples are on the way to Emmaus (v. 13). One is later (v. 18) identified as Cleopas. He is not otherwise known but probably comes within the group of disciples among whom Joseph Barsabbas and Matthias are named in Acts 1:23 and two unnamed in John 21:2. As they go they are talking about "all these things that had happened" (Luke 24:14) which it later appears refers to the career and death of Jesus rather than to the story about the tomb in the previous verses. The reader is then told that "Jesus himself" joined them but "their eyes were kept from recognizing him" (vs. 15–16). The Greek used here, *ekratounto tou mē epignōnai auton,* means that their eyes were closed to the recognition of Jesus; they were *prevented* from seeing who it was. The implication is that until some disclosure had been made they were incapable of knowing the new companion to be Jesus simply on the basis of their previous knowledge of him. To know the Risen Christ, more was involved. This is one of the most interesting verses in all the resurrection narratives and fits, as we have seen, one of its constant motifs.

The question Jesus asks about their conversation brings them to a standstill, sadly astonished that anyone could have been in Jerusalem and not known of the recent events. Their questioner, thinks Cleopas, must be the only one (vs. 17–18)! It is the purpose of the story, by the device of Jesus' asking, "What things?" to require the disciples to express the way in which they have understood their experience of Jesus and his death. Its terms are intended to be noted (vs. 19–20). The events were concerning Jesus the Nazarene: he was a prophet who showed his power by word but also by deed, before God and in the presence of the whole people. This, then, according to Luke or his source, is the impression gained of Jesus' public career, but it does not satisfy what was expected of him. He was taken to be something more than *a* prophet, no matter how powerful. They then describe (v. 20) how Jesus had been condemned and crucified by the church and state ("the chief priests and our rulers"). There was the tragedy, because they had continued to hope (*ēlpizomen*) that he was the one who was about to deliver Israel (v. 21). To them he had not been merely a prophet but the one on whom their Messianic hopes were set, hopes that had been destroyed to their complete bewilderment by his execution. There was nothing left for them to do but to leave the scene.

We must pause to remark that Luke's vs. 22–24 may be an interpolation, either by Luke or an editor, to bring the passage into harmony with the rest of the account (cf. vs. 1–11, with 12 omitted from Codex Bezae, and v. 34). If this were so, we would probably have to include the last part of v. 21, "Yes, and besides all this, it is now the third day since this happened." Alone, these words could be taken to mean that there was no hope, Jesus was really dead. They can also be interpreted to mean that in view of the "passion predictions," taken to refer to a resurrection promise (but see Chapter Five, above), the promise had not been fulfilled. This would be difficult taken with the verses that follow. In any case vs. 21b to 24 are a distraction to the movement of the story itself.

Jesus' reply introduces the reinterpretation, or the new understanding of the Scriptures leading to a new conception of the role of the Anointed (the Christ). The disciples fail by being slow to understand that the Anointed One had to suffer before he could "enter into his glory" (vs. 25–26). The new interpretation covers the Torah, the Prophets, and the "Writings," that is, the whole Old Testament (v. 27). The church undertook to show that the suffering of the Messiah and his "rising" to glory are "in accordance with the Scriptures" (I Cor. 15:4). We learn, in Luke 24:32, that Jesus' discourse, this "opening" of the Scriptures, had "kindled" (*kaiomenē*) their minds as they walked. This, then, is the first step necessary before the obstacle can be removed to their seeing the Risen Christ for who he is, before their eyes can be opened to know him. The term "Jesus himself" in v. 15 is probably used by Luke to indicate the continuity of their companion with the Jesus they had known before. Now, however, in order to recognize him at all, there is first of all necessary the reinterpretation of the Scriptures and, according to vs. 6–8, which refer back to the "passion predictions," the recall and new comprehension of Jesus' own words. We find here the clue to the form in which the "passion predictions" are now found.

The story continues to the second and final stage of recognition. Jesus, their companion, acts as if he has a longer journey in view and would leave them at their destination (v. 28, and see the same intention in Mark 6:48, Chapter One, above). Yet they persuade him to be their guest (Luke 24:29). The invitation is key to what follows, for here, as in the other story from Mark 4:35 ff. discussed in Chapter One, they treat Jesus as an ordinary person, one whom they can invite to stay with them. So Jesus is seated with them at supper as guest. The climactic moment now arrives (Luke 24:30) when he, and not one of his hosts, but *he* takes and blesses and breaks the bread and gives it to *them*. That is, he, the guest, acts as the host. He undertakes, as by right, the functions of the head of the household. This action, this reversal of role, finally enables them to see immediately that he whom they assumed to be their guest is actually their host. Clearly that is the clue to the disclosure, not some imagined peculiarity in Jesus' handling of the bread. Some idiosyncrasy might attract attention but it would not explain why the guest acted as host. On the other hand, his assumption of this prerogative would recall his acting with the same right at the "feeding" by the lakeside and at his table in the upper room. At this point the Christ cannot be detained. He vanishes. The Jesus of the lakeside and the upper room of Galilee and Jerusalem cannot be kept in that form nor understood by that means alone, although he cannot be "known" at all without them.

So it was by the opening of the Scriptures and by *his* breaking and giving of the bread that their eyes were at last enabled to see who he was; the inability of v. 16 was removed. They report this double process in v. 35: "what had happened on the road" (the Scriptural discourse) and "how he was known to them in the breaking of the bread." The Greek here may be read, "by the breaking of the bread" and in context means that they knew Jesus by the fact that he did the breaking.

The Emmaus story gives the clues we need to the process

by which the death of Jesus was accepted, and more than accepted, was transformed by the new understanding of the Scriptures. That new reading embraces a new comprehension of the movement of history, of the story of Israel itself. Indeed, as my colleague Dr. Harvey Guthrie has put it, it reaffirms God's involvement in history (see "Notes to Chapter Eight," par. 5). Also, as a consequence, we have the initiation of that dual ministry which informs the earliest traces of liturgical worship. Its duality was recovered (where it did not go from one extreme to the other) by the Reformation and is being restored in the post Second Vatican Council Church, namely, the coordinate ministry of "Word and Sacrament," the ministry of the Lord's gospel and of the Lord's Table.

INFLUENCE ON THE GOSPELS

By the time the Gospels were available to read or to be heard in the Christian assemblies, the resurrection recovery had already diffused the telling of the story and, further, has already begun to appear in places as a transposition. In Chapter One it has already been suggested that the scene of the walking on the water is in essence a resurrection story. Also, the call of Peter in Luke, ch. 5, is a transfusion into the Marcan story, the call to be "fishers of men," of a resurrection motif available in a different form in John, ch. 21. In the Matthean form of the first story and the Lucan form of the second, Peter is crucially involved, a fact that requires further study. Before we do this, however, we return to one aspect of Dr. Dodd's analysis of the resurrection story form. In it Jesus appears as one unknown until he declares himself. This proves, by application, to be a useful means of helping to distinguish between what are primarily resurrection stories and what are not. We have seen in Chapter One how, in the story of the stilling of the storm, Jesus is quite familiar from the beginning. In the other boat and storm scene he appears quite otherwise—as a "phantom" which causes fear—and has to speak before he is known. The latter shows a resurrection form, the other does not.

The same may be said of the transfiguration in Mark 9:1 ff. and parallels. As said in Chapter Five, above, it is a postresurrection story of the anticipation of the Parousia, a proleptic vision of the ultimate exaltation of Jesus, closely related to his determination to go to Jerusalem. Its form shows it to be not a misplaced resurrection story, though it shows signs in the various versions of being in process of becoming one (rather, I think, than of having been one which has been modified for its place in the ministry). In it the whole point is that Jesus is well known in the ascent of the mountain and he is *transformed* into a figure of awe and then back again into the Jesus they know, prepared to set out on his journey. Even amid the scene of glory Peter can make a suggestion (which has embarrassed Mark and Luke; see Mark 9:6; Luke 9:33) and it is not until the cloud of glory encloses them that the Voice from heaven intervenes to reaffirm Jesus' anointing and to draw attention to his teaching (Mark 9:7; Luke 9:34). The vision of glory remains a glimpse, a lifting of the corner of the curtain, to be ratified and consummated beyond Jerusalem and death, not a present possession as in the resurrection. Though Peter speaks in the transfiguration scene, it is probably not the "lost" account of an appearance to Peter, especially since James and John also share it. If it is without the resurrection form, it is also without the consequences produced by the resurrection—there is no sign of results in the later chapters and there is no charge to go on mission (cf. Luke 9:36 and Mark 9:9 f.||Matt. 17:9).

The tendency for Peter to act as spokesman is found occasionally in the Gospels (Luke 5:5||Mark 8:29||10:28) but is still more prominent in the early chapters of Acts (chs. 1:15; 2:14, 38; 3:6, 12; 5:3, 8). It may be that Peter was the natural leader or that he was treated by Jesus as such. There might be another factor which accounts for the Gospel passages, namely, that Peter's experience was crucial to the resurrection story and the form it takes, the first and most important witness. It may therefore seem surprising to suggest that he was, on the New Testament evidence, a reluctant one, not easily won over.

THE HUMAN STORY OF PETER

To understand this we must review briefly what the Gospels have to say about Peter, since he is the prototype of the Christian disciple as well as of the apostle. When we compare the Gospels, Mark contains a much more "natural" picture of Peter and the others show a tendency to spare him (Luke, who relieves him of some of his "bluster," and Matthew, who begins the development toward a legend). We may ask, Why is *Peter* accorded this treatment? That he has received it in Matt. 16:13–19 has, in view of the papal claims associated with it, led to a good deal of controversy and exegetical maneuvering. The Peter story in the Gospels is not an easy one but it is basically a human one. The first "apostle" he may be, but the appendix to the Fourth Gospel (John 21:15–23; cf. ch. 1:40–42) as well as such passages in Paul as Gal. 2:6–14 show that Peter's preeminence did not go unchallenged.

The story starts, in Mark 1:16–20, with his call to be one of four "fishers." The term, I have argued, changes its meaning with the postresurrection understanding (see "Notes to Chapter One," par. 5). We learn that Peter is married. He becomes the beneficiary of Jesus' ministry when his mother-in-law is healed (ch. 1:29–31). He observes the power of Jesus' healings to draw the crowds and emerges as the leader when we read, "Simon and those who were with him" in v. 36. His enthusiastic interest meets its first obstacle when Jesus expresses his intention of leaving Capernaum for a wider proclamation rather than staying as a thaumaturge. This need for a revision of Peter's interest in Jesus becomes the significant underlying theme in his development. The appointment of the Twelve and their mission to Israel (see Chapter Four) again puts Peter in the first place (cf. Gal. 2:7–9). Here in Mark the name Peter is given to Simon. Matthew introduces it at the call in ch. 4:18; Luke's doing so was discussed in Chapter One. The Marcan stories of the stilling of the storm and other incidents make no special mention of Peter except as he appears in Mark 5:37 as one of an inner group with James and John.

The key scene in which Peter appears as leader is the incident at Caesarea Philippi discussed in Chapter Five, above (Mark 8:27-33). The incident of the sacramental meal by the lake as the revision of an expectation may be read as having failed with the disciples as well as with the crowd. The comment on this comes at the end of the boat scene in Mark 6:51-52: "They were utterly astounded, for they did not understand about the loaves, but their hearts were hardened"—that is, their minds were closed as yet to a new possibility. It is again in a boat (ch. 8:13-21, in the section of "doublets") that they fail to understand except on a plain level of forgotten bread. Whatever Jesus had done, they had failed to comprehend, or his comments on it. They shared with the crowds the refusal to accept Jesus except on their own terms.

The Caesarea Philippi scene is a watershed in the treatment of the question of Messiahship in the Synoptics. The town may be taken as a decisive point from which Jesus must either abandon Israel or turn back to Israel. Peter is the spokesman, in a sense, for Israel as well as for the disciples. The rebuke Peter receives in Mark (ch. 8:30, 33; for the Matthean version, see below) indicates that his designation of Jesus as "Christ" (Anointed One) is rejected. We have seen that it has been modulated by means of the expression "Son of Man." That Jesus belongs in a special place Peter does see, but as yet he does not see clearly. It has often been suggested that the preceding incident of the man whose eyes are partially opened is an anticipatory comment on Peter's "confession" (Mark 8:22-26). We can only suppose that Peter's use of "Christ" contains a meaning in context which does not fit Jesus' intention—this rather than that Jesus knew himself to be Messiah but wanted it kept secret. This is not the "Christian" way of reading the incident, but underlying Mark throughout there is clearly the sense that Peter and the rest of the Twelve have not yet understood Jesus. Nor do they to the end—a surprising fact in a Gospel that emphasizes Jesus' teaching of the disciples, but that is part of the paradox. Jesus teaches with authority but in no wise compels belief.

The distance between Jesus and Peter becomes apparent in the scene of Peter's "denial" in the high priest's courtyard. The accusation made against Peter is that of "guilt by association" (Mark 14:67, 69, 70 and ‖s). "You also were with the Nazarene, Jesus" (cf. Acts 4:13). The bystanders are aware that Jesus has been taken into custody as a disturber, possibly a Messianic leader with a Galilean following (v. 70), and Peter responds in that vein. The possibility of an uprising, if it existed at all, was now over. Peter, in Mark's version, denies that he understands the charge, denies he is one of the band and, finally, that he knows Jesus at all. Mark's placing of this denial brings out the pathos. It comes immediately after the confrontation between Jesus and the high priest where Jesus has, not unambiguously, admitted to being Messiah but has turned attention at once to the "Son of Man" and his exaltation (Mark 14:61–62)—as he had done when Peter "recognized" him as Messiah. Peter is denying association with a cause that Jesus himself does not avow. It is an unreconstructed Peter, still believing Jesus to be a Messianic claimant, still unable to understand. Matthew has followed this arrangement but Luke has put Peter's defection before the interview with the high priest and before the mocking (Luke 22:54–65), thus to some extent lessening the pathos and lightening the blame.

Between Caesarea Philippi and the courtyard there is the transfiguration scene shared by Peter, but no results are apparent. Peter has claimed that leaving all to follow Jesus should provide some reward, since he and the others are astonished to learn that the wealthy can only with difficulty enter the Kingdom. Jesus' reply is enigmatic, even in its developed form (Mark 10:28–31). Peter has shared in the indignation over the request of James and John for positions of honor—but by no means repudiates their request (Mark 10:35–41). In Mark, Peter is the witness to the withering of the barren fig tree, since he recalls Jesus' words about it (ch. 11:21). He is again one of the original four "fishers" as audience for Jesus' eschatological discourse over Jerusalem (ch. 13:3). On the

way to Gethsemane, in response to Jesus' warning of the
disciples' defection, Peter vehemently repudiates the possibility
that *he* would desert, even after the explicit warning that he
would not last until dawn (ch. 14:29–31). In Gethsemane,
Jesus reproaches Peter that he could not be vigilant even in
this crisis (v. 37). It is only in John 18:10 that Peter is identified as the one who took action with the sword (but John also
knows the name of the victim). The most significant comment
on the whole story is that of Luke who, in ch. 22:31–34, has
put the protest of Peter at the Last Supper rather than on the
road. Here Peter, addressed by his old name, "Simon, Simon,"
is warned that the Adversary is to "sift like wheat" (the Baptist metaphor!) the whole group, but that Jesus has prayed
for *Peter* (the plural pronoun changes to the singular). Jesus'
prayer is that Peter's faith will not fail. Peter's *conversion* is
then anticipated and he is charged, when this happens, to establish the others: "And you, when you are turned around
(*epistrepsas*), settle ("confirm," *stērison*) your brethren."

PETER AND THE RESURRECTION

Luke's comments are always worth considering as they often
prove to be more detached, even objective, about past events. It
is clear from the several mentions of Peter's experience of the
resurrection, never described, that he played the leading part
in accepting Christ's presence and took the lead, according to
Acts, in the new assembly based upon it. It is true that John,
ch. 21 (with ch. 20:1 ff. interpolated into most texts of Luke
24:12), represents a later disposition, in a particular area of
the church, to dispute this in favor of "the beloved disciple."
Even that necessity reveals the importance of Peter. As said
above, it is surprising that Matthew, for whom the legend of
Peter is important, does not mention Peter's prominence in the
resurrection. Is this only apparent?

The tradition as we have it is in a developed form, involving
apologia of a probably antidocetic type, and a tendency to

dispute leadership. None the less it suggests that Peter was indeed the leader in the recognition of the resurrection. He did, as Luke anticipates, convince and establish his brethren in it, but also, that ability did not come about instantly, without some hesitation, perhaps struggle. Peter had Messianic ambitions for Jesus and rebuked his Master for his suggestion that he might be rejected and die before entering his "glory." He may have offered a show of force to prevent Jesus' arrest, and yet wanted to disassociate himself from a lost cause. This Peter was not easily converted to a Christ who had suffered ignominy and a traitor's death in spite of a revelation that he was living and exalted as the heavenly Son of Man. The evidence suggests that all the same, Peter was converted, the great reversal in him did take place, and that it was in the nature of a crisis. It is surprising, as with other aspects of the paradox, that anything of this should still be apparent, and yet it is.

It is an old theory that Mark did not end his Gospel with ch. 16:8: "They said nothing to anyone, for they were afraid." Various suggestions used to be made to show how the ending might be reconstructed in ways other than the patently later additions in vs. 9–20. In view of ch. 16:7, "Tell his disciples—and Peter," one would expect an appearance to Peter to be reported. It would be an interesting speculation, nothing more, that there was such a conclusion which described the difficulty and hesitancy with which Peter accepted the appearance of the Risen Christ.

Apart from this kind of speculation, we have more reliable indications. The controversy over leadership has produced the story of Peter and "the beloved disciple" and their visit to the tomb. John 20:6–7 says that Peter went into the tomb, but no suggestion is made that what he saw convinced him. By contrast, the other disciple then entered "and he saw and believed." The addition to Luke (ch. 24:12) bears this out by saying ambiguously only that Peter (there alone) "went home amazed at the happening." We can too easily assume that the introduction of the empty tomb motif was a convincing proof. It may have been an early strand in the tradition, rather than a later, but only as an element of confusion and mystery which had to be turned into a "sign."

When we turn again to the story of the "walking on the water," we find another clue. On the theory that here Jesus' appearance on his own initiative, going about his own purposes, unrecognized but awesome to the rowers (see Chapter One, above), is a resurrection appearance introduced into the precrucifixion gospel, we have what is apparently missing from Matthew later. The addition made by Matthew to this story (ch. 14:28–31) concerns Peter's response to Jesus' disclosure of himself. Peter's challenge, "Lord, *if it is you*, bid me come to you on the water," is in effect a demand for a "sign" (see the temptation retrospect below). The sign is granted, but Peter's faith is inadequate to the occasion, for though he "came to Jesus" he was put in terror by the storm, began to sink, and had to call on the Lord to save him. "Why did you doubt?" the Christ asks, and this is a reference to *Peter's request*, not to his failure to carry through. To demand a sign, a proof, is itself a mark of inadequate faith (cf. Thomas in John 20:24–29). When all are in the boat, then they "worship" Jesus with the words, "Truly you are the Son of God"—the answer to the test proposed in the wilderness to Jesus and rejected (Matt. 4:3, 6 || Luke 4:3, 9). That verse is missing from Mark who has tied the scene more closely to its wider context with the reference to the bread (ch. 6:51–52).

We note that this incident is missing from Luke, so that we must refer again, instead, to his version of the call of Peter (ch. 5:1–11) referred to also in Chapter One, above. There, too, Peter offers an act of worship, made conscious of his sinfulness by the manifestation of the Lord (v. 8). As said above, the story is a conflation of the call of the four in Mark 1:16–18 and a resurrection appearance, at its base related to the scene in John 21:1–12. In John, Peter is unaware that the figure on the shore is Jesus until so informed by the "beloved disciple" (v. 7, one of the "other disciples" of v. 2). In the Lucan version, as observed earlier, Peter moves from a familiarity with Jesus (Luke 5:1–5) in which he addresses him as "Master" (*epistatēs*), to a recognition of him as "Lord" (*kyrios*)—a fair, if cryptic, description of the effect of the resurrection on Peter.

In the gospel tradition, then, apart from Mark, we have various indications that Peter had a priority and leadership in the resurrection faith in Christ but that he did not reach it easily. It became, however, the new impetus for the followers of Jesus and saved them from despair. On its basis they could discover what the Scriptures really implied about the Anointed of the Lord and interpret Jesus' death and his appearance in exalted form in accordance therewith. So the passage Matthew has introduced into the Caesarea Philippi scene (ch. 16:17–19) emerges as a responsible claim to the importance of Peter's faith in Jesus as the (Risen) Christ based, not on his recognition of the full meaning of Jesus in mid-career, but on his acceptance of the resurrection and its implications. Truly this faith, by the means of the resurrection, was not revealed to him "by flesh and blood" (v. 17). On the rock of the resurrection faith, in which Peter has priority, Jesus' ecclesia is built. Because it depends on something more than human events, "the powers of death" will not shift it (v. 18).

This aspect of the resurrection has been explored in some detail because the upheaval in Peter's experience is so easily underestimated or ignored. He apparently was not easily converted. Yet his conversion was most likely the human turning point in the cause of Christ. It is true that Paul's conversion was a violent reversal and essential for the mission to the Gentiles, which is described as its purpose. Peter's change of heart and outlook would also appear to have been a tremendous reversal, obscured by the reverence later paid him by the church, represented in different ways by Matthew's Gospel and The Acts of the Apostles. Yet, as in so many instances at which we have looked, the traces of the actual experience are still there, a part of the paradox. Peter's response to Jesus, the response Jesus could not obtain on the road to Jerusalem, was obtained by the resurrection—as was Paul's on the road to Damascus. The resurrection faith is itself the response to the whole experience of Jesus, though we are unable now to describe what the cause of that response was. It was an act of God (Matt. 16:17: "For flesh and blood has not revealed this to you, but my Father who is in heaven") revealing that the whole event of Jesus' life and death was the evidence of God's new undertaking, for something more than Jonah or Sheba, something more than Moses or Elijah, is here. God has shown himself to be at work still for man's redemption.

Peter's response, therefore, would seem not to have been won against his will; he was free to struggle against it. Christian faith as a response to the new disclosure of God at work in Christ must be freely offered. The Emmaus story is one kind of retrospect on the work of Jesus and now we must turn to another which earlier we deferred—the story of the "temptation" of Christ.

THE PARADOX AS RETROSPECT

Mark's brief reference to the wilderness struggle (ch. 1:12–13) is elaborated by Matthew and Luke in an account which may have come from Q, though the order of items is varied, affording in each a different climax (Matt. 4:1–10; Luke 4:1–12). Mark's version, part of his introduction to the Christian reader, recalls the ancient promise of a victory over evil that would involve even the animal creation (see Chapter Three, above). The same motif of a victory over turbulent nature may be suggested in the storm stories discussed in Chapter One. Matthew and Luke use another series of motifs which provide a three-point explanation of the way in which this victory was achieved. But it is a *proleptic* story, anticipating and commenting upon what is to follow. That is, it could not have been written until there was the knowledge of Jesus' career upon which to base it. To try to explain it as historical, an account of an event between Jesus' baptism and his public appearance, produces an unconvincing theory that at some time Jesus recounted the experience to his disciples. This cannot be disproved. As a psychological account it is fitting, but again involves a knowledge of Jesus' *modus operandi*. It is, rather, the Christian discovery, on consideration of his work and words, that Jesus' career did in fact involve the rejection of certain approaches to Sonship, certain attitudes toward his anointing, which should therefore remain closed to the Christian church as the new "Son," the new "Israel."

Such a judgment appeared particularly true, since "the way Jesus had walked" had led to the cross and this denouement had paradoxically confirmed his whole mode of life. Jesus' death could be attributed directly to his refusal to go the way his contemporaries approved, the way they endorsed as official, and it only confirmed the literal fatality of his going his own way.

In the temptation narrative is summed up three great rejections, now understood in retrospect, since they could be observed in Jesus' actions and made proleptic on the assumption that Jesus, filled with the Spirit, could find no room in his purpose for those temptations to follow the traditional and popular way—an assumption not unnatural or even impossible. Whether he had made these decisions at the outset of his public career is not the important question. What is significant is how his activity revealed that orientation which finds here its anticipatory vindication. The consistency between the temptation decisions and subsequent words and deeds shows that Jesus put no great store in material things, in attracting attention by the performing of wonders, or in the resort to force; but it is a consistency seen in retrospect.

The Form of the Temptation Narrative

We come near the mind of the Evangelists when we consider the Old Testament background to the stories and their built-in pattern of concern and pronouncement. They are essentially those which we associate with "the school of Matthew" (in Stendahl's phrase). If we have difficulty in thinking that Luke has copied and rearranged Matthew, we may yet assume that he had access to the work of that school. The basic tradition is that which interprets Jesus as the recapitulation of Israel, a people that must worship and serve the Lord alone (Matthew's climax). As Israel had come out of Egypt as God's "Son" (cf. Matt. 2:15), so had Matthew's Jesus. As Israel had passed through the waters of the Red Sea, so had Jesus through the waters of baptism (cf. Paul's use of the term "baptized" in I Cor. 10:1-4). Therefore, as Israel in the wilderness for "forty years" had been tempted to put God to the test, so Jesus, as himself the New Israel, for forty days undergoes the same experience, and Israel must not "test" the Lord its God (Luke's climax).

It is easily seen that the words of Jesus to the Adversary (Satan) are from Deuteronomy, itself a commentary on the accounts in the book of Exodus from earlier sources (see Deut. 8:3; 6:16; 6:13 and, in turn, cf. Ex. 16:1 ff.; 17:1 ff.; 32:1 ff.). The quotations from Deuteronomy are given in reverse order while the incidents on which they are based appear (in Matthew) in the Exodus order. It is the history which is followed and which Jesus is made to follow by his refusals. Where Israel failed, he triumphs. Yet no positive answer is given to his own solution of the problem of implementing "Sonship"—how the expected One could solve the problems of his people if not by the age-old (and, sadly, still relied upon) methods of material prosperity, provision of wonderous spectacles, or the use of force. "Bread and circuses" backed by troops and police is not a solution confined to ancient Rome in these days of the welfare state, moon shots, tear gas, napalm, and atomic missiles.

The impression of consistency is a correct one, but retrospective. The recapitulation of Israel is not carried through in the Gospels. The story of the temptations of Jesus prior to his ministry is a reflection based on his actual work which in turn interprets what anointing by the Spirit meant. The fact that no positive decision emerges from the temptations suggests what is apparent elsewhere, that the issue is not predetermined —it is left to God. Obedient response is not compelled; it is an offering; since it is costly, a "sacrifice."

THE PARADOX OF POWER AND FREEDOM

In retrospect, therefore, there is one important observation that arises from analysis and reflection. If we should ask, as we should, why solutions are rejected which, in one form or another, men still pursue, we find the answer that in them man is deprived of his manhood. In trying to save himself he is dehumanized. In essence the demonic answers, which constitute a demand that God offer proof, reduce man below his manhood by diminishing his freedom. The misapplication of power in one form or another, more especially power attributed to the Spirit of God, must meet, respect, and respond to that spirit in man which is itself the gift of God and exhibits itself in his desire and search to be free to respond (cf. Rom. 8:12–17). "Bread" can be a potent weapon, a bribe; marvels can bypass the reason; power can override every consideration. For bread men may, often must, surrender their freedom. To gape at wonders and be bemused by the wonderworkers who have a power not open to the many may demand an abandonment of reason and reasoned choice. The worship of force is all too easily documented even, indeed spectacularly, in the twentieth century. Each temptation is a different form of power, all of them, in the Gospels, attributed to that access of Spirit which came to Jesus at his baptism. So, in history, it does not matter whether the power be military, scientific, or magical, control of the land or the cash or tools, or even ecclesiastical; from one side a triumph of manhood, on the other it is a threat to that very humanness. Even the power of God, the power to heal and exorcise, the power of the resurrection itself must leave man, must leave a Peter, free to say yes or no.

It was of great interest to discover, when I first read Fyodor Dostoevsky's *The Brothers Karamazov*, that he had grasped this more clearly than most commentators and preachers. The scene in Part II, Book V, Chapter v, entitled "The Grand Inquisitor," has often been used in sermons, but usually only its least effective part. What Dostoevsky has done is to claim, by the Inquisitor's discourse, that the church has sided with Jesus'

opponent in the wilderness and found it inexpedient to follow
Jesus' rejection of the devil's proposals. The church, on the
contrary, has found it expedient to use "miracle, mystery, and
authority," even in Christ's name. Thus where Christ has loved
the common man, the church has despised him. The smell of
burning victims was still in the air and the testimony to the
value of the Inquisition's methods was the unshakable domina-
tion the church had achieved. No reappearance of Jesus, holding firm to his rejection of those methods which deprive man
of his humanity, could be allowed to interfere—even for
Christ's own sake.

The Grand Inquisitor has cowed the populace and visits
Jesus, whom he has thrust into a dungeon, in the dead of night.
Two passages will convey Dostoevsky's insight:

> "Is it Thou? Thou?" But receiving no answer, he adds at once,
> "Don't answer, be silent. What canst Thou say, indeed? I
> know too well what Thou wouldst say. And Thou hast no right
> to add anything to what Thou hadst said of old. Why, then, art
> Thou come to hinder us? . . .
>
> "Thou mayest not add to what has been said of old, and
> mayest not take from men the freedom which Thou didst exalt
> when Thou wast on earth. Whatsoever Thou revealest anew will
> encroach on men's freedom of faith; for it will be manifest as a
> miracle, and the freedom of their faith was dearer to Thee than
> anything else in those days fifteen hundred years ago. Didst
> Thou not often say then: 'I will make you free'? But now Thou
> hast seen these 'free' men," the old man adds suddenly, with a
> pensive smile. "Yes, we've paid dearly for it," he goes on, look-
> ing sternly at Him, "but at last we have completed that work in
> Thy name. For fifteen centuries we have been wrestling with
> Thy freedom, but now it is ended and over for good. Dost Thou
> not believe that it's over for good?"

The penetration of Dostoevsky's treatment is seen where he
suggests that in the story of Jesus' temptations the devil's
three questions are those that still tempt man to "final" solutions.

"And could anything truer be said than what he revealed to Thee in three questions which Thou didst reject, and which in the books is called 'the temptation'? And yet if there has ever been on earth a real miracle, it took place on that day, on the day of the three temptations. The statement of those three questions was itself the miracle. . . . For in those three questions the whole subsequent history of mankind is, as it were, brought together into one whole, and foretold. In them are united all the unsolved historical contradictions of human nature." (See "Notes to Chapter Eight," par. 13.)

Throughout the Gospels are the marks of a consistency in refusing to be seduced by the shortcuts to power over people, in the temptations proleptically represented as a prior decision that to succumb meant to put God to the test rather than to rely entirely on him. That was a negative program, but it finds its positive summation in the scene in Gethsemane where Jesus, in agony of spirit, submits himself to God's (as yet undisclosed) will.

FREEDOM AND COMMITMENT IN THE GOSPELS

It is clear that Jesus' exorcisms and healings were attributed to a superhuman, or extrahuman, power. The question posed was whether that power was demonic or divine. Jesus rephrased the problem but left it to men to decide for themselves (Mark 3:22; cf. the parallels in the Q passage, Matt. 12:27 f.; Luke 11:19 f.). The places in which Jesus commands silence about his works of mercy may be interpreted in the same way. Large-scale success might well be taken as permitting man no choice. The same may be said for his silencing the demons, for their testimony, regarded as supernatural, might well have been taken as leaving no option but to believe. That something more than this, some "sign from heaven," was demanded before those in authority would accept him before the people, is indicated by such passages as Matt. 21:38 ff. and parallels.

We may compare the attitude of the Fourth Gospel in its interpretation of this aspect of the Synoptics from a very different interest in Jesus' self-disclosure. The crowd admits that Jesus has performed "signs": "When the Christ appears, will he do more signs than this man has done?" (John 7:31; cf. for the hierarchy, ch. 11:47). Yet all of this was insufficient; something more spectacular was demanded than healings and exorcisms, or the clearing of the Temple court. "The Jews then said to him, What sign have you to show us for doing this?" (ch. 2:18). "Then what sign do you do, that we may see, and believe you?" (ch. 6:30). Signs in themselves, even in John, do not demand or compel belief, at least not the acts Jesus did, taken as such (ch. 12:37). They were more likely to cause divisions (chs. 2:23; 6:2; 12:18; cf. 12:37 and Jesus' comments, chs. 4:48; 6:26) or to produce partial belief only, as with Nicodemus (ch. 3:2), to whom they mean "God is with him," or with the people who are willing to accept him as *the* promised prophet (Moses?) in ch. 6:14, or the formerly blind man who contends that Jesus must be a prophet (ch. 9:16 f.).

THE FREEDOM TO BELIEVE IN JOHN'S GOSPEL

The whole theme of freedom to choose and Jesus' refusal to compel belief by the acceptance of any unambiguous title or by pointing to his works as more than evidence of the drawing near of the Kingdom of God, is engagingly elucidated in the story of John, ch. 9. Its setting is the turn-of-the-century danger that anyone who attributes divine power to the Christ of the Christian church would be expelled from the synagogue (vs. 22, 34). Here the striking thing is the inability of the man to whom sight was granted to say for certain by what power this change has been effected. The passage is not without its touches of humor in the unexpected independence displayed by the man and his parents in the face of this synagogual inquisition.

The story then bears out Jesus' point, but it is of the greatest importance to note how it does. The man can bring no overwhelming proof (in that sense of a "sign") such as would convince his enemies and those of Jesus. He himself can give no conclusive answer. Certainly he will not accept the answer that Jesus is in league with evil powers, especially not on the extraneous grounds that it was the Sabbath (vs. 16 f., 24 f., 30–33). He will not be stampeded into a decision. All he knows is that for the first time in his life he can see and that Jesus had made this possible. But he is not yet able to see *who* Jesus is.

Quite possibly the exchange (v. 12), " 'Where is he?' . . . 'I do not know' " leaves open the surmise that some nonhuman factor is involved. The healer may have been only an "appearance" or may have been magically transported. If so, the direction of the story is the answer to that possibility as well. Jesus is real enough. Jesus' presence, whether in the flesh or at work in the church, did not compel belief but raised live options. There was no such thing as an undeniable "sign."

The blind man, when pressed, has himself a partial solution, like the man in Mark 8:22 ff., who saw what at first might be trees in motion but turned out to be people. "He is a prophet" —at least that, and perhaps it was said because it would not be open to censure (cf. Mark 11:32 and ||s). But the issue cannot remain in that indeterminate state (in the beginning of the second century it cannot). When "the Jews" have checked on the facts and tried to intimidate the parents, they are reminded that as an adult the man has to decide for himself and be willing to abide by his decision and its consequences (John 9:21–23, 34). The reiteration of what Jesus has done, what has happened, prevails over the question of the source of the power. It is upon what has happened that Christian faith is built, because apart from what Jesus has done the question which faith answers does not arise.

By the man's reply, "Yet he opened my eyes," we know they are not talking about Nazareth (they know he "comes" from there; cf. ch. 7:41–43, 52) but about what is behind him, of what power Jesus is an emissary. We see that by constantly pressing the man to admit one conclusion he is being moved toward another. He moves from "prophet" to the confession that God has listened to Jesus (made his power available) because Jesus not only worships God but does God's will (ch. 9:31). Hence the power to do the unheard of (to give sight to a man *born* blind) is the power of obedience, previously expressed in the Johannine view of the sent One who is "at one" with the Father (cf. chs. 5:19 f., 30; 6:38; 10:30, 37 f., etc., and the centurion in Chapter Four, above). The conclusion, therefore, is that Jesus must be "from God." But the opponents here revert to the question Jesus had put aside in v. 1 and say the man is not qualified to judge such issues—for himself (v. 34). So they excommunicate him.

It is at this point that Jesus finds the man and asks the question of faith in the words, "Do you believe in the son of man?" The chances are that John does not mean this to be read directly in lowercase, "Do you believe in the man who did this for you?" but has already moved beyond that point without abandoning it. It most likely means, "Do you believe there is such a deliverer as is known as 'The Son of Man'?" The man's reply reflects the confusion indicated elsewhere in John (see John 12:34 and Chapter Five, above) and in effect says, I would like to believe in such a one, but who is he? Jesus' answer is, "You have seen him"—that is, he is the one who opened your eyes—and, "He now speaks to you" (John 9:37). The one in whom faith may be reposed is already known to him. Thus the man, after all the confusion and pressure, is urged not to doubt, not to fail to trust his experience. Now, therefore, the man can say, "Lord."

The fascinating thing which makes close study of this subtly elaborated story worthwhile is that it makes the same point as the Synoptics, though it is applied to a clearly later and more specific situation, the expulsion of Christians from the synagogue. The charge against the Christians really was that they have presumed to judge for themselves on the basis of the work of Jesus, apart from any determinative decision by the authorities, that the power which had worked in Jesus was "from God." The stages of the debate in John, ch. 9, with all its shifts and subterfuges which endeavor to avoid the inevitable conclusion, show that there was no overwhelming compulsion about Jesus' acts; they bore no sign designating them "acts of God" apart from man's response, his recognition. That response involved a choice between two alternatives, to which a man must move on his own at the risk of opposition and penalty, until he was ready to accept Christ as the agent of God's restoring power.

What the story of the temptations, of the challenge to give a sign which will clearly show supernatural and divine interposition, points to is Jesus' refusal to use his works of mercy or acts of power or the available titles as *inescapable* answers to the questions his activity and teaching raised (see Chapter One above). The Johannine story and the temptation story are together a commentary on two facts—Jesus' own words and work and his refusal thereby to compel men, and the way in which men come to believe in him by their own free will. The resurrection itself, as suggested above in the story of Peter and the other hints of unreadiness to grasp it, was not an overwhelming "sign" but a response to something much more enduring than the reports of a tomb empty of a human body. The paradox remains in all its elements and there is no facile resolution. The Christology to which the Gospels lead is a Christology of commitment. Upon this act of commitment the Christian life rests without any more "certainty" than what Jesus offered his followers, what he himself could find in Gethsemane, the certainty that God's word is the first— and the last. And so it is seen, eventually, that Jesus *is* that "Word."

NOTES TO CHAPTER EIGHT

1. The story of the discussion of the resurrection can be traced in the following:

P. W. Schmiedel, "Resurrection-and-Ascension Narratives," in *Encyclopedia Biblica* (The Macmillan Company, 1903), Vol. IV, cols. 4039 ff.

K. Lake, *The Historical Evidence for the Resurrection of Jesus Christ* (G. P. Putnam's Sons, 1907).

P. Gardner-Smith, *The Narratives of the Resurrection* (London: Methuen & Co., Ltd., 1926).

S. V. McCasland, *The Resurrection of Jesus* (London: Thomas Nelson & Sons, 1932).

R. H. Niebuhr, *Resurrection and Historical Reason* (Charles Scribner's Sons, 1957).

L. Goppelt, H. Thielicke, H.-R. Müller-Schwefe, *The Easter Message Today*, tr. by S. Attanasio and D. L. Guder (London: Thomas Nelson & Sons, 1964).

W. Künneth, *The Theology of the Resurrection*, tr. by James W. Leitch (London: SCM Press, Ltd., 1965).

C. E. Braaten, *History and Hermeneutics*, contains a summary of the modern discussion in Ch. IV, "The Historical Event of the Resurrection."

2. For a literary analysis and theory of I Cor. 15:1–9, see M. H. Shepherd: "Paul and the Resurrection Tradition," *Journal of Biblical Literature*, Vol. 64 (1945), pp. 227 ff. On the expression used by Paul, see J. Munck: "Paulus tanquam abortivus (I Cor. 15:8)," in Higgins, ed., *New Testament Essays*, pp. 180 ff.

3. The use of the terms "objective" and "subjective" has, with the displacement of metaphysics by epistemology, been abandoned or has given place to other terms. In the text they are retained in default of any others as clear to the common reader. They may serve to point to a distinction implied in the resurrection references. On the one hand is a reaction to something unexpected and having its "cause" outside and apart from the person experiencing it. On the other hand is an experience more clearly originating in inward reflection, in the mind or emotions—as Renan said, "That which resurrected Jesus was love." (It is well to present the actual quotation: *"L'incident matériel qui a fait croire à la résurrection n'a pas été la cause véritable de la résurrection. Ce qui a ressuscité Jésus, c'est l'amour. Cet amour fut si puissant qu'un petit hasard suffit pour élever l'édifice de la foi universelle."* [*Histoire des Origines du Christianisme*; II, "Les Apôtres," p. 44.]) Over against it is another much quoted phrase of Keim describing the experience as a "telegram from heaven" (see Schmiedel, in *Encyclopedia Biblica*, col. 4077).

4. On Galilee or Jerusalem, see R. H. Lightfoot, *Locality and Doctrine in the Gospels* (Harper & Brothers, 1938).

5. For the reaffirmation of history by the coming of Christ, see H. Guthrie, *Wisdom and Canon* (Winslow Lecture, 1966, Seabury-Western Theological Seminary).

6. A curious sidelight on passages where the Risen Christ eats is found in C. S. Lewis' discussion of "The Mistake About Milton's Angels," Ch. XV in *A Preface to Paradise Lost* (London: Oxford University Press, 1942).

7. A discussion of the Petrine material is found in O. Cullmann, *Peter: Disciple, Apostle, Martyr*, tr. by Floyd V. Filson, 2d rev. ed. (The Library of History and Doctrine, The Westminster Press, 1962). He suggests (p. 184) a passion-story connection with Peter's denial for Matt. 16:17–19. He mentions the theory that it was a saying of the Risen Christ transferred to the life of Jesus (p. 181). Of theories about the transfer of appearances to Peter to various points in the ministry he says, "We cannot here attain complete certainty" (p. 62).

8. A clear statement of the difference between the transfiguration and the resurrection narratives is found in R. H. Lightfoot, *The Gospel Message of St. Mark*, p. 43.

9. After the suggestion came to mind that Matt. 14:28–31 turns the resurrection story of the walking on the water into the "missing" appearance to Peter, I find it is remarked in several places (probably many more) but, except for Bundy, without the suggestion of a demand for a sign. Cullmann, *Peter: Disciple, Apostle, Martyr*, p. 62, mentions it with a reference to H. Sasse. It is discussed, without his usual references, in Bundy, *Jesus and the First Three Gospels*, p. 270. He says: "Matthew's form of the story, including the Simon episode, has equally close affinities with the resurrection tradition." He refers to John 21:7 and to "Simon's scepticism and desire for proof" as "typical of the disciples' frame of mind in the resurrection tradition," and adds, "In fact, Matt. 14:28–31 might be a remnant of the lost appearance of the Risen Christ to Simon." Gardner-Smith, *The Narratives of the Resurrection*, p. 18, says: "In some circles the tradition of an appearance to Simon may have survived in stories relating to an earlier period of the ministry (Matt. xiv. 25 ff., John vi. 19 ff.)." McCasland, *The Resurrection of Jesus*, p. 201, n. 25, writes that Mark 6:45–52 may be "a survival of the first or subsequent appearances of the risen Jesus" but does not note the Matthean addition of Peter's demand for a sign. A reference to the empty tomb as "an ambiguous sign" (but not to Peter's demand for one) I now find in Goppelt, *et al.*, *The Easter Message*, p. 45.

10. What is preserved of The Gospel of Peter offers no help,

since it ends as Peter and his friends resume their fishing. See M. R. James, *The Apocryphal New Testament*, p. 94; E. Hennecke, *New Testament Apocrypha*, Vol. I, p. 187. Non-Christian parallels to the walking on the water are not relevant to the point under discussion. G. D. Kilpatrick, *The Origins of the Gospel According to St. Matthew* (London: Oxford University Press, 1946), pp. 41, 82, 95, holds the pericope to have been built up by stages as a "reflection of a Resurrection story."

11. R. H. Niebuhr, *Resurrection and Historical Reason,* pp. 29 f., in discussing the apostolic testimony, says: "We cannot make the experience of the primitive church the vicarious bearer of our faith, unless our faith also has roots in the experience of the present community of faith." Also, "Without the testimony, the life of the community would have been shapeless; it would not have borne the impress of the historical Jesus."

12. On the temptations and the use of Deuteronomy, see, e.g., J. A. T. Robinson, "The Temptations," in *Twelve New Testament Studies* (Studies in Biblical Theology, No. 34), pp. 53 ff. For K. Stendahl's view of the Matthean process see his *The School of Matthew* (Lund, 1954).

13. The quotations from F. Dostoevsky, *The Brothers Karamazov,* are the translation of Constance Garnett. Renewed interest in this aspect of Dostoevsky's chapter is indicated in an essay by W. Hamilton, "Banished from the Land of Unity," in T. J. J. Altizer and W. Hamilton, *Radical Theology and the Death of God* (The Bobbs-Merrill Company, Inc., 1966), pp. 53 ff.

Living with the Paradox,
Then and Now

What more can be said? In the nature of the case presented in the last chapter the reader must put the parts together in his own way, make his own decision and response.

We have pointed to the paradoxical nature of the Gospels, which are at one and the same time about Jesus from Nazareth and Christ from heaven, about the faith of the church at stages in its early development and the event of Jesus' brief career seen through the lens of the resurrection. The paradox consists in the necessity of explaining the Christian faith in ways which transpose the happenings into responses without losing touch with the event. One way of putting it is to say that the proclamation of the gospel of Christ, the kerygma, has always included a recollection and recital of the kind of person Jesus was, the sort of things he said, and the path he followed. When the churches forget this and Christ becomes a theological myth, those who take the following of Christ and the understanding of God through him to be Christianity will be found outside the churches—but perhaps not outside the "church."

We have examined in detail selected passages and the interconnections between them, allowing one section to throw light on another, in order to uncover the paradox of unfulfilled expectation which was yet fulfilled, the discontinuous continuity which cannot be ignored. The Baptizer who was baptized, the conception of an Anointed One who remains himself, was taken as the germ of all the rest—the paradoxes noted in the chapter headings, representative of many more which would be but variations on the same themes.

The overall paradox is that of a historic man who came to be worshiped as, in a special and changing sense, Son of God, Word of God, the Second Person of the Divine Trinity. Here is a man who would seem to have claimed no title, unless the most enigmatic one current, made no pretensions to rule from an earthly throne, demanded no predetermined belief in himself, who died the victim of the power structures and the uncertainties of his own friends. A human fate indeed. Yet a man who was remembered as embodying a mystery that let neither friend nor foe rest, whose invitations were imperious, whose words sprang from authority, and whom to follow involved total abandonment and complete commitment.

Two concepts of the times, one Jewish and one Hellenistic, have entered into the presentation of the story: the *theios anēr*, or "divine man," and the Messianic figure who attests his claim by "signs." Yet the evidence points to a person, humanly speaking, endowed with remarkable gifts of healing for mind and body, of intellect and penetrating insight, a charisma that could at the least be attributed only to possession by the Spirit of God. "Of God," not of the gods, for the God presupposed is the Biblical God in whom mercy and judgment, love and power, mystery and knowledge, demand and freedom, are all as one. A person is revealed whose death in no way diminished his power to reach men, to call them, to lead them, to enlighten them, or to convey to them some measure of his own power to bring others within the orbit of his Spirit, his obedience. This fact has transformed what might have been reminiscences or a biography into Gospels—a new form of literature, *sui generis*, indispensable to Christian faith, life, and worship.

From a primitive time we can, on the basis of early second-century evidence and of hints in the New Testament itself, assume that there was in the Christian assemblies, as in the Jewish, the practice of "recital" of the works of God—now renewed in Christ. In all probability worshipers heard incidents and teaching patterns like those now in the Gospels every first day of the week. They probably discussed them on other occasions and the application of them to their affairs under the

direction of "teachers," a class of persons mentioned by Paul
(I Cor. 12:28; cf. Rom. 12:7; reflected by the Paulinist in Eph.
4:11). There was in all probability a Christian catechesis that
embodied the same kinds of material.

The Gospels do not represent the tradition itself as recited,
though such recital, especially when it took the form of preaching, could hardly have been a catalog of "plain unvarnished
tales." We can, again, overemphasize what are helpful clues to
a type of literature that has no exact precedent as we should
do if we explained the forms in the Gospels as entirely the
product of preaching or as if they were shaped completely by
"theologians."

Undoubtedly, each Evangelist is an incipient theologian, but
the term so generally connotes a systematic undertaking that it
can lead to misapprehension. The parables as well as much
else that has survived of Jesus' teaching warn us that system
was already beginning to be imposed on what was originally
occasional and "situational." The teachers and prophets of the
church have added to and modified the tradition before the
Evangelists applied their editorial skills. Each Evangelist has
his own point of view, pressures from his own situation to ac-
commodate, and the product can, in essence, be called "theological."

Fundamentally, it reveals a Christological problem. The
paradox we have discussed is the expression of the factors
with which it deals. A good deal of modern elucidation of the
redactional work of the Evangelists produces impressive, if
sometimes hard to follow, results but they owe a good deal to
"prior understanding" and to the commentators' skill in seeing
esoteric patterns. There are many such schemes proposed, most
of them equally feasible, all of them helpful as meditations on
the gospel tradition. In view of the paradoxical nature of the
fundamental tradition it is probably unwise to look for too
much consistency, even within any particular Gospel. Mark,
Matthew, and Luke, no less than John, had each his own time
and place with its needs to satisfy. Each had his own method,
tendencies, and line of reasoning which are capable of analysis

and definition, and they add up to what may loosely be described as a theological viewpoint. It is paradoxical material with which they deal and as such has resisted all attempts entirely to remove that paradox or to resolve it. Hence the need for a new array of commentators and theologians in every generation, for they do but continue, in a derived sense, the work of the Evangelists. A serious sense of the radical changes represented by the twentieth century in every aspect of life should set us free from solutions offered in ages vastly different from our own. In the resulting need initially to "stand back" from our systematic theological inheritance, a grasp of the paradoxical nature of the Gospels and of him of whom they speak is a releasing factor.

It would be unwise to consider the Evangelists "theologians" before understanding them as "apologists," for the one grows out of the other. We come close to the fact and difficulty of the paradoxical element when we understand the task faced by the early Christian preachers, teachers, and Evangelists in the need for a reasoned defense and explanation of a gospel having to do with an obscure Jewish condemned criminal. We tried to indicate its weight in Chapter Seven. The problem was serious for the Evangelist whose written document would be available for study by the intellectual and cultured world, as the prefaces to Luke and Acts make clear. Yet it is to their credit that the Gospels (Mark notably and to some extent the others) while works of art are also, as the form critics insist, less than literature in the classical sense. That they are predominantly folk literature is still evident. All the same, they editorially undertake to meet a situation and state a case. The wonder is that in so doing they have not entirely obscured or removed the paradox which occasioned the effort. Their only partial success as apologists in the sophisticated sense (even in the case of Luke) suggests that, in the nature of the case, they were unable to do so.

Insufficient attention can be paid to the setting of suspicion and danger in which the first-century Christian movement developed and its relation to the fall of Jerusalem with the destruction of the Temple. Though sources are scant and Josephus is a biased witness, the Gospels are difficult to explain without taking into account the Jewish War and the unrest that accompanied it from A.D. 6 until A.D. 135. The radical upheaval in the Jewish church that led to the disappearance of sects and the dominance of the Pharisaic school of Jamnia and, no less, the disruption of the Jerusalem and Palestinian church with very little trace, must be kept in mind in reading every page of the New Testament. Quite apart from the controversies with the Synagogue, the problems posed for the church by the Roman efforts to deal with the problem of religion cannot be ignored. The internal strife among the Jewish factions, the incompetence and sometimes the venalities of the procurators of Judea, the self-seeking of the puppet rulers with their urgent desire to keep favor with Rome, and the frequent outbreaks of violent resistance were no tempest in a teacup.

The gravity of the situation is indicated, if by nothing else, by the fact that two or three legions of the best Roman troops in addition to local auxiliaries had to be diverted from vital tasks elsewhere at a time of internal upheaval at Rome, along with some of the most competent and crucially important leaders such as Vespasian and his son Titus. The defeat of a Roman legion under the legate C. Gallus could not be taken lightly. It could not have been of small concern to the Roman military and civil authorities that disputes and disturbances should involve them in such heavy commitments and in the radical and costly action which led to the final overthrow of Jerusalem. Even after A.D. 70 a constant state of suspense would have to be assumed in view of the second Jewish War and the rise of a leader hailed by some as Messiah.

It could not have been easy for the Romans to grasp just what the Jewish movement centered upon, especially in its Messianic forms, when religion, politics, and economics were so intimately interwoven as they were among the Jews. We tend to forget how vast a majority of the Jews lived in the Diaspora, in centers such as Rome and Alexandria, and the repercussions the war would have had upon them. The report found in Suetonius that disturbances in the Roman Jewish community prompted the emperor Claudius about A.D. 50 to expel them from the city is usually read by eyes anxious to find any secular reference to Jesus. Suetonius says, "Since the Jews constantly made disturbances at the instigation of Chrestus, he expelled them from Rome." It is very probable that he did not understand "Chrestus" to refer to a particular person but to disputes over Messiahship, the Messianic role and program. It may well have included disputes generated by Christians present with their claim for Jesus, but we must allow for a wider context in view of the reports reaching the community from Jerusalem. "Messianic" unrest at Rome or wherever found could not be ignored. The confusion of terms used, their lack of a uniform definition, the tendency to avoid the term "Messiah" in favor of others, may be explained on the basis of Roman watchfulness. The holocaust in Jerusalem and the tedious sieges that culminated at Masada in A.D. 73, in cost of Roman lives alone, besides military equipment and private, commercial, and religious property, and the disruption of agriculture on which Rome was so heavily dependent, cannot be regarded as incidental. In the years that followed, with the sporadic outbreaks of persecution of Jews as well as Christians, with the difficulty of deciding just how the sect of the Nazarenes was related to the recognized Jewish faith, the suspicion and uneasiness would not readily diminish.

It is chiefly W. R. Farmer in America and S. G. F. Brandon in England (see "Notes to Chapter Seven," pars. 1 and 2) who have taken the Jewish Zealot movement and the fall of Jerusalem with utmost seriousness for the study of the New Testament. Brandon's solutions, much more those of Eisler and Schonfield, may not be acceptable, but Brandon has the virtue of bringing into the foreground elements that were pervasive in the background of the Gospels. It has long seemed to me that the reasons offered by critics for dating the Gospel of Mark before the fall of Jerusalem are, to say the least, tenuous. It seems a much more natural explanation of the appearance of a "Christian apocalypse" like that in Mark, ch. 13, and of the whole problem of a deferred Parousia, to suppose that it was the Jewish War and its culmination in the fall of the Holy City to a pagan power without the intervention of God that prompted the writing of Gospels—both the fact of their being *written* and the form they take.

The whole matter needs a great deal more serious research than it has received, even since the discovery of the Qumran literature with its War Scroll. It has been suggested earlier that apologia entered into the Gospels. Attention to this aspect has often centered on the "trials" and the execution of Jesus which are seen to have definite apologetic tendencies. Yet the attempt to justify the Christian viewpoint and movement, including its use of the term "Christ," has entered more widely into the Gospels than into the passion narrative alone. In view of the conditions of the time, it is surprising that this apologetic is not more throughgoing and obvious than it is.

The modulation from "Messiah" to "Son of man" at two crucial points in Mark is undoubtedly the key to the Christian defense. But it is not a purely Christian invention. The combination of nationalistic ambitions with apocalyptic hope of supernatural intervention can be widely documented. It suggests that Jesus had been treated, even by his followers, as a Messiah or had been under pressure to assume that kind of leadership. Though he was held by the church to be the Christ in fact, in fact also he was not. He had not claimed to be such a Christ as would be a direct threat to Roman rule and order and to the freedom the Imperial Government granted to local traditions. The claim of the Gospels, and by implication that of Jesus, lay in an immediately more "religious" realm, where its threat to worldly rule was more eschatological than instantly political and military. That the apologia is not more throughgoing is a testimony to the paradox we have discussed—the facts put a limit even to the defense of the faith. The Evangelists are willing to admit that there was a Messianic tendency among Jesus' followers, that there were attempts to capture him for the cause, that he was arrested on suspicion of being a potential disturber, and that he was executed on the charge of sedition, of lese majesty, with others of the same order. An attempt is made, somewhat halfhearted from a thoroughgoing point of view, to shift blame from the Roman Government to the Jewish hierarchy (in Matthew to the people). Involved with the apologia to Rome is entangled controversy with the Jews and persecution, perhaps mutual—which would appear to the Romans as internal strife among sects of Jews.

The question necessarily arises whether the apologia is of such a character that the Gospels represent a complete rewriting of history in that Jesus was, in fact, a Messianic claimant as charged, had led a militant band of Galilean "zealots" to Jerusalem and threatened to take over the Temple if not the city. Brandon and others, it would seem, put an emphasis and interpretation on the tribute-money incident (Mark 12:13–17 and ||s) it will not bear and they exaggerate the "triumphal entry." Scientific study of the Gospels—unless all students can be accused of complicity—has shown no real basis for a supposition of "thoroughgoing Messianism." The probability dealt with in Chapter Six, that Jesus entered Jerusalem at the Feast of Tabernacles, that it represented no planned invasion and was ignored by the authorities for months, makes the assumption of a Messianic incursion at least unfounded. The Tabernacles probability is found by recovering a tradition older than that of the present Gospels. The confinement, in the oldest tradition, of the cleansing of the Temple to the Court of the Gentiles lends no support. That Jesus expected some divine intervention is not impossible, but it is a hope which finds no clear expression in the later chapters and while the Gethsemane story and the cry from the cross may indirectly support such a view, they more directly indicate the abandonment of any such hope as an immediate prospect. There is throughout the Gospels abundant evidence of how Jesus approached the crisis toward which he apparently saw his people headed, especially in the parables. Here and elsewhere his teaching speaks against a violent solution by human hands and it would deny the competence of critics to deal with this type of tradition if it were dismissed as an apologetic invention of a "pacific Christ" (Brandon). It has entered too integrally into the paradoxical material to be nothing more.

This still does not answer the lay question as to what actually happened, nor can it be answered definitively. In "placing" Jesus it is clear that he had close affinities with the Pharisees. In treating his teaching, allowance must be made for the absence from the Gospels of an immediate sense of the severely agitated conditions amid which Jesus lived and spoke (see *The Jesus of the Parables* where an attempt was made to supply this). Under these conditions of urgent expectation with its insistence upon a "final solution," with the concurrent suspicions of sectarian listeners, the words of Jesus would be heard with much more relevance to the crisis than they now appear to have. It is true they often assume the form of "wisdom" sayings, but in view of the explosive nature of the times they can hardly have seemed to the hearers to have been the calm contemplations or the dispassionate words of a reflective philosopher discoursing in an academy. Sadducees, Pharisees, Zealots, Essenes, "the poor," the ʽam haʼaretz, the outcasts, all would have heard with their own ears and applied what they heard from their own impassioned viewpoint. The Evangelists have succeeded in rescuing the words of Jesus from confinement to that past situation and released them in a form available for constant reapplication.

It is clear that Jesus was taken to be some sort of Zealot and indeed, so far as the Zealots held a passionate regard for the righteousness of God, for his absolute rule and for the sanctity of the Temple, Jesus could be classified with them. This would be true from the religious side of the movement and at a stage when the Zealots themselves had by no means all reached the point of assuming that the resort to arms was inevitable. Jesus' warnings were not all "after the event" and some features of his parabolic and other teaching, in the conditions of the time, counsel against the danger of losing the ultimate function of Israel in seeking the immediate redressing of its legitimate grievances. We have also to weigh the evidence of the Gospels that he was deeply sympathetic to the common man (having been one of them), shared their burdens, their woes, and their hope for a solution. At the same time we have the paradox that he associated with those who were anathema to the Zealots, the tax collectors and religious outcasts who were considered little more than collaborators. Even if he had given up hope of the Temple's fulfilling its proper function, he may originally have shared the devotion of the Zealots for the Temple ideal. Yet, if Mark 11:17 can be trusted (see "den of brigands," in Chapter Six), he viewed with repugnance its use as a fortress—which it soon came to be at their hands. This could be a reflection of later apologia but it is by no means impossible that it goes back to Jesus' acute reading of tendencies already at work.

Jesus' faith in the ultimate purpose of God and divine intervention seems to have been tied to no timetable for apocalyptic or human activity, not even his own, yet there is a sense in which his preaching of the critical imminence of God's Kingdom and the need for immediate response implies, in the outcome, the crucial factor of his own presence apart from the usual kind of Messianic plotting. That Zealots among his followers and sections of his public read this otherwise may well account for the reaction of the Jerusalem authorities and the measures they took to end what was then a danger and was to become in the decades that followed one that no responsible official could ignore. The Roman interventions which led inevitably to the war of A.D. 66 proved the wisdom of trying to prevent occasions for just such involvement. The Gospels are at pains to show as an apologetic gesture that in the period between A.D. 70 and 135 Jesus was mistakenly identified with this form of Zealotry. To say so is far from proving that the basis of the apologia is not itself a correct recounting of the actual facts and person.

It is an interesting and convincing point that Luke, and following him, John, feel freer than Mark to bring into the open the charges upon which Jesus was condemned and to discuss more freely the issue of "kingship." We have seen above also that Matthew can ignore Mark's careful treatment of the term "Son of David." The way in which Luke makes the charges explicit and John causes Pilate and Jesus to discuss together the nature of his claim show that toward the end of the century and at the beginning of the next it was possible to deal with the remembered facts with less hesitation and to explain what lay behind them. As suggested above, the confusions and apparent irregularities are accepted as having been part of the original events. In the process the Romans are, it is true, absolved of any intention to do away with a person now viewed as Son of God, but the confusion is allowed to remain and the Roman procurator does not emerge flawless.

Undoubtedly the attempt to move from the politically dangerous term "Christ" to the more open-ended one "Son of Man" must be seen as having apologetic *value*. Its roots, however, go deeper than that and reach down into a paradox which could not (and cannot) be resolved in any simple manner. The fact that, in spite of all, the term "Christ" persisted, no matter how filled with new meaning, is testimony in itself to a paradoxical situation in which the issue had to be admitted while its meaning had to be safeguarded. There is not far below the surface in the Gospels enough evidence to show that the paradox was not a postcrucifixion phenomenon alone. It was part also of the explanation of the picture of Jesus' followers in the Gospels, who show a divergence from Jesus freely admitted to have existed during his lifetime and which was dealt with only by the outcome in the resurrection faith. It is a departure from the Gospels to make Peter and the rest saints before their time or to assume that being "one of the twelve" (cf. Mark 14:10) was simply by association with the human Jesus a transformation of character.

It was this paradox with which the early Christians had to live—and so do we. The Evangelists had to contend with it, and so do our own theologians and preachers. Too often the Gospels are taken in a simplistic sense with no attempt to distinguish between the various Evangelists, in which the Fourth Gospel is taken on a par with, sometimes as a guide to, the others. There is thus disturbance of a proper assessment of the New Testament in which the preaching of the church suffers. We can no longer assume that those who attend churches or hear preachers elsewhere are unaware of at least some of the results of modern study of the Gospels, and to discount this fact leaves the preacher with less credence than before. Nor can relief be found in treating the Gospels as simply repositories of Christian theology, kerygmatic collections as ready to be preached now as they were when first used. In a period when we cannot even assume faith in God—when the term itself is part of mythology—the need is for honesty even to the confession of ignorance rather than dogmatic reiteration amplified by electronics.

Christianity is no myth because Jesus was no myth. Nor was he the invention of the kerygma without historical reality, definition, or necessity. Where the Gospels need demythologizing (including "dedemonizing") it can be done to some extent by restoring Jesus to his proper humanity in the actual setting of the times, leaving, it is true, the substructure of a mythological faith in God to be dealt with then as now. The result will be neither a twentieth-century distortion (like the nineteenth-century "Jesus of history") nor a first-century grotesque incomprehensible to anyone outside a library. The Christ of the Gospels paradoxically can be neither extracted from the Gospels nor shut up in them.

In presenting the proclamation of the gospel of Christ the Evangelists have had to deal with the Jesus from whose life and death the faith arose, and this has determined the character of their products. The influence of Jesus on the Gospels (if one may put it that way without being facetious) is paramount. Gerhard Ebeling has properly insisted on this point in his *Theology and Proclamation.* The sheer fact of the name "Jesus" in the kerygma is the basic evidence. Of the Christological titles he says, "[Rather,] they only receive a definite meaning when they are applied to Jesus. By comparison with their original sense they are all to some extent transformed through their being applied to Jesus. It is just this process of reinterpretation which represents the decisive kerygmatic event in such statements about Jesus" (p. 51). Further, he writes, "Statements such as 'Jesus is Christ' or 'Jesus is risen' cannot be fully interpreted merely by examining their predicates. Even if one interprets all that is predicated of Jesus with reference to the eschatological event as the lowest common denominator it still remains unclear what this means, if we leave out of account the fact that they are intended as statements about *Jesus*. Only by reference to him can the meaning of the predicates themselves become clear" (pp. 51–52, Ebeling's italics).

One may be dubious about "quests for the historical Jesus" as if thereby the paradox could be avoided. We have to live with it. Yet the actual Jesus who lived also lives within the proclamation of the gospel of Christ, and Ebeling comments upon it in this way: "At this point, it becomes necessary to speak of Jesus. Our reflections on the kerygma have led us to this in two ways. Firstly, we saw that the clarity (*Eindeutigkeit*) of Christological statements depends on their being understood as statements about Jesus. And further we noticed that the intelligibility of Christological statements depends on the situation being qualified as kerygmatic, i.e., depends on that which constitutes the basis and necessity of the Christological kerygma. Now the Christological kerygma itself points us most clearly to this basis. One cannot escape the persistence with which it uses the name of Jesus. Nor is this only because the kerygma happens to make Christological statements about Jesus, it is also—and this is really one and the same thing—because it constantly claims Jesus as its authority" (pp. 54–55).

Attempts, which tend to reappear, to reduce Christianity to respect for a man who once lived, no matter how exalted the respect, without Christological, if not theological, implications equally do violence to the nature of the Gospels. In the period of reconstruction in which the twentieth century lives, the pulpit must take the lead (or some substitute for the pulpit), for that is the avenue by which the work of students of the Bible and the theological revisers will be mediated to the people. A new kind of apologia is a need which no one can overestimate. The examination above of the apologetic task of the early church should be a spur to the constant need to relate the gospel to the demands of the time while at the same time holding a caution that there are limits beyond which apologetics deny the actual situation, paradoxical though it is.

Since we have to live with the paradox, the twentieth century is as well equipped to do it as any other, perhaps better. Events have freed us sufficiently that we properly suspect facile solutions. As suggested above, no resolution of the paradox of Jesus in the Gospels is available, or ever was, which does not involve a commitment. Christology, seeking a basis in the Gospels, is incomprehensible apart from personal involvement. Such commitment cannot exist until it is wholeheartedly prepared to follow a road without a map, yet a road already traveled, a freely chosen resolve to move and trust the God to whom Christ committed himself. By doing so, it is possible to prove that there is a way. Finally, there is the supreme paradox in which all lesser ones are taken up into a reality of life and intensity of personal existence which is, at root, what we mean when we venture to speak of God. It is a venture, especially when we speak of "the God and Father of our Lord Jesus Christ." To this God the Gospels represent the man Jesus as having had a relationship of particular clarity and even intimacy. His address to God as "Father" makes room for the response along with him (or "in Christ") of all who come to be willing to share his trust. Not less does it make room for all those, as a community, who in discovering Jesus to be "the Christ of God," discover each other anew, as brothers, and forever.

Notes to Postscript

1. On the technical debate about kerygma, multiple kerygmata, the "Jesus of history," historiography, existential and faith knowledge, etc., see N. Perrin, *Rediscovering the Teaching of Jesus*, (London: SCM Press, Ltd., 1967), especially Ch. V, "The Significance of Knowledge of the Historical Jesus and His Teaching," and Bibliography, No. 9.

2. For a strong view of the preservation of the oral tradition, see H. Riesenfeld, *The Gospel Tradition and Its Beginnings* (London: A. R. Mowbray & Company, Ltd., 1951).

3. For books on the political apologia, see "Notes to Chapter Seven," par. 1.

4. On the Gospels as folk literature, see the opening chapter of M. Dibelius, *From Tradition to Gospel*, tr. by Bertram Lee Woolf (London: Ivor Nicholson & Watson, Ltd., 1934).

5. The Suetonius text is given in the Loeb Classical Library: *Suetonius, II*, "Divus Claudius" XXV.4: *"Iudaeos impulsore Chresto assidue tumultuantis Roma expulit."* Cf. Tacitus, *Annals* XV. xliv: *"Vulgus Christianos appellabet. Auctor nominis eius 'Christus'."*

6. A balanced summary of the method needed for study of the Gospels in view of the "debate" referred to in the Preface has now appeared in O. Betz, *What Do We Know About Jesus?* (The Westminster Press, 1968); see pp. 16–27.

Index of Names and Subjects

Anointed, the, 32, 61–68, 121, 162, 172–176, 189, 192, 194, 199, 213

Anti-Semitism, 162 f., 180n4

Apologia (apologists), 30, 45, 53 f., 57 f., 70n3, 74, 76, 101, 117, 138, 141, 143, 157n4, 161 f., 172–174, 183, 196, 216, 219 f., 222 f., 225, 227n3

Apostles, 32, 74, 78, 84–87, 90, 97n5, 128, 161, 184, 193, 199

Ascension, 51, 60, 95, 116 f., 182, 185, 209n1

Authority, 23, 26, 45 f., 77, 92, 100, 121, 139, 144, 146, 194, 204, 214

Baptism, 31 f., 34–42, 46, 49n5, 51–54, 56, 59, 60–62, 65–69, 71n3, 74 f., 78, 81, 116, 121, 126, 134, 156, 179, 202 f.

Barabbas, 169–172, 175

Caesarea Philippi, 100, 119, 127 f., 134, 140, 194 f., 199

Christ, 12, 16, 19, 32, 34, 37, 46, 128 f., 140, 159, 179, 194, 199 f., 204, 206, 209n1, 214, 219, 223, 225 f.; Risen, 91, 95, 184, 187, 189, 197, 211n6

Christology, 18, 30, 48n2, 52, 58 f., 61, 68, 72n11, 100, 173, 179, 181n9, 209, 215, 224–226

Church, 12, 29, 30 f., 34 f., 38, 44 f., 48, 52 f., 55, 68, 77, 79–82, 84, 86, 94 f., 101, 106, 123, 127 f., 134, 142, 144, 147, 158 f., 166, 175, 199, 201, 203 f., 207, 212n11, 217, 219, 223, 226

Claim (of Jesus), 57, 83, 101, 124, 126, 138, 150 f., 154–156, 159, 161, 174 f., 189, 213 f., 220

Coming One, 38, 43 f., 48, 109, 131n10

Commitment, 24 f., 99, 119 f., 138, 156, 179, 209, 214, 226

Consistency (of Jesus), 25, 27n6, 201 f., 205

Crucifixion, 19, 23, 32, 55 f., 60, 87, 89 f., 103, 112, 117, 120, 124, 127 f., 134, 137, 140, 152, 155, 158, 160, 161 f., 168 f., 170 f., 175–177, 181nn., 187 f., 201, 220

Day of the Lord, 47, 107, 124, 148, 154

Demythologizing, 13, 57, 224

Elijah, 47, 54, 107–109, 113, 115, 126 f., 131nn10, 11, 200

Enoch, 108 f., 115, 127, 131n11, 132n13

Eschatology, 41, 45, 47, 56, 62 f., 76, 83, 85 f., 93 f., 96,

97n10, 104, 107, 110, 114, 123–125, 131nn., 146, 151 f., 154, 175, 178, 195, 219, 225

Essenes, 42, 63, 221

Evangelists, 20, 31, 35, 45, 51, 56, 58–62, 66, 68 f., 73–76, 81, 86, 93, 95 f., 100 f., 113, 117, 122, 127 f., 153, 161, 172, 174, 201, 215 f., 219, 221, 223

Exorcism, 25, 77 f., 80, 132n16, 203, 205 f.

Expectation, 43–45, 47 f., 51, 64, 66, 68, 101, 124, 127, 148, 152, 155, 186, 189, 194, 213, 221

Faith, 11, 15, 18, 25, 33, 60, 137, 140, 160, 176, 179, 196, 198 f., 200, 204, 207, 212n11, 213 f., 222–224, 226n1

Fire, 35–37, 48, 51 f., 64 f., 69

Flesh, according to the, 23, 120, 144, 155, 175 f.

Fourth Gospel, 32–35, 47 f., 48n3, 49n7, 50, 53, 64, 85, 87 f., 90, 116–118, 122–124, 128, 130n7, 143, 147, 153 f., 164 f., 174 f., 177 f., 186 f., 193, 196 f., 205 f., 208 f., 222 f.

Freedom, 24, 200, 203–209, 214

Fulfillment, 43 f., 46–48, 51, 54 f., 60, 63, 66, 110, 123 f., 150, 153, 156

Gentiles, 73–75, 83, 88 f., 92–95, 98n14, 113, 143, 145 f., 151–153, 179, 199

Gethsemane, 173, 179, 196, 205, 209, 220

Herod, 41 f., 105–107, 112, 125, 139, 165

Incarnation, 29–31, 68 f., 176 f., 182

Integrity (of Gospels), 43, 46 f., 50, 54, 73, 102, 128, 156

Jericho, 134 f., 137–139, 147

Jerusalem, 22 f., 74, 84, 89 f., 109, 113, 121, 126 f., 134, 136–138, 141, 144 f., 148, 152–154, 156, 166 f., 180n1, 192, 195, 210n4, 216–218, 220, 222

Jesus, 12, 22–26, 31–35, 44–46, 128, 136 f., 155 f., 158, 166, 172 f., 175 f., 184, 187, 199, 213, 218–226

Jewish Wars, 217–219, 222

John the Baptist, 31–35, 37–48, 51–54, 59, 62 f., 66, 68 f., 76, 83, 94, 106–108, 113, 154, 165, 180n1, 196, 213

Judgment, 37 f., 40, 43, 45 f., 48, 64 f., 83, 109, 115, 176

Kerygma, 11, 19, 30–32, 44, 48, 67, 69, 74, 100, 102–104, 111 f., 122, 127 f., 159, 173, 175, 182, 213, 215, 224 f., 226n1

King (kingship), 59, 62 f., 65–69, 121, 123, 127, 134, 141, 143, 146, 148–152, 155 f., 162, 171, 222

Kingdom of God, 68, 77, 83, 86, 130n1, 132n17, 139, 148, 172, 187, 195, 206, 222

Lord, 18, 21 f., 44, 69, 84, 88, 127, 141, 143, 148, 152, 155 f., 161, 176, 185, 199, 202, 208, 226

Lord's (Last) Supper, 86, 122, 124 f., 176–181, 196

Melchizedek, 109, 127, 131n11

Messiah (Messiahship), 47, 69, 70n1, 99, 101, 114, 120 f., 138–142, 144, 161, 174 f., 180n1, 194, 217–219

Messianic: Banquet, 86, 124; consciousness, 57, 100, 114 f., 119, 127, 151; disturbance, 123, 189, 195, 220 f.; Kingdom, 58, 65, 105, 117; mission, 45, 110, 136; secret, 111 f., 142, 194

Mightier (Stronger) One, 36–39, 43–45, 50, 66 f., 156

Miracle, 17, 20, 24, 97n3, 122, 135, 138, 142, 146, 156, 204 f.

Mission, 77–80, 82, 84 f., 87–89, 91–96, 192

Moses, 108, 115, 126 f., 131n11, 200, 206

Opposition, 77–79, 87, 90, 154, 158, 175, 204, 209

Outcasts, 26, 83, 90, 137, 176, 221 f.

Parables, 12, 20, 24–27, 38, 47, 48n1, 71n9, 85, 90–92, 94, 96, 98n13, 99, 129 f. nn., 144, 147, 154, 215, 220 f.

Paradox, 12, 19 f., 23, 29, 30 f., 34, 40, 42, 48, 52, 57, 68–70, 76, 84, 93, 95 f., 99–101, 117, 127, 129, 144, 148, 155 f., 158–160, 162, 165, 172, 177, 179, 182, 194, 197, 200 f., 203, 209, 213 f., 216, 219, 221, 223, 225

Parousia, 125, 165, 192, 219

Passion predictions, 58, 101–103, 111–117, 119, 127, 129, 130 f. nn., 134, 140, 186, 189 f.

Passover, 147, 153, 159, 166–168, 178, 180n1

Paul, 44, 60, 74, 81, 92, 155, 162, 165, 176, 183–185, 187, 193

Pentecost, 51, 87

Peter (Simon), 18, 21, 32, 110 f., 119–121, 128 f., 140, 146, 173, 175 f., 180n3, 184,

187, 191–199, 203, 209, 211nn., 212n10, 223

Pharisees, 26, 99, 105 f., 142 f., 221

Pilate, 171 f., 175, 178

Power, 45–48, 51, 61, 77, 80, 92, 149, 156, 188, 203, 205, 207–209, 214

Prayer, 122, 128

Preaching (proclamation). See Kerygma

Prophets, 106, 108, 126 f., 153, 189, 206 f., 215

Qumran, 42, 63, 67, 70n3, 83, 109 f., 132n13, 219

Recapitulation, 54 f., 61 f., 202

Recognition (acclamation), 99, 140, 146, 209

Recognition of Christ, 16–18, 20–23, 26, 75, 100, 136, 138, 186, 188–191, 195, 199

Redemption, 178, 200

Repentance, 34, 38, 41, 47

Resurrection (Easter), 11 f., 17–22, 31 f., 35, 44, 51 f., 60, 63, 68, 75, 89, 95 f., 102, 107–117, 119, 125–129, 132n14, 155 f., 160 f., 174 f., 179, 182–192, 196–200, 203, 209–212nn., 213, 223

Rome (Roman), 72, 92, 104, 112, 128, 154, 160–162, 164–166, 168, 170, 172, 180n5, 202, 217–220, 222 f.

Samaritans, 90 f., 99

Sanhedrin, 23, 103, 113, 162, 164 f.

Savior, 11 f., 67, 73, 94, 141, 160

Secular, 29, 99, 106, 165

Servant, Suffering, of Yahweh, 55–57, 103, 113, 116 f.

Seventy, the, 88 f.

Signs, 24, 45, 94, 150, 187, 198, 205–207, 209, 211n9, 214

Son of David, 135 f., 138–144, 157n3, 222

Son of God, 18, 34, 54–61, 63, 66–69, 71n3, 117, 121, 126, 155 f., 173, 175, 179, 198, 201 f., 214, 223

Son of Man, 46 f., 70n1, 86, 101, 103, 108–110, 112–118, 120 f., 126 f., 131 f. nn., 156, 174 f., 194 f., 208, 219, 223

Spirit, 34–36, 38, 41, 48, 49n6, 51–53, 56, 59, 61–64, 90, 95, 120, 153, 175–177, 201–203, 214

Synagogue, 23, 61, 74, 77, 79, 81, 84 f., 87, 89, 117, 128, 147, 162, 166, 206, 208, 217

Symbolism, 12, 20, 22, 26, 93, 124, 150 f., 153 f.

Tabernacles, Feast of (Booths), 71n6, 88, 98n12, 145–147, 150–153, 156, 160, 166 f., 220

Temple, 56, 75, 95, 127, 134, 139, 144–147, 151–157, 166, 171, 179, 206, 217, 220–222

Temptation(s), 27n6, 62, 65, 156, 159, 179, 198, 200–203, 205, 209, 212n12

Transfiguration, 113, 125, 129, 133n18, 134, 145, 192, 195, 199 f., 210 f. nn.

Twelve, the, 31, 77–88, 96 f. nn., 100, 104–107, 110–112, 114, 119–123, 125, 127 f., 135, 139, 167, 169, 178, 184, 193, 223

Withdrawal, 17, 79, 93, 122, 125

Women, 26, 89–91, 123, 143

Worship, 11, 19, 122, 152, 160, 177, 191, 198, 208, 214

Zealots, 170, 172, 180nn2, 7, 218, 220–222

Index of References

to Scriptures and Josephus

OLD TESTAMENT

Genesis
2:7 64
5:24 109
11:6 ff. 51
12:3 94
14:18–20 109
25:22–26 41

Exodus
4:22 .... 70n1
16; 17; 32 202

Numbers
11:16–25 88

Deuteronomy
4:24 64
6:13, 16 .... 62, 202
8:3, 7–12 .... 202 f.
18:15, 18 108
32:48–53 108
34:5–6 108

I Kings
22:17 123

II Kings
1:9, 11, 13 123
2:11 f. 108

II Chronicles
18:16 123

Psalms
2 ..... 34, 56, 58 ff.,
109, 116, 146
22 .... 160, 177
110:4 .. 60, 109, 143
118 .... 136, 145 ff.,
155 f.

Isaiah
11:1–9 ... 64 f., 146
29:18 f. 45
35:5 f. 45
42:1 .... 56 f., 71n3
49:6 94
53 113
56:6 f. 95, 152
61:1 .... 45, 63

Jeremiah
6:3 f. 123
7:11 152

Ezekiel
37:9 ff. 51

Daniel
7:10–14 .. 64, 70n1,
109

Joel
2:28–32 56

Amos
4:7 85

Micah
5:2–4 123

Zechariah
9:9 ..... 146, 149 f.,
151
14 .... 146, 151, 153

Malachi
3:1 ff. 47, 54,
107, 154
4:1–6 .... 47, 107 f.,
151

APOCRYPHA

Ecclesiasticus
48:10 108

I Enoch
12:1; 48:2; 62:7;
69:26; 70; 71:1,
14 109

IV Ezra
6:26 109

Testament of Judah
24:2 .... 56, 59

JOSEPHUS

Wars
II.254; IV.504 .. 170

Antiquities
XIV.159 f. 170
XVIII.v.2 41
XX.160 f., 167 .. 170

New Testament

Matthew

1:1–17 ..... 55, 142
2:1–15 ..... 55, 93,
              123, 202
3:1–6 .... 32, 39
3:7–10 .. 39, 40, 92
3:11 f. .... 35 f., 38
3:13–17 .. 34, 54 ff.
4:1–11 .. 55, 62, 159,
              198, 200 ff.
4:12–17 .. 55, 75, 76
4:18 ff. 193
4:23 81
5:1–11 55
5:47 95
6:32 95
8:5–13 92
8:28–34 93
9:27–31 142
9:35 to 10:16 ... 81,
         82, 84, 85, 123
10:24–34 ... 87, 116
11:1 81
11:2–6 .. 43, 45, 159
11:7–19 .. 45, 47, 54
12:22–37 .. 38, 142,
                  205
12:38–42 95
13:24–43 85
14:22–36 .. 18, 198,
                211n9
15:21–28 ... 89, 91,
                  143
16:13–23 .. 121, 193,
           199 f., 211n7
17:9–13 .... 47, 192
18:10–14 91
19:28 ...... 86, 116
20:29–34 .. 135, 142
21:1–9 .... 143, 149
21:10–17 .... 147 f.
21:26 46
21:38 205
22:1–14 92

23:37–39 156
24:30 116
25:31 116
26:13 93
26:15 169
26:55 171
26:60–64 .. 116, 154,
                 173 f.
27:15–26 162,
               171 f.
27:33–43 .. 169, 177
27:51–53 179
27:62–66 183
28:1–10 ... 183, 186
28:16–20 ... 73, 95,
                  186

Mark

1:1–6 ... 32, 34, 39,
                 53 f.
1:1–8 ...... 35, 38,
             49n5, 51
1:1–13 ..... 34, 36,
                 49n4
1:9–11 ...... 34, 56
1:12–13 ... 62, 65,
                  200
1:14 f. .... 65, 76 f.,
             78, 192
1:16–20 .... 21, 23,
           27n5, 83, 87,
           91, 104, 193,
                  198
1:21–34 .... 23, 45,
           77, 87, 193
1:32–38 .... 77, 193
1:39–45 .. 15, 77, 81
2:1 to 3:6 .. 77, 105,
             134, 154
2:14 ...... 23, 192
2:38 192
3:6 .... 105, 192
3:7–12 ..... 77, 79,
             93, 192
3:13–19 ... 23, 77 f.,
             80, 83

3:19–35 .. 38, 77 f.,
                  205
4:1 79
4:8, 29 85
4:35–41 .. 12 ff., 190
5:1–20 93
5:37 193
6:1–6 .... 23, 79, 81
6:7–13 .... 23, 80 ff.
6:14–16 ..... 105 ff.
6:17–29 42
6:30–45 ... 78, 82,
             85, 122 f.
6:45–52 ..... 12 ff.,
           122 ff., 126,
         190, 194, 198,
                211n9
7:24–30 .... 89, 91,
                  143
8:1–26 .... 107, 134,
                  194
8:22–26 .... 89, 140,
             194, 207
8:27–33 .... 100 ff.,
         107 ff., 119 ff.,
         125, 192, 194
8:34 to 9:1 116,
           120, 125
9:2–8 ...... 125 ff.,
             145, 192
9:9–13 ..... 47, 101,
             113, 129
9:30–32 ... 101 ff.,
     112 ff., 125, 131n7
10:17–31 .. 86, 135,
             192, 195
10:32–34 ... 101 ff.,
      113 f., 127, 131n7,
                 134 f.
10:35–45 .. 101, 113,
         121, 126, 134,
             136, 195
10:46–52 .... 134 ff.
11:1 to 12:12 ..
      98n12, 144 ff.,
                156n1

11:1–11 ...... 142, 144 f., 147 ff.
11:12–14 .... 145 ff.
11:15–19 .. 95, 145, 147, 157n7, 222
11:20–25 .... 146 f., 195
11:27–33 ...... 46, 146 f., 153, 167, 207
12:12–17 .. 167, 220
12:35–37 142
13 ... 87, 154 f., 195
13:9–12 .... 84, 97n8, 131n7
13:26 116
14:1–2 .... 103, 147, 167
14:9 .... 93, 98n14
14:10–11 .. 103, 223
14:12–16 .... 148 f., 167
14:26–31 .. 173, 196
14:32–42 ... 131n7, 173, 196
14:43–52 .. 103, 171
14:53–72 ..... 116, 154, 173 f., 181n9, 195
15:1–15 ...... 103, 171 f.
15:21–32 .... 158 f., 162, 169, 177, 179
15:34 177
15:37–39 .. 56, 177, 179
16:1–8 .... 186, 197
16:9–20 .... 73, 186, 197

Luke
1; 2 .... 71n5
1:1–4 87
1:17 108
1:41 f. 41
2:4, 11 141

2:32 94
2:41–52 75
3:1–3 32
3:7–10 .... 38 ff., 92
3:16–17 ... 35 f., 38
3:19 f. 76
3:21 f. ... 34, 56 ff., 71n4
4:1–14 .... 62, 159, 198, 200 ff.
4:16–30 ..... 45, 63, 89
5:1–11 .... 20 f., 91, 129, 191 f., 198 f.
6:15 170
7:1 ff. 92
7:18–23 ..... 43 ff., 159
7:24–35 ..... 47, 54
7:36 ff. 93
8:22 21
8:26 ff. 93
9:6 81
9:10 86
9:18–22 128
9:26 116
9:28–36 ... 126, 192
9:51 to 18:14 ... 61, 71n5, 90
9:54 f. 64
10:1–4 ..... 82, 85, 88 f.
10:25–37 90
11:14–23 ... 38, 205
11:30 f. ...... 94 f.
12:8 f. 116
13:1 171
13:28 f. 92
13:24 f. 156
14:16 ff. 92
15 91
16:16 47
17:11 ff. 90
18:8 116
18:38 f. 143

19:1–10 137
19:28–38 .... 143, 147 f.
20:6 f. 46, 153
20:41 ff. 143
21:12 ff. 84
21:27 116
21:36 116
22:6 169
22:14–20 178
22:28 ff. ... 86, 116
22:31–34 196
22:35–38 89
22:52–56 .. 171, 195
22:69 .... 116, 174
23:2 170
23:17, 19 171
23:32–49 ...... 159, 170 f., 177
24:1–12 .. 186, 189, 196 f.
24:13–35 .... 20, 186 ff.
24:36–49 ..... 94, 186 f.

John
1:1–14 ...... 30, 32
1:19–23 108
1:29–36 .. 34, 44, 53
1:40–44 ... 87, 193
2:18–22 ... 154, 206
2:23 206
3:2 206
3:18 f. 48
3:22–30 ..... 34, 50
4:1 f. 50
4:23 154
4:35 85
4:48 206
5:19–24 .... 48, 208
5:30 208
6 122
6:2–15 .... 87, 108, 122 f., 139, 206
6:16–20 ..... 211n9

6:26–38 ... 206, 208
6:63 48
6:64, 71 ..... 131n7
7:31 206
7:32 167
7:37 153
7:40–44, 52 48,
                167, 207
8:16, 47 48
9:1–38 .. 48, 206 ff.
9:39 48
10:19 48
10:24–39 .. 111, 208
11:47–52 .... 164 f.,
                206
11:53, 57 167
12:1–8 .. 93, 131n7,
                169
12:12–19 .... 147 f.,
                151, 206
12:22 87
12:34 ... 116 f., 208
12:37 206
13:1–30 122,
                131n7, 169
14:22 111
18:1–14 .... 131n7,
                165, 180n5
18:28–38 ... 131n7,
                142
19:11, 16 .... 131n7
19:18–30 177
20:1–10 186,
                196, 198
20:14–25 .... 186 f.
20:19–30 .. 20, 51,
            64, 95, 186 f., 198
21:1–14 ... 21 f., 91,
            95, 186, 188, 191,
            196, 198, 211n9
21:15–23 21,
                131n7, 193

Acts
1:1–5 ...... 63, 187
1:6–11 ..... 90, 187

1:13 170
1:15–26 .... 31, 67,
    169, 182, 185, 187,
                192
2:1–4 51
2:14–38 32,
        131n7, 182, 192
3:6 192
3:11–26 ... 32, 182,
                192
4 .... 60 f.
4:8–13 .... 32, 182,
                195
4:24 ff. .. 32, 61, 67,
                182
5:1–11 192
5:29–32 .... 32, 182
7:45 61
8:4–8 90
8:14–17 90
9:3–9 .... 184 f.
10:34–43 ... 32, 44,
        61, 67, 111, 182
11:15 f. 63
13:16 ff. ...... 60 f.
22:6–11 185
22:22–29 165
26:9–23 185

Romans
1:3–4 .. 52, 142, 155
4 40
8:12–17 203
12:7 215

I Corinthians
1:23 161
3:13, 15 65
10:1–4 202
15:1–9 .. 183 f., 186,
            189, 210n2

II Corinthians
5:1–17 176
8:9 30

12:1–4 183

Galatians
1:12–16 183
2:6–14 193
3:6 ff. 40
3:13 162

Ephesians
4:11 215

Philippians
2:5–8 ...... 30, 177

II Thessalonians
1:7 f. 65

Hebrews
1:3, 5 60
2:9–15 .... 30, 177
4:8 61
4:14 to 5:10 ... 60,
                109, 179
6:19 f. 109
7:1–10 109
7:28 ...... 60, 70n3
9:6–14, 24–25 .. 179
10:19–22 179
10:26 f. 64
12:29 64

James
5:13–16 81

I Peter
1:7 65

II Peter
3:7 65

Revelation
1:13 f.; 2:18; 3:18;
8:4; 9:17; 10:1; 11:5;
13:13; 14:18; 16:8;
19:12, 20; 20:9, 10,
14 f.; 21:8 64
14:15 f. 85